OECD Proceedings

Institutional Investors in Latin America

PUBLISHER'S NOTE
The views expressed are those of the authors
and do not necessarily reflect those of the Organisation or of its Member countries.

D1377779

ORGANISATION FOR ECONOMIC CO-OPERATION AND DEVELOPMENT

ORGANISATION FOR ECONOMIC CO-OPERATION AND DEVELOPMENT

Pursuant to Article 1 of the Convention signed in Paris on 14th December 1960, and which came into force on 30th September 1961, the Organisation for Economic Co-operation and Development (OECD) shall promote policies designed:

- to achieve the highest sustainable economic growth and employment and a rising standard of living in Member countries, while maintaining financial stability, and thus to contribute to the development of the world economy;
- to contribute to sound economic expansion in Member as well as non-member countries in the process of economic development; and
- to contribute to the expansion of world trade on a multilateral, non-discriminatory basis in accordance with international obligations.

The original Member countries of the OECD are Austria, Belgium, Canada, Denmark, France, Germany, Greece, Iceland, Ireland, Italy, Luxembourg, the Netherlands, Norway, Portugal, Spain, Sweden, Switzerland, Turkey, the United Kingdom and the United States. The following countries became Members subsequently through accession at the dates indicated hereafter: Japan (28th April 1964), Finland (28th January 1969), Australia (7th June 1971), New Zealand (29th May 1973), Mexico (18th May 1994), the Czech Republic (21st December 1995), Hungary (7th May 1996), Poland (22nd November 1996) and Korea (12th December 1996). The Commission of the European Communities takes part in the work of the OECD (Article 13 of the OECD Convention).

OECD CENTRE FOR CO-OPERATION WITH NON-MEMBERS

The OECD Centre for Co-operation with Non-Members (CCNM) promotes and co-ordinates OECD's policy dialogue and co-operation with economies outside the OECD area. The OECD currently maintains policy co-operation with approximately 70 non-Member economies.

The essence of CCNM co-operative programmes with non-Members is to make the rich and varied assets of the OECD available beyond its current Membership to interested non-Members. For example, the OECD's unique co-operative working methods that have been developed over many years; a stock of best practices across all areas of public policy experiences among Members; on-going policy dialogue among senior representatives from capitals, reinforced by reciprocal peer pressure; and the capacity to address interdisciplinary issues. All of this is supported by a rich historical database and strong analytical capacity within the Secretariat. Likewise, Member countries benefit from the exchange of experience with experts and officials from non-Member economies.

The CCNM's programmes cover the major policy areas of OECD expertise that are of mutual interest to non-Members. These include: economic monitoring, structural adjustment through sectoral policies, trade policy, international investment, financial sector reform, international taxation, environment, agriculture, labour market, education and social policy, as well as innovation and technological policy development

FOREWORD

Over the past few decades the number of institutional investors has grown dramatically in advanced market economies and, more recently, Latin America as well, largely influenced by the development of private pension systems in the region. The experience in advanced market economies suggests that the investment activities of institutional investors will have a significant impact on the development of financial markets of these countries.

The OECD Centre for Co-operation with Non-Members (CCNM) and the Commission of the European Union organised, in co-operation with the government of Chile, a workshop on "Institutional Investors in Latin America". The workshop took place in Santiago in September 1999, with the participation of policy-makers, academics and private sector representatives of 15 Latin American and OECD countries. Participants assessed the current state of development of institutional investors in Latin America and examined how Latin America and OECD countries might benefit from each other's experience in broadening the role of institutional investors.

Many of the discussions signalled a risk of tension between choice and competition objectives on the one hand and prudential and protective objectives on the other. Regulations and constraints that sought to protect investors, consumers and workers also have the potential to hamper competition in the institutional investor sector. Choice and competition can entail certain benefits for these individuals by offering a wider selection of financial instruments with different risk-return characteristics, lower commissions, and greater control over firms' corporate governance, and hence, over returns to financial assets. Yet, competition can have a downside. For example, consumers in Latin America are paying higher fees as pension fund administrators devote significant resources to advertising, marketing campaigns and sales forces.

This publication, prepared by the Directorate for Financial, Fiscal and Enterprise Affairs, brings together selected papers by experts who attended the Santiago meeting. Part I assesses the current state of the institutional sector in Latin America while part II examines OECD policy experience in the area of institutional investors. Part III contains the conference proceedings

This publication should stimulate further debate and assist the formulation of policy priorities for the growth of institutional savings in Latin America. The views expressed are the sole responsibility of the authors. They do not reflect the views of the OECD or those of its Member countries. This book is published on the responsibility of the Secretary-General of the OECD.

Eric Burgeat
Director
Centre for Co-operation with Non-Members

TABLE OF CONTENTS

Part I

INSTITUTIONAL INVESTORS IN LATIN AMERICA: RECENT TRENDS AND REGULATORY CHALLENGES

Part II

THE INSTITUTIONAL SECTOR IN THE OECD

Part III

SUMMARY OF CONCLUSIONS BY THE OECD SECRETARIAT

INTRODUCTION

by
Carmen Villegas-Caballero[*]

The OECD/EU workshop on Institutional Investors in Latin America assessed the current state of development of institutional investors in Latin America, both as providers of financial services and as holders of financial assets. Prior to the onset of the Asian crisis in 1997, the growth rate of assets under management by domestic institutions had been fairly strong in many Latin American countries, in some cases comparable to or even exceeding those in advanced market economies. For most countries in the region, however, the institutional investors sector does not yet have the same bearing on overall financial market activity as its counterparts in more advanced market economies. A number of factors explain this discrepancy, including the fact that, in some countries, the relevant legal and regulatory frameworks have been created only recently. Accordingly, as an additional objective, the workshop tried to identify any remaining obstacles to the further growth and development of the institutional sector in participating countries and suggested policies to address the problems, including ways to improve the financial infrastructure.

The project built upon previous work on this topic, especially the OECD horizontal projects on Institutional Investors and Capital Market Development in Transition Economies. It moved the discussion forward by bringing together policymakers and private-sector representatives from both Latin America and the OECD area. The following is an introduction to the various issues that were discussed during the workshop. It is divided into four sections, coinciding with the four main sessions of the workshop. A summary of the various presentations and the conclusions from the workshop are contained in Part III of this publication.

---

[*]   Consultant, OECD.

1. The institutional sector in Latin America – Assessment, experience, comparison

In Latin America, the importance of institutional investors is steadily increasing. In particular, pension reform has been an important factor in developing a domestic institutional sector in some Latin American economies, and pension funds are more developed than other categories of institutional investor in the region. Total pension fund assets in Latin America were estimated at around US$137 billion as of 1998, compared with $2 198 billion and $5 766 billion respectively for Europe and North America for the previous year. They are projected to increase to as much as $981 billion by 2015. As in more advanced market economies, demographic change has been a major factor driving the increase in pension fund assets. Societies in some emerging market economies are ageing even more rapidly than those in more advanced economies. In Latin America, for example, the proportion of the population over 60 years of age is expected to increase by almost 90% by 2025. The need for pension reform has been pressing for some time, and Latin American countries have been at the forefront in making the transition to systems that will be sustainable over the longer term.

Chile, in 1981, became the first country to radically change its pension system, replacing its public pay-as-you-go (PAYG) system with a privately managed, fully funded model. Upon introduction of the system, persons already employed were presented with the option of remaining with the public system or switching to the private one. As of 1997, only 8.5% of the Chilean work force had stayed with the public system. The great majority of the working population is enrolled in nine private pension fund companies known as *administradoras de fondos de pensiones (AFP)*. The AFPs collect 10% of an employee's gross monthly salary and invest the money, mainly in domestic bonds and stocks. They also collect 3% of salaries to cover insurance premiums and administrative expenses. The assets under their management - $32 billion at the end of 1998 - are equivalent to 40% of Chile's GDP, and by 2000 that figure is expected to rise to 45% of GDP. AFPs own more than 10% of all Chilean equities and are responsible for about one quarter of all transactions on the country's stock exchange. The Chilean pension fund system has attracted much attention, not only in Chile, but also abroad. In 1998 the government increased the limit for pension fund investments abroad to 12% of the portfolio. This increase is expected to amount to more than $7 billion by 2004.

Mexico, Bolivia and El Salvador adopted a similar privately managed system in 1997 and 1998. In July 1997, Mexico partially privatised its provisions for old age. As of 1998, around 85% of the eligible workers, or 12.6 million people, had enrolled in the pension system. This makes Mexico the largest country in Latin America in terms of number of affiliates. Since its inception, assets have grown at an average rate of 52 % per month, and there are high growth expectations for the coming years.

In Argentina, a multi-pillar system replaced the former public social security system in 1994. The first pillar continues the public PAYG tradition. Workers also contribute to a second pillar, which can be either a private defined-contribution scheme or a public defined-benefit plan. By end 1997, approximately 70% of the employees had opted for the private *Administradoras de Fondos de Jubilaciones y Pensiones* fund. Uruguay introduced a similar model for old-age provision in early 1996, and Venezuela enacted a law in 1998 providing for such a system. In Colombia (1994) and Peru (1993), the private pension-fund system provides an alternative to the public PAYG system. Employees can freely choose the system to which they will subscribe and, within certain time limits, can transfer from one system to the other. As in Chile, private insurers cover the pension funds' disability and death risks, and offer annuity insurance.

Brazil has one of the largest private pension systems in Latin America, despite the lack of a national, private pension fund system. At the end of 1998, total pension assets under management were equivalent to 10% of the country's GDP. Three types of complementary private system coexist with the government's pension plan: closed pension funds, which are established by companies solely for their employees; individual retirement funds; and open pension funds to which any worker can belong. The potential for pension fund asset growth in Brazil is thought by most analysts to be great, given the regulatory changes being implemented and the privatisation of state-owned companies. Other countries with a similar complementary system are Costa Rica (since 1985), Ecuador (since 1995), Guatemala, Honduras and the Dominican Republic (since 1998).

In most of these countries, differences in the investment portfolios of the individual *Administradores de Fondos de Pensiones* are small. Several factors may be involved, including direct and indirect regulatory restrictions on investments and the still limited availability of investment instruments in incipient capital markets. In some cases, for example in Mexico, pension funds have not been allowed to invest in equities; thus, the portfolios of pension funds in the country consist entirely of fixed-income securities. This restriction is currently under review and may be changed shortly. In most countries in the region, investment in foreign securities has been either negligible or disallowed, at least during the start-up phase of private pension systems. Even in Chile, where more than 10% of assets may be invested abroad, the share of foreign securities in the portfolio had typically not exceeded 4% until last year. As domestic returns fell, pension funds reacted by increasing their exposure to foreign securities, to as much as 6% by December 1998.

Compared with pension funds, the mutual fund sector in most Latin American countries is somewhat underdeveloped, relative to GDP and income per capita, but the potential for growth is believed to be quite high, especially for the larger economies. In some cases, the low degree of penetration of the mutual fund sector reflects the success of pension funds, which have captured a large share of savings. In Chile, for example, which has a well-established private pension system, the ratio of mutual fund assets to GDP is extremely low by international standards. The degree of penetration of the Argentine mutual fund sector is even lower, well below that of other countries in the region. Brazil is the lone exception in the region in the sense that its mutual fund industry is well developed, and penetration is high by international standards. There are approximately 2 500 funds operating in Brazil with nearly $120 billion in assets under management, amounting to roughly 13% of GDP. An impetus to growth in this sector was given during the years of hyperinflation, when short-term fixed-income mutual funds offered an alternative means to preserve value.

The Latin American insurance market has changed dramatically in the 1990s. During this period, all the major markets in the region and many of the smaller country markets were reformed by new legislation and regulations that reversed the earlier pattern and laid the foundations for modernising the industry. Important reforms have been carried out in many countries, concerning not only the pension sector but also health insurance, which has passed, in whole or in part, to the private sector. These reforms have begun to produce growth, diversity in coverage, competition-driven pricing, and globally oriented markets that should greatly benefit their respective national economies.

Thus far, ten countries in Latin America have freed insurance markets: Chile, Colombia, Peru, Argentina, Mexico, Venezuela, Panama, Brazil, El Salvador, and Bolivia. The process followed by each of these countries has been very similar: it includes such measures as removing restrictions on local and foreign investors, freeing rates, eliminating most filing and policy approval, freeing brokerage and reinsurance, accepting foreign investment—with up to 100% equity ownership in some cases—and introducing solvency margins and minimum capital requirements for insurance company operations. These changes, which have won widespread recognition, are contributing to a new respect for the Latin American insurance markets and their potential.

Between 1990 and 1998, total insurance-premium volume more than doubled in Latin America from $15 billion to $37 billion, contributing just under 2% to the region's GDP in the latter year. Even though this is still a very low level of penetration compared with the 7% to 10% contributions generated by insurance in most European economies, the United States, and industrial Asia, the potential in Latin America is very high, with expectations of a $90 billion premium volume for the next decade. Whatever the extent of insurance growth, however, this change will bring a significant expansion in the region's permanent stock of capital. Moreover, insurance company capital and reserves offer a means to address the challenging problems posed by the current dependence on highly mobile short-term investment flows.

Further expansion of the insurance industry will depend on a number of factors: building up an adequate infrastructure in the sector (including disclosure of companies' financial performance and solvency); further improvements in regulatory systems (in some Latin American countries, the insurance sector is still over-regulated); reforms in social-security systems; and the economic development of the region as a whole.

2.   The institutional sector in the OECD area: Lessons for policymakers

The experience of advanced market countries clearly shows that institutional investors have an impact on the overall structure of financial markets. For instance, countries with large funded pension schemes (*e.g.* the United Kingdom and the United States) tend to have highly developed securities markets, while such markets are less developed in countries with smaller pension fund sectors (*e.g.,* Germany and Italy). The second session provided background for the study of global trends in institutional investment, focusing in particular on the key factors that have been driving the growth of institutional investors' activities in OECD countries. Participants discussed how the factors responsible for this growth can stimulate the further development of the domestic institutional sector in Latin America.

In 1996, the most recent year for which complete data are available, assets of institutional investors as a share of national income varied widely among OECD countries. The United Kingdom, the United States, the Netherlands and Sweden occupy the highest positions ranging between 120 and 193% of GDP. Asset holdings of institutional investors in Australia, Canada, France and Switzerland stood at between 80 and 100% of GDP in 1996. An exceptionally high rate was observed in Luxembourg due to its position as an international centre for institutional investment. Growth in assets under management has been quite rapid in the 1990s.

Pension funds and insurance companies have traditionally been the biggest institutional investors in OECD capital markets but, in recent years, the growth in assets of investment companies, especially mutual funds, has been especially striking. Also noteworthy is the gradual trend towards internationally diversified portfolios, especially of pension funds, as evidenced by a rise in the share of foreign-security holdings. That said, the analysis of general trends and developments in this sector is complicated somewhat by the fact that, increasingly, there are a number of institutional and functional overlaps among the various categories of institutional investors.

World-wide deregulation in the financial services sector along with technological advances have brought about a wave of consolidation among banks, other financial intermediaries and securities market participants, which makes it difficult to separate out growth trends. For example, increased competition between and among banks and other financial institutions in the OECD area has encouraged banks to move *en masse* into both the mutual-fund industry and the insurance business. Moreover, in many OECD countries, mutual funds play an increasingly important role in managing pension fund assets. Despite these overlaps, it would not be correct to view institutional investors as a monolithic group: some statutory barriers remain in place (*e.g.* banking restrictions in the United States), and there are noteworthy operating differences as well. Institutional investors have different investment objectives and fiduciary mandates, operate under different regulatory and tax regimes and have different risk tolerances. The nature of the liabilities of the different types of institutional investors is a key determinant of their behaviour, including their investment activities.

Although each category of institutional investor has had its own specific influences, there are a number of major structural factors driving the growth of institutional investors as a group. They include:

Deregulation of the financial sector

Deregulation of the banking and securities industries since the beginning of the 1980s has heightened competition between and among banks and other OECD financial institutions. New capital standards for banks were introduced in the same period, and the abolition of cross-border restrictions on capital flows has further increased competition. In response to these pressures, banks have massively moved into the insurance and investment-fund businesses, in search of new activities that generate earnings in the form of commissions and fees without necessarily absorbing additional capital.

Liberalisation of the institutional sector

Liberalisation of the activities of institutional investors, both in terms of the production and distribution of their respective products and the investment of their assets, has also contributed to the expansion of the institutional-investor sector. A significant aspect of this process has been the relaxation of regulatory constraints on cross-border activities and investments.

Demography, pension systems reform and financial markets

The growing needs of a rapidly ageing population for retirement income, in conjunction with an increase in the number of more sophisticated and wealthier private investors, has boosted the demand of private households for the retirement benefits offered by the different types of financial institutions.

Advances in communications and information technology

Technological advances in computers and telecommunications equipment have greatly enhanced the capacity of the financial sector, professional fund managers, and the international investor community to capitalise on the opportunities available in the more liberalised institutional environment. Advances in technology have enabled funds to be managed at lower costs. These advances have also led to more efficient and reliable clearing and settlements systems for securities and payments and have fostered the creation and use of complex new financial products for risk management purposes. The result has been a more complete integration of capital markets which has been one of the important factors underpinning the spectacular growth of the managed assets of institutional investors, in particular mutual funds.

The increasingly active role of the fund-management industry.

Individuals and institutional investors have increasingly delegated the management of their portfolios to professional fund managers. The total volume of funds managed by them is now larger than the portfolios of the "traditional" regulated institutional investors. Fund management companies are also involved in the management of the portfolios of "high-net worth" individuals, the non-pension fund money of non-financial enterprises, foundations and endowment funds, and non-pension fund money managed by banks, as well as banks' and securities firms' own portfolios. The role of the fund-management profession is therefore a key factor in analysing the relationship between institutional investors and financial markets.

Financial integration

The pace of financial integration has been and continues to be quite rapid, fuelled by financial market liberalisation and modernisation, advances in information and communications technology, and the international diversification of portfolios of the OECD institutional sector. In addition, major policy initiatives, such as NAFTA and EMU, have been launched in recent years. They have given a major push to financial integration, initially at the regional and subsequently at the global level.

The expansion of the portfolios of institutional investors in the OECD area has been the driving force behind the portfolio flows to emerging markets of the 1990s. Net private capital flows to emerging markets exceeded $265 billion in 1996, nearly six times what they were at the beginning of the decade. Among institutional investors, mutual funds have led the rapid growth of investments in emerging market equities. However, it is increasingly the expansion of the OECD pension sector that is the main financial muscle behind the continued flow of capital into emerging markets, investing either through mutual funds or directly on their own account.

3. The regulatory and supervisory framework and the financial infrastructure

The establishment of an adequate regulatory and supervisory framework and a level competitive playing field in the institutional market has been an integral part of the overall reform process undertaken by the countries that have been most successful in developing an institutional sector. In Latin American countries, pension fund regulations extend from traditional prudential controls to specific rules affecting industry structure, performance and investment. In contrast, the insurance industry has been subject to a more liberal regulatory regime, and entry into the industry tends to be more competitive.

Financial security and rights of beneficiaries

A critical objective of regulations governing institutional investors is to ensure that investors, and, in some cases, the general public, are adequately protected against incompetence, negligence, fraudulent practices on the part of managers, and any other factors that may impair the soundness of these institutions. In the case of pension plans, the primary objective is to protect beneficiaries from the effects of a sponsor's insolvency, insufficient funding of the pension plan because of improper technical and/or investment decisions, misappropriations by managers, or default by other financial entities involved in the provision of benefits.

While the new Latin American pension systems are based on a defined-contribution formula (fully funded, by definition), the need to ensure the financial security of pension benefits is patent, because, in most cases, these plans have become the main providers of pension benefits. Insurance, though still largely voluntary (*e.g.* annuities, life insurance), also requires careful

16

control by regulatory agencies. In particular, funding levels need to be enforced to ensure the solvency of participant companies.

Two of the most important risks related to DC plans are the investment risk to the beneficiary and the related risk of not having an adequate level of benefit at the time of retirement. Since, in these plans, investment risk is, in principle, borne by the employee, training in financial matters is of paramount importance (at least when DC plans allow beneficiaries to choose investments). Risk also affects the adequacy of benefits at the time of retirement, measured in relation to the previous standard of living and final salary, or to a minimum subsistence level. This risk is partly dependent on investment choices, but also on the contribution record, the administrative costs charged by pension fund administrators (employers or financial institutions), and access to annuities markets. DC plans, even if they offer a high return, may not always permit the payment of an adequate pension, as a result of either high costs in the management of the plans themselves or adverse selection in annuities markets.

The OECD has suggested a set of regulatory principles to safeguard the financial security of pension plans and the rights of members[1]. It covers licensing, asset separation, information requirements, self-regulation, investment rules, supervisory effectiveness and transparency. The Latin American countries that have reformed their pension systems have made considerable progress in developing a solid regulatory and supervisory framework for private pension funds, but important issues remain to be resolved. Among the most important is the structure of the industry (defined-contribution plans, with a single account per affiliate, managed by specialised financial institutions) and the impact this structure has on administrative costs. Other important unresolved issues include the adequacy of regulations imposed on the performance of pension funds and on their investment regimes.

The OECD has defined a similar set of principles for insurance regulation which may be relevant for Latin America[2]. It covers licensing, supervision of insurance companies, investments, competition, accounting, contract law and taxation. A source of great controversy in OECD countries is the regulation of the investment regime of insurance companies. Investments by insurance companies are generally governed by more stringent regulations than those of pension funds. Many types of restrictions have been identified, most of them set ceilings or (less frequently) floors and include provisions regarding currency and maturity matching. Although it seems that greater consideration ought to be

---

1. See *Maintaining Prosperity in an Ageing Society*, OECD: Paris, 1998

2. See *Insurance Guidelines for Economies in Transition* OECD: Paris, 1997

given to the possibility of liberalisation in this area, a regulatory framework should be in place to ensure that financial institutions invest prudenty.

The source of greatest concern, however, is the weakness of regulatory and supervisory frameworks of voluntary employer-pension plans, especially in the two largest economies, Brazil and Mexico. Since such plans are often based on a defined-benefit formula, they require specific vesting and portability standards, minimum funding rules, appropriate methods for calculating valuation and funding, using actuarial techniques and based on comparable standards, favourable tax treatment of over-funding and surplus, and ways of providing insolvency insurance without incurring moral hazards. The development of occupational plans as a complement to existing public defined benefit or individual capitalisation regimes will be thwarted unless regulations are modernised and adequate supervision is exerted.

Another matter for concern is the lack of control over the pension funds and investment companies that are sprouting up in countries that have yet to develop the necessary legal and regulatory frameworks. These are essentially the countries that have not as yet reformed their public pension systems along sustainable lines. As the confidence of private investors can be permanently damaged by failure of these institutions, it is imperative to develop an adequate regulatory and supervisory framework for them.

Financial infrastructure

Government regulatory actions can do much to either mitigate or aggravate the dysfunctional aspects of financial innovation; an important example is the role of regulators and supervisors in setting standards for institutional investors' management of risk. Among the main functions of the regulatory framework have been:

- Ensuring an accurate disclosure of all material information. Differences in disclosure requirements among countries are significant, partly due to differing legal systems.

- Adopting insider-trading legislation. Markets should try to eliminate insider trading by relying on the full range of sanctions (civil, administrative and criminal) rather than on criminal prosecution alone.

- Ensuring fair treatment of all shareholders, including minority shareholders, and establishing effective mechanisms for corporate governance so these shareholders participate in key corporate decisions.

4. Opportunities for growth of the institutional sector in Latin America: A policy challenge

A critical policy challenge in both OECD and Latin American countries is ensuring the adequacy of a pension system. This adequacy should be examined in a broad context, taking into account existing government systems and the expected role of private schemes. This applies not only to the level of benefits but also to the degree of population coverage. It is important to note that, in countries where the public systems do not provide sufficient levels of benefits, a substantial part of the population does not benefit from coverage by private schemes either. Some OECD and South American countries have sought to tackle this problem by making private pension schemes compulsory or providing substantial tax incentives. Nevertheless, some segments of the population seem to have fallen through the net, as shown by the informal sector problem in Latin America. This situation is bound to pose serious problems for governments in the long run as they may be called upon to provide old-age income support for these people. Government authorities must pay attention to the adequacy of private pension plans, as, if benefits turn out to be insufficient, the state will in the end have to provide relief through public systems. Preventing problems from occurring requires that plan members be properly informed and that well-defined rules designed to protect them against abuse be implemented.

The expansion of the institutional market can have a significant impact on the development of the financial sector. The OECD experience demonstrates how the growth of the institutional market can contribute to the modernisation of, and a stronger role for, the financial sector. An expansion of the domestic institutional market in Latin American economies could be expected to give a similar impetus to the development of the domestic financial sector. Although progress has been made in Latin America, the policy agenda remains full. The potential for the expansion of a domestic institutional investor base is enormous.

Part I

**INSTITUTIONAL INVESTORS IN LATIN AMERICA: RECENT
TRENDS AND REGULATORY CHALLENGES**

INSTITUTIONAL INVESTORS IN LATIN AMERICA: RECENT TRENDS AND REGULATORY CHALLENGES

by
Juan Yermo[*]

Institutional investors are playing an increasingly important role in both OECD and non-OECD countries[1]. This trend is the result of interest on the part of both the public and private sectors in institutional forms of savings and insurance. Governments reconsidering their social welfare systems are turning towards private pension funds and insurance companies as a supplement, and sometimes alternative, to their public systems. The mutual fund business, meanwhile, is growing rapidly: there is increased demand for professional asset management on the part of retail investors who are moving away from low-risk assets, such as bank deposits, in the hope of achieving higher returns on their financial portfolios. Increasingly too, mutual funds are offering their services as asset managers for pension funds and insurance companies.

This study analyses the role of institutional investors in providing financial services in Latin America. It must be realised, however, that their impact extends into the financial markets and the macro-economy. Institutional investors have been credited, for example, with raising domestic savings rates, though conclusive evidence is still elusive. On the negative side, they have been blamed for increasing the volatility of capital flows and causing contagion effects. Institutional investors can also be both a source and a result of financial sector development. They can become large holders of long-term assets, such as equities and corporate bonds, and can be prime investors in risk capital and private infrastructure. Indeed, the linkage between institutional investment, savings and growth is most likely to be channelled via the effect that the former has on capital market development (Holzmann, 1998). In a region like Latin America, which has suffered from chronically low savings rates, underinvestment, and severe capital flight, institutional investors could play a

---

*　　　　Consultant, Insurance and Private Pensions Unit, OECD.

critical role in raising savings by investing resources in domestic capital markets.

As past experiences of hyperinflation and loose government spending are left behind, the demand for institutional investment vehicles in Latin America is rapidly growing. Individuals are gaining confidence in local markets and financial institutions, and institutional investors are both broadening their domestic client base and, increasingly, moving to overseas markets. This renewed impetus to expansion of the sector has been aided by a process of institutional reform, which has led to the establishment of modern regulatory and supervisory frameworks for institutional investors. The process, however, is far from complete, and some Latin American countries are still dealing with the consequences of living with financial markets that lack the resilience necessary to serve their respective economies well.

The study focuses on the regulatory environments in which Latin American institutional investors operate. The adequacy of existing regulations is analysed from the perspective of two basic objectives: first, preventing systemic risks in the financial system and, second, ensuring the provision of adequate financial services to the population. The role of institutional investors as holders of financial assets and their impact on capital market development is also touched upon. The impact of regulations on this linkage is evaluated, with a view to determining to what extent rules need to balance objectives of financial security with those of financial development.

Regulations considered include not only prudential and protective rules that have become standard in most modern financial systems, but also certain restrictions on the operation of institutional investors and different forms of mandatory savings and insurance. These other forms of government intervention, in addition to having an impact on the two basic objectives of financial regulation, can also affect the quality and the cost of financial services. An evaluation of the role of the financial regulatory framework is incomplete without taking these effects into account.

The institutions considered are pension funds, insurance companies, and mutual funds or investment companies. From this definition are excluded government funds, such as development funds, social security funds and other related funds, like the capitalisation fund in Bolivia, which is actually administered by the new private pension funds[2]. This report also largely ignores pension funds linked to employer pension plans in all countries except Brazil, mainly because of lack of information. The order of magnitude of these funds, however, is quite small relative to the new pension funds in the larger countries and cater mainly for civil servants and military personnel[3].

Given the expected growth of pension funds in the region, as a result of the establishment of mandatory private pension plans, the study concentrates on institutional investors in countries having such plans, including Argentina, Bolivia, Chile, Colombia, El Salvador, Mexico, Peru, and Uruguay. It also includes Brazil, a country which has had a large, voluntary private pension system since the mid 70s. In addition to the largest economies in the region, the sample covers countries (such as El Salvador and Bolivia) with very little capital-market development as well as those with the most developed markets (Brazil, Argentina, and Chile). Specific reference is also made to some countries that have a significant presence in an industry (e.g. Venezuela in insurance).

The study is structured as follows. Section 1 provides an introduction to institutional investors and their relative importance in the economy. Section 2 looks at the role of laws and regulations in ensuring an efficient functioning of the institutional sector. Sections 3, 4 and 5 concentrate on pension funds, insurance companies, and mutual funds, respectively. Section 6 provides a summary of the main controversies surrounding the regulatory framework for insurance companies in Latin America. Section 7 looks at specific regulatory issues regarding the role of institutional investors in the development of capital markets. The last section presents some conclusions.

1.   Overview of institutional investors

The development of the institutional market in Latin America has been very uneven, both across time and countries. In some countries mutual funds emerged early, in the late 1970s, only to suffer a severe setback as a result of adverse market conditions. Pension funds have been a much more recent development, except in Brazil and Mexico, where funds linked to employer plans have existed since the mid-70s. The pension fund industry was given a substantial boost with the introduction of a mandatory private pension system in Chile in 1981. In most other countries, the development of the industry has also been linked to reform processes in social security in the 1990s. Finally, market penetration in the region's insurance industry, measured as the ratio of premiums to GDP, is still relatively low (less than 2%). The industry, which has traditionally been concentrated in the non-life sector, has gained much importance with the establishment of private pension systems. In countries with mandatory defined-contribution (DC) schemes, insurance companies have emerged as critical players in annuities markets and as providers of disability insurance. They have also taken advantage of the general trend towards private sector sources of retirement income by promoting other life insurance products.

As of December 1998, there were approximately US$ 300 billion in assets[4] in the ten largest Latin American countries (see Table 1). For Latin America as a whole, the total amount of funds managed by institutional investors may be as high as US$ 330 billion. In the ten countries considered, almost half of total assets managed (US$ 136 billion) are held by pension funds. Mutual funds hold a similar amount, US$ 148 billion, while insurance companies hold US$ 35 billion. Overall, the Latin American market represents a small fraction of the world institutional market. As a comparison, the estimated assets held by institutional investors in OECD countries in 1998 were approximately US$30 trillion, of which over half were held by US investors. Hence, in the global financial system, institutionally held assets in Latin America represent 1% of those held in OECD countries. The relevant measure of industry development, however, is the ratio of assets to GDP. While the ratio in Latin America is less than 10%, in OECD countries it is over 100% (OECD, 1998).

Brazil accounts for over 60% of all assets held by institutional investors in the ten countries reported. Brazilian pension funds account for over half, insurance companies for less than 30%, and mutual funds for more than 80% of all assets held by the respective industry. Brazil, therefore, has a very similar relative weight in the institutional market of Latin America as does the US in OECD countries.

Table 1 **Assets held by institutional investors in Latin America**
US $ billion (December 1998)

	Pension Funds	Insurance	Mutual Funds	Total
Argentina	11.53	4.55	7.19	22.46
Bolivia	0.33	0.04	0.24	0.62
Brazil	78.31	9.43	121.70	182.03
Chile	31.34	10.48	3.57	44.45
Colombia	2.12	1.53	0.34	3.99
El Salvador	0.05	0.10	0.00	0.15
Mexico	10.59	6.73	14.00	31.33
Peru	1.70	0.41	0.36	2.35
Uruguay	0.37	0.22	0.20	0.79
Venezuela	0.00	1.22	0.10	1.32
Total	136.34	34.72	147.71	289.49

1. The numbers do not necessarily add up because the total assets held by pension funds in mutual fund accounts are deducted from the total.
2. Assets held by the Bolivian capitalisation fund are not included.
3. Mutual fund assets are estimated based on September 1998 figures.
Source: National securities commissions, pension fund regulators, insurance supervisory agencies, Goldman Sachs, Salomon Smith Barney, ASSAL.

Table 2 **Assets held by institutional investors in Latin America**
as a percentage of GDP (December 1998)

	Pension Funds	**Insurance**	**Mutual Funds**	**Total**
Argentina	3.3	1.3	2.1	6.4
Bolivia	3.9	0.5	2.8	7.2
Brazil	10.2	1.2	15.9	23.7
Chile	40.3	13.5	4.6	57.2
Colombia	2.1	1.5	0.3	4.0
El Salvador	0.4	0.8	0.0	1.3
Mexico	2.7	1.7	3.6	8.0
Peru	2.5	0.6	0.5	3.5
Uruguay	1.3	0.8	0.7	2.8
Venezuela	0.0	1.4	0.1	1.5
Average	7.2	1.8	7.8	15.3

1.   The numbers do not always add up because the total assets held by pension funds in mutual fund accounts are deducted from the total.
2.   Assets held by the Bolivian capitalisation fund are not included.
3.   Mutual fund assets are estimated based on September 1998 figures.
Source: World Bank Development Indicators, Salomon Smith Barney.

In relative terms, however, Chile has the most developed pension fund and insurance industries of the countries considered. As shown in Table 2, Chilean pension fund assets represent over 40% of GDP, while insurance company assets represent over 13% of GDP. The difference between Chile and the other countries can largely be explained by the presence of the private pension system since 1981. All other countries, except Brazil, only began to accumulate pension assets after their pension reforms in the mid and late 1990s. In Brazil, a pension fund industry has existed since 1977, but unlike that of other Latin American countries, it is voluntary. Hence, coverage has remained very low (around 5% of the labour force).

Brazil has the largest mutual fund industry relative to the size of the economy of any Latin American country (nearly 16% of GDP). The gap between Brazil and the other countries cannot be explained, as in the case of pension fund and insurance company assets, by purely chronological factors, since mutual funds have existed in countries like Chile and Mexico for as long as they have existed in Brazil. Furthermore, mutual fund investment is voluntary in all countries. The divergent development can in fact be traced partly to the failure of mutual funds in other Latin American countries during the various financial crises that visited some of these countries in the 1980s and 1990s. In Chile, for example, mutual funds lost popularity after the banking crisis of 1981-2 severely damaged their investments. Similarly, in Mexico, mutual fund assets contracted severely after the 1995 financial crisis had dented the profitability of banks, the principal sponsors of mutual funds. In Brazil, on the other hand, mutual funds emerged as an innovative instrument in the inflationary late 1980s and early 90s by offering inflation-indexed accounts. The popularity of fixed-income mutual funds has remained high ever since.

Chile and Brazil are the only Latin American countries in which total institutionally held assets account for more than 10% of GDP. The ratio in Chile (57%) is very close to that of some OECD countries like Germany (58% in 1997), Spain (56%), and Italy (53%). It is, however, much lower than countries with well-developed capital markets like the US (203%) and the UK (200%). For the ten Latin American countries reported, the ratio of total assets of institutional investors to aggregate GDP was 15% in December 1998. These figures reflect the late and limited development that institutional investors have had in Latin America so far. At the same time, they show that there is much potential for the future development of the industry.

2.   The development of the regulatory and supervisory framework

The development of the regulatory and supervisory framework of institutional investors has followed a very different path over time and between countries. A general trend, however, can be observed in most countries, away from direct government intervention in the form of state ownership of domestic financial institutions or protection from foreign competition, towards an increased emphasis on investor protection and financial solvency. The trend, however, is by no means simultaneous. A modern regulatory regime for pension funds was established in Chile as early as 1981, while other Latin American countries have had to wait till the 1990s. In the largest Latin American financial market, Brazil, pension funds have functioned with a relatively lax regulatory regime. The government, however, is currently in the process of designing new prudential rules and introducing greater protection of consumer and employee rights.

The first industries to be established - insurance companies and mutual funds - were subject to a less onerous regulatory regime during their first years of existence than pension funds, which have been the latest entrants in the industry. Insurance industries were in fact under state control in many countries until the 1990s, when the process of liberalisation took hold in earnest. This process has been accompanied by a modernisation of the regulatory regime that has involved greater emphasis on industry competition and solvency. Even after these reforms, however, pension funds are still subject to a more stringent regulatory framework, including an industry structure that prevents the other institutional investors from providing fund management services and investment rules that are generally much tighter. This difference, while it can certainly be attributed in part to the presence of a more favourable economic and political climate and the slow pace of institutional change, is also clearly a consequence of the mandatory nature of the new private pension systems.

The mandatory nature of private pensions has placed a strong fiduciary responsibility on the government to ensure that the new institutions in charge of administering pensions work to the best advantage of affiliates. The objectives include ensuring that the institutions are free of fraudulent behaviour or other malpractice, that consumers are not exposed to excessive administrative charges, and that the assets managed by these institutions are managed with due care, so that the highest possible returns may be achieved at reasonable levels of risk. Hence, it is not surprising to find that in Latin America pension fund rules affect more aspects of their behaviour and are generally much more strict than those of the other two institutional investors. There is, however, a trend in most countries towards using the regulations applied to pension funds, especially risk-rating, valuation and other prudential rules, as a benchmark for other institutional investors.

3.   Pension funds

While personal pension plans are a new phenomenon in Latin America, mutual associations and occupational pension funds have existed since at least the 1920s in Brazil, Mexico, and other countries. In the late 70s, employer-based pension plans were formalised in Brazil. Such pension plans also exist in Mexico and in some Central American countries like Guatemala, the Dominican Republic and Panama. The recent development of the industry, and its expansion to countries like Bolivia, El Salvador, and Peru, however, is a result of the process of privatisation of social security that various countries, starting with Chile in 1981, have undertaken in recent years. This process has involved the substitution, to different degrees, of pay-as-you-go public pension systems by a fully funded, defined-contribution system, with individual pension accounts managed by pension fund administrators.

So far, eight Latin American countries have reformed their systems along these lines, including Chile in 1981, Peru in 1993, Argentina in 1994, Colombia in 1994, Uruguay in 1995, Bolivia in 1997, Mexico in 1998, and El Salvador in 1998. Of the remaining Latin American countries, Brazil is currently considering some form of pension reform, while the governments of Ecuador, Costa Rica, Venezuela, and the Dominican Republic have submitted pension reform proposals to their legislatures.

While all these new private pension systems are based on the defined-contribution model (DC), Brazil has experienced a significant development of its mainly defined-benefit (DB) employer pension plans. Private pension plans in Brazil act as a complement to the existing social security system, which remains largely unreformed. Moreover, in Brazil, most private pension plans are based on defined-benefit schemes, which is understandable given the history of high inflation experienced in the late 1980s and early 90s, up to the establishment of the Real Plan in 1994.

3.1 Market overview

Market structure

All the new private pension systems that have followed the Chilean example have a simple structure where individual pension funds are managed by specialised financial institutions called pension fund administrators or a similar name[5]. There are nine such administrators in Chile, five in Peru, fifteen in Argentina, eight in Colombia, six in Uruguay, thirteen in Mexico, and two in Bolivia. In all cases except Bolivia, there is free access to the industry as long as certain eligibility conditions are satisfied.

Bolivia's pensions market is restricted to two administrators, chosen in a bidding process. The market is divided between the two companies, with one offering services in the northern part of the country, and the other in the south. The two however, compete in the capital and other large urban areas.

Ownership of pension funds is not very diversified, with large financial institutions, especially banks and financial conglomerates, holding large stakes in pension fund administrators. An example of this structure is shown in Table 3 for the five largest pension fund administrators in Argentina. Chile, Peru, and El Salvador are the exceptions to this structure, since domestic banks and insurance companies cannot own directly pension fund administrators, though they can do so through subsidiaries. Ownership is highly concentrated, nevertheless, in these countries. Foreign companies have a strong representation in most countries. In Bolivia, for example, both pension fund administrators are majority owned by Spanish banks.

The pattern of industry concentration in Latin America is remarkably similar from country to country. The largest firms in Argentina, Chile and Mexico account for around 20-25% of total assets, with the top three holding over half of this amount, and the top five, around three quarters. The situation is similar in Colombia, Peru and Uruguay, where the largest three firms cover 60-75% of total assets.[6] In Bolivia, the two licensed pension fund administrators have a roughly equal share of the market.

In both Chile and Argentina, there has been substantial recent consolidation in the pension funds industry. In 1994, there were 26 funds in Argentina, falling to 18 at the beginning of 1998 and 15 after three recent mergers. In Chile, there were 21 funds in 1994, 13 at the beginning of 1998 and 9 now. Mexico has also experienced substantial consolidation, despite the fact that its private pension fund industry is very young. The number of fund managers has fallen from 17 in 1997 to 13 in 1999, and more mergers are expected soon. In other Latin American countries, reforms are more recent, and there were fewer funds initially (*e.g.*, nine in Colombia, five in Peru, six in Uruguay, and two in Bolivia). Hence, it is not surprising that there has been little consolidation in these countries.

Private pension plans in Brazil form a voluntary complement, or second pillar, to the social security system[7]. This second pillar consists of the so-called Complementary Pension System (*Sistema de Previdência Complementar*), established in 1977 by Law 6435 and the *Fundos de Aposentadoria Programada Individual* (FAPIs), long term investment accounts managed by mutual funds. The complementary system itself consists of closed pension funds (*Entidades Fechadas de Previdência Privada*), and open pension funds (*Entidades Abertas de Previdência Privada*). The closed funds are constituted as employer-sponsored, non-profit organisations covering the employees of a particular firm or group of firms. The open funds are constituted as insurance companies covering any worker who chooses to enrol. Brazil has by far the largest number of pension funds, with 352 closed funds sponsored by a total of 2 092 companies and 47 open funds as of October 1998.

Table 3 **Top shareholders in five largest Argentinean AFJPs**
September 1998

AFJP	Largest owner	Percentage of equity	2nd largest owner	Percentage of equity
Origenes	Banco Provincia Buenos Aires	40.7	Santander Investment, SA	39.8
Consolidar	Banco Frances	53.9	Banco de Galicia	26.9
Maxima	HSBC Banco Roberts	17.0	Banco Quilmes	17.0
Siembra	Grupo Siembra	99.0	U.S. Bank Subsidiary	1.0
Previnter	Bank of Boston AIG	90.0	Bansud	10.0

AFJP: Administratoras de Fondos de Jubilaciones y Pensiones
Source: Salomon Smith Barney, 1998

31

Open pension plans were until recently structured as DB schemes, and took the form of inflation-indexed deferred annuities, though there were some DC plans. Hence, the main players in this market are insurance companies, which carry out the four main services of a pension system: contribution collection, account administration, asset management, and benefit payment. The DB plans offer a guaranteed 6% real rate of return and between 50% and 75% of any actual excess return[8]. At retirement, the investor has the option of drawing partially or wholly the accumulated balance. Open pension plan administrators also offer other benefits, such as life, survivors, and disability insurance.

In 1998, a new form of plan, the *Plano Gerador de Benefício Livre* (PGBL) was created. The PGBL is a DC scheme with flexible contribution and investment options, and without return guarantees. Companies can contract PGBL plans for their employees, as with the 401(k) plans in the United States. Contribution rates may be altered and investors may choose between three different funds: a "sovereign" fund (government securities), a fixed-income fund, and a mixed-income fund. The PGBL administrator can invest contributions in only one of these three funds, which are managed exclusively by mutual fund companies[9]. At retirement the accumulated assets are used by the PGBL administrator to buy an inflation-indexed annuity.

While public companies were the first to organise closed pension plans, the process of privatisation and continuous expansion in the private sector has led to a predominance of funds sponsored by private firms. In October 1998 there were 257 closed-pension funds sponsored by private companies against 95 sponsored by public companies. The latter, however, still hold the vast share of assets (70%) and account for half of all affiliates.

The open fund industry is even more highly concentrated, with one fund, Bradesco, accounting for over half of all pension reserves. The three largest companies account for over 70% of industry reserves, while the five largest companies account for 84% of reserves.

Assets

Pension funds have accumulated a vast amount of assets in all countries where they have been established. Brazil and Chile account for approximately 80% of all pension assets in Latin America, Brazil by itself accounting for over half. The larger size of the private pension industry in these two countries is largely a result of their early establishment. However, relative to the size of the economy Brazilian pension fund assets have grown much more slowly than those of their Chilean counterparts despite their earlier establishment in the late 1970s. As shown in Table 4, pension fund assets in both countries were equivalent to 1%

of GDP in 1980. By 1990, however, Chilean funds had accumulated assets worth 25% of GDP, while Brazilian funds held only 3% of GDP in assets. By the end of 1997, the relative size of the sector in Chile (42% of GDP) was comparable to that in countries with well-developed private pension industries, like the US (73% of GDP), while Brazil lagged far behind, with assets equivalent to 11% of GDP. Brazil, however, compares relatively well with Spain, where there is also a voluntary, employer-based pension system, though it was formally established some time after that of Brazil, in the mid-80s. Spain's pension funds held assets equivalent to only 2% of GDP in 1997.

Table 4 **Pension-fund financial assets** as a percentage of GDP (1980-1997)

Country	1980	1990	1997
Switzerland	51	60	117
Netherlands	46	81	102
UK	23	55	75
US	24	45	73
Malaysia	18	41	55
Brazil	**1**	**3**	**11**
Chile	**1**	**25**	**42**
Spain	0	3	2

Malaysia's 1980 amount is actually 1976. Chile's 1981.
Source: Davis (1995), OECD (1999).

Table 5 **Pension funds, assets under management** million US$, 1994-98

	1994	1995	1996	1997	1998	Growth 1997-98
Argentina	517	2 492	5 323	8 816	11 526	30.7
Bolivia	0	0	0	0	332	N.A.
Brazil	55 806	60 080	70 423	79 600	78 308	-1.6
Chile	23 926	25 358	27 495	30 876	31 336	1.5
Colombia	32	270	809	1 371	2 119	54.6
El Salvador	0	0	0	0	47	N.A.
Mexico	0	0	0	755	10 594	N.A.
Peru			949	1 509	1 700	12.7
Uruguay	0	0	50	191	374	95.8

Source: Pension fund regulators

As shown in Table 5, however, growth in assets has been fastest in the more recently established pension industries, where changes in assets are mainly determined by new contributions, rather than asset yields. In the mature systems of Brazil and Chile, on the other hand, returns are a more important determinant of the growth in assets managed. Since 1994, assets under management have grown more in Brazil (40.3%) than in Chile (31%), despite a fall in total assets in Brazil in 1998.

Investments

Pension fund investment portfolios and returns in mandatory pension systems show very little variation within countries but a large degree of disparity between them. Srinivas and Yermo (1999) report average correlation between pension funds in Chile and Peru as high as 0.95. In Argentina, the average correlation is lower, 0.87. The similarity in returns means that investors gain very little by switching between pension funds in these countries, especially in those countries where returns are subject to maxima and minima. Evidence on correlation for countries that restrict the investment regime significantly such as Mexico, Bolivia and Uruguay is not meaningful, because a short time has elapsed since the start of these systems. Once the figures become available, however, it is likely that the similarity in returns will be even more striking.

While there are few differences in asset allocation or rate of return between pension funds in any one country, there are very marked contrasts across countries. As shown in Table 6, Brazil is the odd country out with 27% of its portfolio of closed funds invested in non-financial assets ("other investments"). This portion of the closed fund portfolio consists mainly of real estate (10.7%), lending to affiliates (6.3%), and lending to the sponsoring company (8.4%). The investment regime of closed funds also differs significantly from that of open funds and the FAPIs, which hold assets worth 5% and 0.1% respectively of the value of those held by closed funds. Open funds had over 89% of assets invested in fixed income securities, including 37% in government securities. The rest consisted of stocks (9.5%) and real estate (1.4%). FAPI portfolios were equally conservative, with over 97% invested in fixed income securities. Another peculiarity of the Brazilian regime is the high investment in mutual funds; almost 30% of the total portfolio for closed funds and 45% for open funds. This compares strikingly with countries having a mandatory pension system. After Brazil, Argentina had the largest investment in mutual funds, representing 7% of total assets.

Despite the fact that pension fund portfolios in countries with mandatory defined-contribution pension systems are fully invested in financial assets, there are significant differences in asset allocation between countries. In fact, in only

34

half the countries considered do pension funds invest in all asset classes. This is because in Uruguay, Bolivia, and Mexico only investments in government bonds and deposits are currently permitted, while in El Salvador, the lack of development of capital markets has forced a high concentration in fixed income securities. However, there are significant differences even between countries with similarly liberal investment regimes. Chile, for example, has a relatively high portion of its portfolio invested abroad (nearly 6% in December 1998, or US$1.8 billion). Peru is remarkable in having a low level of pension-fund investment in government securities (5%), and a high level in corporate bonds and equities. The particularity of the Peruvian regime can be traced to the government bond market's lack of depth and liquidity. Also noteworthy is the allocation to corporate bonds in Colombia, over 40%, slightly higher than that in Peru (35%), but significantly above that of any other country, since in no other case is the allocation to corporate bonds greater than 5%.

Another noteworthy aspect of the investment regime in Latin America is the large portion of fund assets invested in liquid or bank instruments, more than 20% in most cases[10]. This contrasts with the experience of OECD countries where generally less than 10% of their portfolio is invested in such instruments. While it may be possible to attribute the special behaviour of Latin American pension funds to risk aversion, the limited availability of financial products must also be an important factor.

Table 6 Pension fund portfolios (%) December 1998

	Govern-ment Securities	Corporate bonds	Financial institution securities / deposits	Equities	Invest-ment funds	Foreign securities	Other Invest.	Total
Argentina	50	3	21	18	7	0	1	100
Bolivia	68	0	32	0	0	0	0	100
Brazil	7	4	10	19	33	0	27	100
Chile	41	4	32	15	3	6	0	100
Colombia	28	18	50	3	0	0	1	100
El Salvador	74	1	25	0	0	0	0	100
Mexico	95	3	2	0	0	0	0	100
Peru	5	38	23	33	1	0	0	100
Uruguay	75	0	22	0	0	0	3	100

1. Brazilian figures include closed pension funds only
2. Colombian data as of December 1997.
3. Financial institution securities include mortgage bonds.
Source: Pension fund regulators

The asset allocation of the longest running system, the Chilean, has changed substantially over time (see Table 7). During the first five years of the system, the whole portfolio was invested exclusively in fixed- income securities (including mortgage bonds). By 1990, 11% was invested in stocks, a proportion that increased to 30% in 1995. Since 1994, pension funds have also been investing in foreign securities; diversification into overseas markets increased to 6% by December 1998, the largest share for any Latin American country. Since 1994, pension funds have halved their exposure to equities (from 30% in 1995 to 15% in 1998), mainly as a consequence of bad returns in the stock market following the Tequila and Asian crises.

Table 7 Asset allocation of pension funds in Chile (%)
1981-98

	1981	1985	1990	1995	1998
Government securities	28	42	44	39	41
Mortgage bonds	9	35	16	16	17
Time deposits	62	21	18	7	14
Shares	0	0	11	30	15
Investment funds	0	0	0	3	3
Corporate bonds	1	1	11	5	4
Foreign securities	0	0	0	0	6

Source: Superintendencia de Administradoras de Fondos de Pensiones (SAFP).

In other countries with long-running systems (Argentina, Peru, Colombia, and Uruguay), the investment regime has not changed much, partly because of the short time elapsed since the start of these systems, but also because there have been few, and small, changes in portfolio limits in these countries. The most noteworthy change is the increase in the allocation of equities in all portfolios, except in Uruguay, where such investment is still prohibited. Tables 8 to 10 show the investment allocation in Argentina, Colombia, and Peru, respectively. The allocation over time in Uruguay has remained concentrated in government securities, as in Bolivia, Mexico and El Salvador.

Table 8 Asset allocation of pension funds in Argentina (%), 1994-98

	1994	1995	1996	1997	1998
Government securities	50	53	53	43	50
Mortgage bonds	0	0	0	0	0
Time deposits	28	25	14	24	21
Shares	2	6	19	21	18
Investment funds	5	2	2	5	7
Corporate bonds	6	9	8	3	3
Foreign securities	0	1	0	0	1

Source: Superintendencia de AFJPs

Table 9 Asset allocation of pension funds in Colombia (%), 1995-98

	1995	1996	1997	1998
Government securities	29	24	21	28
Mortgage bonds	3	14	11	12
Time deposits	28	11	17	38
Shares	1	0	7	3
Investment funds	0	0	0	0
Corporate bonds	29	47	42	18
Foreign securities	0	0	0	0

Source: Superintendencia de AFPs

Table 10 Asset allocation of pension funds in Peru (%), 1993-98

	1993	1994	1995	1996	1997	1998
Government securities	32	26	22	1	0	5
Mortgage bonds	0	1	1	1	0	0
Time deposits	61	35	28	27	27	23
Shares	0	14	18	32	35	33
Investment funds	0	0	0	0	0	1
Corporate bonds	7	24	31	39	38	38
Foreign securities	0	0	0	0	0	0

Source: Superintendencia de AFPs

In Brazil, the investment regime of pension funds has not changed as much in the past few years, largely because pension funds were allowed from the start to invest in a wide range of domestic assets. Table 11 shows the investment portfolio of closed funds between December 1993 and December 1998. Mutual fund investment has been desegregated by asset class and included under the respective type of asset. The relatively high level of investment in stocks is noteworthy, having reached a record 39% of total assets in 1997.

Table 11 Brazilian closed-fund portfolio allocation, 1993-98

Instrument/Asset class	1993	1994	1995	1996	1997	1998
Govt. Securities	4	3.8	4.4	5.7	3.7	6.5
Other fixed-income secs.	26.8	25.8	31.7	31.2	30.8	36.1
Shares	34.8	39.1	29.5	33.5	39.2	29.4
Real estate	16	14.4	14.9	12.9	10.4	10.7
Lending to participants	4.2	6.5	7.7	7.3	6.4	6.3
Lending to sponsor	7.8	7.8	9.4	6.9	7.4	8.4
Other	6.4	2.6	2.5	2.4	2.2	2.6
Total	100	100	100	100	100	100

Shares include equity investment in sponsoring company.
Source: Secretaria de Previdência Complementar, ABRAPP

Open pension funds, on the other hand, invest in a much more conservative portfolio. As of November 1998, 8.5% of technical reserves were invested in stocks, 1.4% in real estate, and 36% was invested in government securities. The latter contrasts with closed funds, which have rarely invested more than 5% of their assets in such instruments. Of the other investment vehicles, FAPI invest mainly in fixed-income securities (over 95% of the portfolio), while data on the PGBL are as yet unavailable.

Table 12 Brazilian closed-fund investment in mutual funds

	Public fund	Percentage of	Private fund	Percentage of	Total assets	Percentage
	Assets (US$mill)	public assets	Assets (US$mill)	private assets	(US$mill)	Of total
FIF	8 433	14.3	6 093	23.3	14 525	17.0
FAQ	2 517	4.3	3 290	12.6	5 806	6.8
FMI	6 271	10.6	1 889	7.2	8 160	9.6
FII	372	0.6	162	0.6	534	0.6
FEE	16	0.0	6	0.0	21	0.0
FIE	86	0.1		0.0	86	0.1
Total assets	59 028	29.8	26 163	43.7	85 191	34.1

FIF and FAQ are fixed-income investment funds, FMI are mainly equity mutual funds, FII are real estate funds, FEE are foreign investment funds, and FIE are venture-capital funds.
Source: Secretaria de Previdência Complementar.

Another unique characteristic of the Brazilian system is the high level of intermediation of mutual funds in asset management and the high percentage of pension assets invested directly in mutual fund accounts. As of October 1998, 34% of assets were invested in some mutual fund (see Table 12). Private company funds invest significantly more via mutual funds than public funds (43% vs. 30%), despite the fact that external asset management is more extended among these funds[11]. The role of mutual funds in the Brazilian pension system contrasts with the experience in other Latin American countries, which have imposed low limits on investment in mutual funds (between 0 and 15% of the funds' portfolio).

Returns and commissions

To date, gross pension fund real returns have been high, but it is difficult to tell whether they compare positively with domestic benchmarks in view of the short time that has passed. For Chile, the country that has had the longest history, Srinivas and Yermo (1998) found that the 10.4% obtained over the last sixteen years was actually lower than the return that could have been obtained on a market benchmark consisting of a bond market index and a stock market index with the same volatility (standard deviation) as that of the average pension fund return. As shown in Table 13, the highest to-date return was obtained by the Argentinean system, 12.1% annual average in real terms. The lowest was Peru's at 5.1%.

Table 13 **Pension fund real annual returns**

Country	Period	Real return %	Standard deviation %
Argentina	Dec 95–Dec 98	12.1	10.9
Bolivia	Dec 97–Dec 98	7.8	N.A.
Chile	Dec 82–Dec 98	10.4	9.5
Colombia	Dec 95–Dec 98	9.9	N.A.
Peru	Dec 93–Dec 98	5.1	5.5
Uruguay	Dec 96–Dec 98	7.1	1.0

Real returns are annualized cumulative values.
Source: Pension funds regulators.

The returns actually obtained by affiliates depend also on the commissions charged by the pension fund administrators. Commission levels vary across countries, ranging from 1% in Bolivia to about 2.6% in Peru (Queisser, 1998). Commission levels have tended to fall over the past, but can still eat into a significant portion of the gross pension fund return over a long investment horizon. For example, for a forty-year horizon, the commission charged by Chilean pension funds is equivalent to 0.8% of assets, nearly 10% of the average pension fund return between 1981 and 1998.

3.2   Regulation and supervision in the new DC pension systems

Market structure

The new private pillar of the pension systems in Chile, Peru, Argentina, Colombia, Uruguay, Bolivia, Mexico, and El Salvador are all based on the same structure: a defined-contribution account for each worker in which monthly salary contributions are invested. The provision and management of pension accounts and related services are restricted to specialised financial institutions exclusively dedicated to this task[12]. These institutions often collect the contributions as well. In Mexico, however, collection is carried out by a centralised agency. Pension funds cannot offer annuities, but must instead contract them out to insurance companies. They can, however, offer other types of pension benefits, such as disability.

Ownership of pension fund administrators is restricted in some countries. In Chile, Peru, and El Salvador, for example, domestic banks, insurance companies, and mutual funds are prohibited from owning pension fund administrators. The subsidiaries of these financial institutions, however, may invest in them. On the other hand, there are few restrictions in any country on ownership by foreign financial institutions, including pension fund administrators from other Latin American countries. In El Salvador, only foreign companies that do not already own domestic financial institutions are allowed to invest in pension fund administrators. Foreign majority ownership in that country is allowed only if there are national or Central American shareholders. In Colombia, public sector institutions, co-operatives, labour unions, and various "social" funds are also allowed to be shareholders of pension fund administrators. Ownership is also liberalised in Argentina and Mexico.

Licensing

Licensing is carried out by the supervisory agency after compliance with certain conditions, which include a minimum capital, a "fit and proper" test, and maintenance of adequate investment reserves. In Bolivia, however, licensing was carried out by a public bidding process which, in addition to these conditions, required a maximum level for the fees charged by pension fund administrators on individual accounts.

Plan design

Workers in all countries are permitted to invest their monthly pension contributions only in the pension fund accounts. In Colombia, however, the law allows the supervisory agency to authorise alternative capitalisation and pension plans, although this has not happened yet. In most countries, workers are permitted to invest in only one account, though the Mexican and Colombian laws permit two, subject to authorisation by the regulator. Chile too, is considering moving to a two-fund system.

While workers are free to choose their pension fund administrator, the transfer between administrators is restricted in some countries. In Mexico, affiliates may switch funds only once a year. In Peru and El Salvador, they may switch only every six months. Pension fund administrators are allowed to charge additional commissions to departing affiliates, but these are usually determined by the regulatory agency.

Commissions

Commissions have to be set as a percentage of salaries (or contributions[13]) in all countries except Mexico, where pension funds have the freedom to establish commissions as a percentage of assets managed and as a percentage of returns. Some countries have established maximum limits on the fees that pension funds can charge. In Chile the total commission charged (including and insurance premiums) cannot exceed 3%. In Bolivia a bidding contract between the regulator and the pension fund administrator stipulates that commissions cannot exceed 1% of salaries. Charging fees on inactive accounts is also prohibited.

Custody

Custody of pension-fund assets is restricted in all countries to authorised institutions, which in some countries include private companies. In Chile, for example, all securities are under the custody of the *Deposito Central de Valores*, a private entity.

Fund governance and fiduciary responsibility

Fund governance rules require the separation of the fund from the administering company; they also require the establishment of an internal control system and external auditing to ensure the fulfilment of rules on conflict of interest. Regulations on fiduciary responsibility tend to spell out what pension fund administrators may not do in order to avoid conflicts of interest, rather than what they should do to in order to maximise the value of investments. There are no requirements to manage funds with "due diligence" or as a "prudent-person" as in Anglo-Saxon countries. Instead, there is a set of investment rules, a set of prohibitions on the behaviour of pension fund administrators and certain constraints, including:

- A prohibition on revealing reserved information on the investment decisions of the pension funds.

- A prohibition on choosing directors in private companies having a link to pension fund administrators.

- Rules and conditions for the election of directors of the pension fund administrator to ensure that their sole objective is managing the fund as well as possible.

Valuation and risk rating

Valuation of pension fund assets at market prices is carried out by the pension fund administrators in all countries on a daily basis. In Argentina, however, up to 30% of the pension fund's portfolio may be invested in government securities kept in an investment account and valued at maturity prices. This limit was raised in September 1998 from the previous limit of 25%, and the law envisages it being raised to 50%.

Risk rating of pension assets is required in all countries except Colombia. In Chile, Bolivia, and Argentina the minimum acceptable risk category for fixed-income securities is BBB or equivalent. The law in these countries requires that *all* investments - not just fixed-income securities - be rated. In Chile, the rating system for stocks meant that only 30 - mainly blue chip - companies out of a total of approximately 300 listed were eligible for pension fund investment until 1997. The new capital market reform bill, approved that year, extended coverage to more than 200 companies with smaller capitalisation and to other financial instruments, such as project financing, securitised bonds and venture capital.

Investment management and rules

Pension fund administrators are solely responsible for the management of pension funds. Contracting out to mutual funds or other financial institutions is not allowed. Investment is only allowed in formal, recognised markets, although some countries permit some level of investment in over-the-counter instruments (mainly derivatives) and in securitised assets. These investments, however, are restricted by portfolio limits (see below).

In all countries, pension funds are subject to standard prudential guidelines to ensure a minimum degree of diversification and avoid conflict of interest. Table 14 summarises the features of the main prudential guideline.. Restrictions are also imposed on investment in securities of a specific foreign issuer, and in a specific investment fund. There are also rules to limit conflict of interest. In Chile, for example, investment in securities of an issuer linked to the pension fund administrator cannot represent more than 0.5% of the fund's assets. The maximum for all issuers so linked is set at 5%.

In all countries tight restrictions are imposed on the percentage of a company's capital that a pension fund can hold. These limits, however, vary widely between countries. For company stock, the lowest limit is in Argentina (5%), while the highest is in Peru's at 15% of the total stock.. For bonds of the same series, the range of limits is less wide, the highest being Peru's at 25% of the total issue.

In addition, pension funds are subject to quantitative limits on their investments by asset class. Table 15 describes the most important portfolio limits in Latin American countries. All countries have tight portfolio limits, but the most flexible systems currently are in Chile, Argentina, Colombia, and Peru (probably in that order). They are the only countries that permit equity and foreign investment (Chile has the highest limit on shares - 37% - and on foreign assets - 12%). In Bolivia, although the legislated limits on shares and foreign assets have been set at relatively high levels (50-90 and 10-50%, respectively), funds have to invest at least a minimum amount in government bonds. In the first few months of the system, this was set at $180 million per annum, only just below the actual flow of funds into the funds. Even though space for alternative instruments was soon created, pension funds have only been able to invest in time deposits, since no private sector capital market instruments have as yet been risk rated[14]. In general, the limits encourage government debt holdings at the expense of equity and foreign assets.

Table 14 **Prudential Investment Guidelines in Latin American Pension Systems**

	Bonds of same Issuer	Shares of same company	Specific risks
Argentina	Lowest of: (i) 5% of fund, (ii) 20% of bond series.	(i) 2.5% of fund. (ii) 5% of company's public capital	Various rules by risk of assets including, e.g. minimum risk rating for fixed-income securities BBB.
Bolivia	(i) 5% of fund, except government securities (10%). (ii) 20% of same bond series.	(i) 5% of fund, except government securities (10%). (ii) 5% of company's public capital.	Various rules by risk of assets including, e.g. minimum risk rating for fixed-income securities BBB.
Chile	Lowest of: (i) 7% of fund times risk factors, (ii) 20% of series.	Lowest of: (i) 5% of fund times concentration factor times liquidity factor times accounting assets factor; (ii) 7% of company's public capital.	Various rules by risk of assets including, e.g. minimum risk rating for fixed-income securities BBB.
Colombia	(i) 10% of fund, (ii) 10% of bond series.	(i) 5% of fund. (ii) 10% of company's public capital	Not regulated.
El Salvador	(i) 5% of fund, (ii) 20% of bond series.	(i) 5% of fund. (ii) 5% of company's public capital	Not yet established
Mexico	(i) 10% of fund, (ii) 10% of bond series.	Equity investment not permitted	Issues must have been awarded two highest rates. (three for maturities shorter than a year).
Peru	(i) 10% of fund, (ii) 25% of bond series.	(i) 7.5% of fund. (ii) 15% of company's public capital	No specific limits
Uruguay	Not regulated	Equity investment not permitted	Not regulated.

Source: Pension fund regulators

Uruguay and Mexico have the most restrictive regimes, although, as in Bolivia, they are supposed to be only temporary. In Uruguay, pension funds are subject to both minimum and maximum limits on investment in government securities. The band is expressed as percentage of the portfolio, and there is a phased programme in which the band is to fall from 80-100% in 1996 to 40-60% in 2000. The laws allow the amount above the band to be invested in any security, but only time deposits have so far been approved. In Mexico, the regulator has so far approved only fixed-income instruments (largely government securities).[15]

Table 15 **Portfolio limits in mandatory pension systems**
(%), December 1998

	Argentina	Chile	Bolivia[a]	Peru	Colombia	Mexico	Uruguay	El Salvador
Government securities	50	50	Min. $180m No max.	40	50	100	Min.75 Max. 85[b]	100[c]
Corporate bonds	40	45	30-45	49	20	35	25	30
Financial inst. Sec./deposits	28	50	50	30	50	10	30	40
Shares	35	37	20-40	35	30	0	25	5
Investment companies/ mutual funds	14	10	5-15	15	5	0	0	0
Foreign Securities	10	13	10-50	10	10	0	0	0
Hedging instruments	2	9	0-5	10	0	0	0	0

a.   Bolivia has not issued regulations for the actual limits. The bands are those established by law.
b.   Up from 80 to 100 in 1996. The legislated limits were 70 to 90 in 1997, 60 to 80 in 1998, 50 to 70 in 1999, 40 to 60 in 2000, 30 to 60 in 2001 to 2005.   The difference can be invested in securities not issued by the central state.
c.   Limit includes investment in Fondo Social para la Vivienda (max 40%), Banco Multisectorial de Inversiones (max. 30%), central government securities (30%), and Central Bank securities (30%).
Source: Pension fund regulators

Investment guidelines for pension funds have tended to become more liberal over time, permitting and extending investments in equities, foreign assets and less liquid assets, such as real estate and venture capital. Changes in portfolio limits in Chile, the country with the longest experience, are shown in Table 16. Investment in equities was not allowed until 1985, while investment in foreign securities was not permitted until 1992. Both limits have gradually been increased, from 30 to 37% of the portfolio in the case of stocks, and from 9 to 12% of the portfolio in the case of foreign securities. Meanwhile, limits on fixed-income securities have been lowered. Investment in government securities was capped at 100% in 1981, but in 1998 it stood at 50%. In the case of mortgage-backed securities the limit has been reduced from 70% in 1981 to 50% in 1998. The limit on corporate bonds has fallen from 60 to 45% over the same period.

Table 16 Evolution of portfolio limits in Chile (%), 1981-1998

Asset	1981	1982	1985	1990	1992	1995	1996	1997	1998
Government securities	100	100	50	45	45	50	50	50	50
Corporate bonds	60	60	40	40	40	40	45	45	45
Convertible			10	10	10	10	10	10	10
Mortgage-backed securities	70	40	40	50	50	50	50	50	50
Letters of credit	70	40	40	50	50	50	50	50	50
Fixed term deposits	70	40	40	50	50	50	50	50	50
Shares, public companies			30	30	30	37	37	37	37
Mutual funds				10	10	10	10	10	10
Real estate funds				10	10	10	10	10	10
Venture capital funds							5	5	5
Credit funds							5	5	5
Foreign securities					3	9	9	12	12
Fixed-income						9	9	12	12
Variable-income						4.5	4.5	6	6
Hedging instruments						9	9	9	12

Source: Superintendencia de Administradoras de Fondos de Pensiones

Performance rules and guarantees

Some countries - Chile, Argentina, Peru, Uruguay, and Colombia - require pension funds to achieve rates of return above a prescribed minimum, typically calculated relative to the industry average (Table 17). In addition, Chile, Argentina, Uruguay and Colombia impose a maximum on pension fund returns, which is also calculated as a percentage of the industry average. Argentina and Chile define their profitability band in relative terms: the minimum of 2 percentage points and 50% (Chile) or 30% (Argentina) above and below the average annual return of the industry[16]. The supervisory agency monitors compliance with the minimum on a monthly basis. All fund administrators have to establish a reserve fund with their own capital (invested in the same way as the pension fund). If the reserve is insufficient to top up the fund's return to the minimum, the government guarantees the minimum return.

Table 17 Pension fund performance regulations and government guarantees in Latin America

	Minimum rate of return	Maximum rate of return	Government guarantee
Argentina	Relative to average	relative to average	Yes
Bolivia	——	——	No
Chile	Relative to average	relative to average	Yes
Colombia	Relative to average and market benchmark	——	Yes
El Salvador	Relative to average	relative to average	Yes
Mexico	——	——	No
Peru	relative to average and minimum absolute return (0 per cent real over 5 years)	——	No
Uruguay	Relative to average (2 per cent real for República)	relative to average	yes

1)	Maximum removed in Peru in November 1996. Minimum legislated but regulations not yet issued
Source:	Pension fund regulators

In Peru the minimum return was calculated in the same way as in Chile up to 1997, but it was not guaranteed by the government. In 1997 the floor was lowered further to 25 percent of the average return or 3 percentage points below the average, and the period of calculation was increased to 60 months. In addition, an absolute minimum return of 0 percent in real terms was introduced, also calculated over a five year period. There is no maximum return: the ceiling was eliminated in November 1996. In Uruguay, the guarantee is expressed in both absolute and relative terms. The state-managed fund guarantees a minimum real return of 2% a year, while private pension administrators have to create a guarantee fund (similar to the reserve fund in Argentina and Chile). This fund is drawn down if the return falls below the average of the industry by more than 2 percentage points. There is also a limit on the maximum return that funds can earn. Because the state-managed fund - *República* - dominates the market average (56% of total assets in May 1998), other pension funds are also forced to reach the 2% real return. In Colombia, the minimum return is calculated as the arithmetic average of the return of the pension fund industry over three years and the return over three years on a market portfolio[17]. No ceiling is placed on the returns. The regulator checks compliance with the stipulated minimum return on a three-month basis.

Retirement phase

In all countries except Uruguay, workers have at least two basic benefit options. They may draw down the balance in a programmed withdrawal, or buy an annuity. The programmed withdrawal method is subject to restrictions on the portion of the accumulated balance that can be drawn every year. The purchase of an annuity is only open to pensioners who have enough funds in their balances to guarantee a minimum pension. Some countries, like Chile, offer a third option, the deferred annuity, in which part of the accumulated balance is consumed and another part is left invested up to a programmed date, when an annuity is bought. The value of the portion of the accumulated balance that is consumed is regulated. In Chile, for example, affiliates may not buy deferred annuities that involve the consumption of more than 50% of the accumulated balance before purchase of the annuity. In Uruguay, the purchase of annuities by retirement workers is mandatory.

Information to affiliates

By law, the pension fund administrators are requested to send regular statements to their affiliates on the amounts contributed, total account balance, returns, and commissions and insurance premiums charged. Such reports are sent on a monthly basis in most countries. In Colombia, however, the minimum frequency is quarterly. In addition, regulations require pension fund managers to publish annual reports on the firm's activities and governance structure.

Supervision

Control and supervision of the operations of pension-fund administrators is based on daily reports of their investment transactions and monthly reports on their financial position and overall performance. In some of the Latin American countries that have set-up private pension industries, the supervisory agency is autonomous and is financed mainly from a supervision fee levied on the pension funds (see Table 18).

Table 18 **Institutional characteristics of pension-fund supervisory agencies in Latin America**

Country	Area of government	Administration	Funding source
Argentina	Ministry of Labour and Social Security	Autonomous	Supervision fee
Bolivia	Treasury	Not autonomous	Supervision fee
Chile	Ministry of Labour and Social Security	Not autonomous	National budget
Colombia	Central Bank	Not autonomous	Supervision fee
Mexico	Secretary of Treasury	Autonomous	Supervision fee (partial)
Peru	Ministry of Economy	Autonomous	Supervision fee
Uruguay	Central Bank	Not autonomous	National budget

Source: Demarco and Rofman (1998)

3.3   *Regulation and supervision of pension funds in Brazil*

Vesting and portability

There are no formal vesting or portability rules for closed funds. Open pension-fund plans have immediate vesting and offer full portability. The legislation establishes a maximum period of two years between a request for liquidation and the actual closure of the account (and transfer of funds, if required). The degree of portability is, in practice, restricted in traditional plans by the penalty fees charged by open-fund administrators if the plan is cancelled before the scheduled date. For one of the largest plans, the fee is 4% of accumulated assets if the plan is cancelled after one year, 3% after two years, and 2% if cancelled at any other date. Hence, transferring plans is a costly option. These fees are not regulated.

Funding rules

Closed funds are subject to minimum funding-levels, but the methodology for their calculation is not specified. The accumulated benefit obligation (ABO) must be fully-funded, while up to 70% of the projected obligation must be covered[18]. The remaining 30% can be covered with assets held by the sponsoring employer. The method for managing funding deficits and surpluses is not specified either. Funding rules for open funds are much tighter, and more severely enforced, than those for closed funds.

Minimum capital, fiduciary responsibility, governance

Open funds are subject to minimum capital requirements similar to those of insurance companies; these vary depending on where the company operates. A fund that operates nationally requires a minimum capital of R$ 4.2 million. One that operates in the Sao Paulo region requires only R$ 2.1 million. Insurance companies that own open funds, however, are subject to additional capital requirements if they operate in other insurance sectors (see section on insurance companies). Closed funds must be set up as foundations and be legally separate from sponsoring employers. The law also provides for the use of independent custodian institutions. The existence of large automated clearing centres for the three major types of securities (government bonds, corporate bonds, and corporate equities) makes the offer of custodian services easier and more economical.

Investment regulations

Unlike pension funds in other Latin American countries, those in Brazil (both open and closed) can contract out asset management to mutual funds and other financial institutions. Investment is subject to prudential rules. The investment regime that was put in place in Brazil in 1994[19] includes limits by asset class and individual security, but does not include limits by risk or liquidity. Prudential rules are similar to those in other Latin American countries: pension funds may not invest more than 10% of their portfolio in the equity of a given company or in the securities of any single issuer.

The investment regime by asset class, on the other hand, is more liberal than that in other Latin American countries (see Table 19). In addition to investing in bank deposits and securities, Brazilian closed pension funds can lend up to 10% of their portfolio to the sponsoring company and another 10% to affiliates. They can also invest up to 19% of the portfolio in real estate. Open funds can lend up to 10% of their portfolio to affiliates and can invest up to 10% in real estate. These investments are banned in other Latin American countries.

Investment rules for FAPIs and PGBLs in Brazil are broadly similar to those of other Latin American countries. Lending and investment in real estate is not allowed, and investment in mutual funds is limited to 10% (5% fixed income, 5% equity mutual funds). The investment limit on stocks however is as high as that of traditional pension funds, namely 50%. These individual pension funds, therefore, have the most liberal portfolio limits of any Latin American country.

Table 19 **Brazil: Closed and open pension fund portfolio limits(%), December 1998**

	Open funds: minimum capital	Open funds: technical reserves	Closed funds
Govt. Securities	100	100	100
Other fixed-income secs.	60	80	80
State and municipal debt			50
Shares, plcs	50	50	50
Real estate	0	30	19[2]
Real estate funds			10
Venture-capital funds			5
Lending to participants	0	10	10
Lending to sponsor	0	0	10
Foreign securities (1)			10
Hedging instruments			5

(1)   Investment permitted via mutual funds only.
(2)   Ceiling programmed to fall to 18% in 1999, 17% in 2000, 16% in 2001, and 15% in 2002.
Source: Secretaria de Previdência Complementar, SUSEP

Benefit and return guarantees

Neither closed nor open funds are subject to statutory benefit or return guarantees, but minimum-return regulations are in place. The minimum rate of return is 6% in real terms but while, in the case of closed funds, this is used as the reference discount return when calculating funding levels, it is used as the actual return on portfolios of traditional open plans.

4. Insurance companies

The insurance business is divided into two main sectors: general and life insurance. General insurance covers risks on auto accidents, theft, fire, and natural disasters (such as earthquakes). Traditionally, the business of insurance companies in Latin America has concentrated on general services. As a result of the reform of pension systems in the region, however, the life insurance sector has been given a new impetus. The new systems, since they are DC schemes, involve insurance companies in the retirement phase. Participants are given the option of purchasing an annuity provided by insurance companies with the totality or a portion of their accumulated assets. Insurance companies also contract disability and survivor's insurance in all countries that have reformed their pension systems except Mexico, where the task has been retained by the *Instituto Mexicano de Seguridad Social*.

Currently, most insurance company-activity in the new pension systems is limited to the active period, in other words, coverage for disability and survival risks. The exception is Chile, where today the insurance sector also offers life annuities coverage to the passive sector. This is a consequence of the establishment of the DC system in 1981. As other DC systems begin to mature in the coming decades, a surge in the life- insurance sector may be expected. In addition, insurance companies are increasingly tapping the voluntary savings sector with new life insurance products that allow investors to reap rewards from investment in capital markets.

Private health-care insurance may also be given a boost by health-care reform, as it is slowly unfolding in the region. Chile and Colombia abolished their state health-care monopolies when they carried out pension reform (1981 and 1994, respectively). In both countries employees make mandatory contributions for health services that complement basic state health care. Contributions are paid into the privately managed funds, administered by managed care organisations. Employees are able to choose freely between private providers. Reform is also under way in Argentina, Mexico, and Venezuela.

4.1 Market overview

Market structure

Unlike pension products, which tend to be homogenous, insurance products vary significantly in design and properties with the type of risk covered. In all cases, however, the agreement consists of a legally binding contract between the insured person or firm and the insurance company. The contract stipulates the conditions under which compensation may be claimed for insured losses. Such conditions vary considerably depending on whether they apply to a life insurance or general-insurance product.

There is a strong presence of foreign companies in Latin America (see Table 20). Chile and Mexico have the most foreign insurers, with the total number of foreign companies very close to that of local firms.

Table 20 **Market structure of insurance industry (1997)**

Country	All insurers	Local insurers	Foreign insurers
Argentina	276	N.A.	N.A.
Bolivia	17	17	0
Brazil	128	102	26
Chile	52	25	27
Colombia	37	24	13
Ecuador	42	39	3
Mexico	60	33	27
Paraguay	45	43	2
Peru	15	10	5
Uruguay	18	18	0
Venezuela	72	N.A.	N.A.
Total / average	769	N.A.	N.A.

Source: International Insurance Council (1998)

Table 21 **Market share, percentage of total market premiums**
June 1998

Brazil		Mexico	
Sul America	19	Hidalgo	20
Bradesco	16	Nacional Provincial	25
ITAU	8	Comercial America	13
Porto Seguro	6	Monterrey Aetna	13
HSBC Bamerindus	5	Genesis	7
Unibanco	4	Banamex	3
AGF	3	Bancomer	3
Paulista	3	Others	16
Golden Cross	3		
Others	33		

Source: National Insurance Federation (Brazil), Actualidad en Seguros y Finanzas, CNSF, Dec. 1998.

Market concentration is relatively low in the largest market, Brazil. The largest company accounts for less than 20% of total premiums, while the largest five accounts for only half the market. In Mexico, concentration is much higher, with the five largest companies accounting for nearly 80% of the market (see Table 21).

Premiums

Total premiums in 1997 amounted to US$ 31 billion in the eleven largest Latin American markets (see Table 22). Of these, Brazil accounts for half of premium income, while four countries (Argentina, Brazil, Chile and Mexico) account for over 85% of total premium income and over 90% of life premiums. The average ratio of non-life to life premiums in the region is approximately 3:1, and in fact in no country except Chile is the ratio less than 1:1. The are, however, huge discrepancies in the distribution of premium income by sector. The highest ratio is Venezuela's, at 48:1, while the lowest is Chile's at 0.6:1. The relatively larger size of the life sector in Chile is due to the maturity of its DC pension system, and the consequent greater development of the annuities market. Among non-life services, motor-vehicle insurance stands out as the largest in terms of premium income.

Table 22 Premiums (US$ million), December 1997

	Total premiums	Non-life-insurance premiums	Life-insurance premiums	Ratio non-life to life premiums
Argentina	4 868	3 487	1 381	2.5
Bolivia	54	47	7	6.7
Brazil	15 029	12 231	2 815	4.3
Chile	2 332	862	1 469	0.6
Colombia	1 929	1 525	405	3.8
Ecuador	248	221	28	7.9
Mexico	4 097	2 700	1 397	1.9
Paraguay	100	95	5	19.0
Peru	508	420	88	4.8
Uruguay	360	236	124	1.9
Venezuela	1 041	1 020	21	48.6
Total / average	30 566	22 844	7 740	3.0

Source: International Insurance Council (1998)

In general, the industry is still relatively underdeveloped, and the level of penetration is low. As shown in Table 23, on average countries in this region have a premium share of GDP of less than 2%, compared with 8.6% in the US or 6.5% in Canada. Chile has the highest ratio of premiums to GDP at 3.3. On a per capita basis, premiums average US$ 65, which contrasts with US$ 2,576 in the US and US$ 726 in Spain in 1997. Differences across countries are relatively smaller in the non-life than in the life sector. Again, Chile exhibits the greatest contrast, where life premiums per capita were more than twice those of any other country. After Chile, the level of penetration in the life-insurance sector is highest in Uruguay and Argentina.

Table 23 **Premium Income in Latin America (1997)**

	Total Premiums/ GDP (%)	Per capita total (US$)	Per capita non-life (US$)	Per capita life (US$)
Argentina	1.54	138	99	39
Bolivia	1.73	7	6	1
Brazil	2.34	95	77	18
Chile	3.33	161	59	102
Colombia	2.79	49	39	10
Ecuador	1.20	21	19	2
Mexico	1.29	42	28	14
Paraguay	1.18	20	19	1
Peru	0.82	21	17	4
Uruguay	1.25	113	74	39
Venezuela	1.55	47	46	1
Total / average	1.73	65	44	21

Source: International Insurance Council (1998), FIDES (1997)

Growth in the insurance market over the past few years has been highest in Brazil, Peru, Colombia and Chile (see Figure 1). On the other hand, premium income has actually fallen in Venezuela and Mexico, largely as a result of the economic crisis experienced by both countries in 1994-5. In Venezuela, the 1994 banking crisis bankrupted many insurance companies that belonged to financial conglomerates. Since then, a restructuring process has taken place, but some companies are still in a special government fund (FOGADE) pending sale or liquidation. Meanwhile, Argentina and Ecuador have seen poor growth, mainly as a result of adverse economic conditions following the Tequila crisis. In Argentina, this was compounded by an internal crisis in the insurance sector triggered by the failing and consequent closure of INDER, the state owned reinsurance company, as local insurers had to contend with unpaid claims. With the return of the region to a growth path in 1999, it is expected that premium income will continue to expand. For the long term, the prospects of the industry are good, as a result of higher longevity in the region, a rapid process of urbanisation, and the greater maturity of the new DC private pension systems, which will require more intermediation on the part of the insurance industry (especially for life and disability insurance).

Figure 1: Average growth in premiums, 1993-7, percent

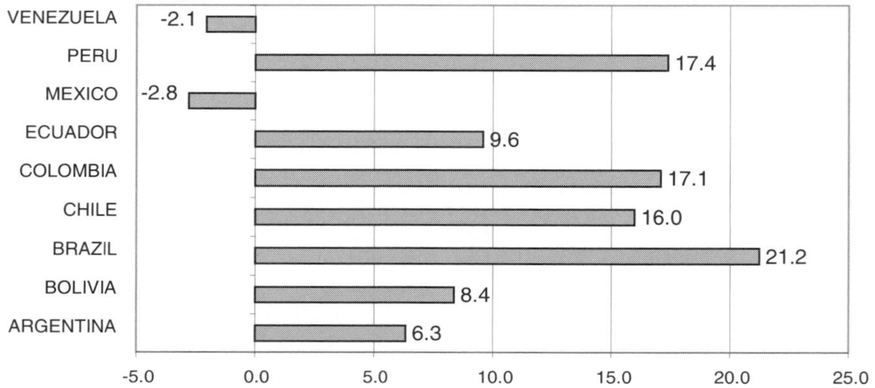

Source: FIDES (1998)

Assets and portfolio investment

Latin American insurance companies had built up assets totalling nearly US$58 billion at the end of 1997 (see Table 24). Over a third of these assets are held by Brazilian insurance companies, 19% by Chilean, 17 by Mexican and 13% by Argentinean companies. Growth in assets was highest in the Southern Cone between 1990 and 1997, while total assets fell in only one country, Venezuela. As a whole, Latin American insurance assets grew by 23% a year between 1990 and 1997.

Total assets of insurance companies can be divided into two main groups: financial and non-financial. The main non-financial assets are real estate and credit entries (such as premiums to be collected) in the insurance company's balance sheets. Most Latin American countries do not separate real estate from financial assets in their statistics. Table 25 contains information on the evolution of financial assets and real estate in the main Latin American markets between December 1990 and December 1998. The picture is similar to that of total assets. The highest growth occurred in Argentina (36.5% annual average), followed by Chile (24.2% annual average).

Table 24 Insurance company financial and non-financial assets
1990-97

	Assets (US$ million)		Growth	% Lat. Am.
	1990	1997	1990-97 (%)[a]	Market (1997)
Argentina	1 860.9	7 255.0	21	13
Bolivia	50.7	72.3	5	0
Brazil	-	21 042.8	N.A.	36
Colombia	1 215.2	4 308.0	20	7
Costa Rica	208.4	516.9	14	1
Cuba	97.4	245.4	14	0
Chile	2 080.0	10 757.2	26	19
Ecuador	86.7	217.0	14	0
El Salvador	118.5	207.8	8	0
Guatemala	73.1	194.4	15	0
Honduras	67.9	110.8	7	0
Mexico	5 063.2	9 580.9	10	17
Panama	305.9	461.5	6	1
Paraguay	26.5	121.7	24	0
Peru	530.0	753.6	5	1
R. Dominicana	134.1	251.1	9	0
Uruguay	189.8	438.0	13	1
Venezuela	1 595.3	1 321.0	-3	2
Total	**13 703.7**	**57 855.4**	**23**	**100**

a.   Average annual growth
Source: Asociación de Superintendentes de Seguros de América Latina (ASSAL).

Table 25 Insurance company investment portfolio, US$ million
1990-8

	1990	1991	1992	1993	1994	1995	1996	1997	1998	1990-98(%)[a]
Argentina	378.4	819.2	1 035.6	1 410.3	1 635.8	2 108.0	2 688.7	3 662.0	4 551.4	36.5
Brazil	-	-	-	3 034.9	4 073.8	7 164.5	10 701.4	12 534.0	9 430.4	N.A.
Colombia	424.6	517.1	587.5	812.9	1 213.0	982.1	1 217.4	1 911.2	1 531.2	17.4
Chile	1 851.6	2 539.5	3 342.1	4 154.7	5 868.8	7 119.9	8 493.0	9 865.5	10 483.4	24.2
El Salvador	56.2	64.2	66.3	83.4	102.0	119.0	110.2	110.7	100.1	7.5
Mexico	3 228.1	4 423.4	5 617.5	6 810.0	4 619.0	4 315.1	5 292.4	6 232.1	6 728.3	9.6
Peru	103.6	151.9	210.9	205.5	217.4	305.1	247.0	353.3	413.1	18.9
Uruguay	98.9	88.3	73.7	119.4	142.7	166.5	198.2	200.7	219.6	10.5
Venezuela	1 028.2	1 307.5	1 332.4	1 304.3	768.9	711.8	774.9	1 086.0	1223.0	2.2
Total	7 169.6	9 911.0	12 266.0	17 935.3	18 641.3	22 991.9	29 723.2	35 955.5	25 250.0	N.A.

a.   Average annual growth
Source: Asociación de Superintendentes de Seguros de América Latina (ASSAL).

Table 26 shows the investment allocation of insurance companies across countries. Certain similarities with pension funds may be noted. Brazil stands out for its high level of investment in mutual funds (36.7%). Investment in foreign securities is very limited, except in Uruguay (3.3%). In most countries, the majority of the portfolio is invested in fixed income securities (e.g. 75% of investments in Argentina), but two countries (Bolivia and Uruguay) have a high concentration of the portfolio in real estate (75% and 33%, respectively). For some countries, statistics also exist for investment by insurance activity. In Argentina, investment in stocks is highest in the life insurance sector (14%), while investment in fixed- income securities is highest in the retirement sector (85% of total assets).

Most countries also report some forms of lending in their investment portfolio. This is the case of Argentina, Bolivia, Chile, El Salvador, and Uruguay. Such assets are reported as "other" in Table 26, and include mainly lending to holders of life insurance policies. In Uruguay, the "other" entry also includes investment for retirement account that has not been desegregated. Hence, the larger figure for this country.

Table 26 Insurance company investment portfolios (%)
December 1998

	Govern-ment Securities	Corpo-rate bonds	Fin. inst. sec. and deposits	Equities	Invest. funds	Real estate	Foreign securi-ties	Other invest.	Total
Argentina	36.3	3.8	34.2	10.3	10.7	N.A.	0.0	4.7	100
Bolivia	0.0	0.0	23.4	0.0	0.0	75.0	0.0	1.6	100
Brazil	46.3	0.6	3.1	7.1	36.7	6.2	0.0	0.0	100
Chile	39.2	7.2	33.8	3.6	10.9	8.4	1.1	2.1	100
Colombia									
El Salvador	17.3	14.7	54.5	0.0	0.0	4.8	0.0	8.7	100
Mexico									100
Peru									100
Uruguay	29.2	1.1	17.5	0.0	0.0	33.4	3.1	15.7	100

Source: Insurance company regulators, Insurance company associations.

Table 27 shows the evolution of the investment portfolio of insurance companies in Argentina since 1994. As with pension funds, there has been a certain reduction in exposure to stocks and an increase in investment in mutual funds and fixed-income securities. Lending too has fallen significantly, from 4.3% in 1994 to 1.6% in 1998.

Table 27 **Argentina: Insurance company investments(%), 1994-98**

	1994	1995	1996	1997	1998
Government securities	24.0	23.4	25.7	28.7	36.3
Stocks	13.9	12.0	14.0	13.7	10.3
Time deposits	53.8	57.4	47.2	40.2	34.2
Corporate bonds	0.2	0.6	1.1	3.2	3.8
Mutual funds				8.7	10.7
Lending	4.3	3.7	4.1	2.4	1.6
Other investments	3.8	2.8	7.8	3.1	3.1
Total assets-$US million	1 636	2 108	2 689	3 662	4 551

Source: Superintendencia de Seguros

As shown in Table 28, the investment regime in Chile has also varied somewhat over time, with an increase in the portion invested in stocks increasing up to 1994, and decreasing thereafter. Total investment in fixed-income securities has remained very high, increasing from 83.8 in 1989 to 88% in 1998. Insurance companies invest less in foreign securities (1.1%) and mutual funds (1.4%) than pension funds do (6 and 3%, respectively).

Table 28 **Chile: Insurance-company investments(%), 1989-98**

	1989	1990	1991	1992	1993	1994	1995	1996	1997	1998
Government securities	31.1	38.5	37.0	39.5	41.4	38.9	39.3	38.4	38.2	39.2
Mortgage securities	15.4	14.0	12.9	12.5	14.7	15.9	18.1	20.7	22.7	25.4
Time deposits	13.6	6.4	5.9	5.1	4.7	3.8	2.8	3.3	1.8	2.6
Stocks	6.8	5.5	9.1	9.5	8.9	11.5	10.4	7.2	5.8	3.6
Corporate bonds	18.4	19.4	19.0	16.7	14.0	12.8	10.4	8.4	6.4	7.2
Bank bonds	1.4	1.8	2.0	2.2	2.0	2.1	1.8	3.7	5.1	5.4
Liquidity	0.7	0.6	0.5	0.6	0.7	0.4	0.5	0.4	0.4	0.4
Other	1.9	1.5	1.8	1.9	1.8	1.2	1.6	1.8	1.9	2.1
Real estate	9.4	10.2	8.9	8.3	7.4	7.8	8.4	7.8	7.4	8.4
Mortgage mutuals	1.3	2.3	2.8	3.6	4.5	5.0	5.6	6.7	7.9	9.5
Mutual funds	-	-	-	-	-	0.6	1.1	1.3	1.4	1.4
Foreign securities	-	-	-	-	-	0.1	0.1	0.3	0.7	1.1
Total (US$ million)	1 308	1 854	2 541	3 342	4 155	5 869	7 120	8 490	9 859	10 483

Source: Superintendencia de Valores y Seguros

4.2   Regulation and supervision of insurance companies

Market structure

As with pension reform, Chile was the first country to liberalise the insurance sector, in 1980. Other Latin American countries have eliminated state insurance monopolies during the 1990s[20]. Countries that still retain a state monopoly in insurance include Uruguay and Costa Rica, though there are already proposals to open the market to competition. In Brazil, there is still a state monopoly of reinsurance activities, although it is expected to be eliminated in 1999. The reinsurance company, IRB, was transformed in 1997 into a public limited company, with 50% ownership by the government, and 50% ownership by Brazilian insurance companies. According to government plans, the company will be privatised and the market opened to domestic and foreign insurers after 1999.

In other countries, the insurance industry is not subject to specific structural or ownership rules. Insurance companies can be owned by other financial institutions, and they can expand their activities to the pensions industry. Most countries have relatively open markets and few restrictions on foreign ownership. Two of the most important exceptions are Brazil and Mexico. In Brazil, the law concerning foreign ownership of local companies states that maximum participation should be 50%, with voting rights being limited to a third. In practice, though, the law is not adhered to, the authorities are more flexible and sometimes permit 100% ownership. The insurance market in Brazil, however, is still relatively closed to foreign firms. Mexico had a limit of 49% on foreign ownership for non-NAFTA members in 1998, but this was increased to 75% in January 1999 and is expected to increase to 100% in 2000. There are no restrictions for NAFTA members.

Countries that have recently liberalised their insurance sector include Argentina and Bolivia. Argentina deregulated the sector on 1st October 1998, eliminating the restriction, which limited entry by foreign companies to the purchase of a domestic firm. Bolivia introduced a new insurance law in June 1998. The new law permits free access by foreign companies and has separated general and life-insurance activities for the first time.

The reinsurance sector has also been liberalised in most of the larger Latin American countries. Insurance companies can freely contract reinsurance agreements in the domestic market or abroad. In some countries (e.g. Peru, Colombia), there are also minimum requirements for reinsurance of catastrophe risks.

Asset segregation, custody, fiduciary responsibility, and governance

All countries require separation of an insurance company's capital from its other assets and require custody of financial assets with recognised financial institutions. Fiduciary rules mainly affect insurance and reinsurance brokers. Fiduciary issues for insurance companies per se mainly have to do with the funding of their technical reserves and investment of their assets. Brokers are subject to various behavioural rules including a requirement to:

- Report on the risks to be borne by the insurance companies, and any risk changes in existing insurance policies.

- Inform the insured person or company of the precise conditions of the insurance policy.

- Ensure that the insurance policy is subject to conditions guaranteeing adequate coverage of the risk.

Minimum capital and solvency rules

Operations in the area of general insurance require relatively low reserves relative to the size of premiums, and therefore the regulatory framework concerns mainly contractual arrangements and insurance premiums. Life insurance, on the other hand, requires the building up of technical reserves that can be several times the annual premiums. Regulation of life insurance activities, therefore, pays much more attention to solvency issues.

All countries impose minimum capital provisions and solvency margins, but the methods for calculating these are not the same (see Table 29). In Peru, insurance companies must at all times have a minimum level of solvency, which is defined as the minimum capital or the solvency margin, whichever is lowest. In addition, insurance companies have to constitute a guarantee fund, equal to 35% of solvency capital.

61

Table 29 **Minimum capital and solvency rules for insurance companies**

	Minimum capital	Solvency margin
Colombia	Life ins: CP 954 million. Non-life: CP 4 273 million (subject to annual inflation adjustment)	Calculated on the total amount of written premiums or losses - whichever is higher
Mexico	Life:NP 9.12 mill. Accident/health: NP 2.28 mill. Non-life: NP 6.84 mill. - 32.8 mill. Depending on # of branches	Calculated using numerous factors, including product lines, assets, liabilities and premium volume
Venezuela	Non-life: Bs. 300 mill. Life: Bs. 500 mill. Composite: Bs. 700 mill. Reinsurance: Bs. 850 mill.	Assets equal to: one year's premium income or three years' claims, whichever is larger.
Argentina	All lines: US$ 5.5 mill. New levels of minimum capital for non-life lines will be introduced in October 1998.	40% of annual premiums for non-life. Whole of the last two months for transit ins., 15% of annual premiums for passenger personal-accident ins. Mathematical reserves for life ins.
Brazil	All lines: US$7.5 million	20% of annual average premium withheld over the last 36 months, or 33% of the annual average of claims incurred over the last 60 months (subtract the largest of the two from net assets)
Chile	Insurers: US$ 2.8 mill. Reinsurers: US$ 3.7 mill.	Maximum debt-to-equity ratio: 15:1 for life insurance, 5:1 for general ins.
Peru	Non life – one line: NS 2 562 265. Life, in addition to the above: NS 3 523 311	Should be higher than minimum capital or solvency margin, measured by premiums or losses

CP: Colombian pesos; NP: Mexican pesos; Bs: Venezuelan bolivares; NS: Peruvian nuevos soles.
Source: International Insurance Council (1998)

Funding and investment regulation

Insurance company assets must match the total of technical reserves, the solvency margin, and any other margins required by the regulator. Regulations impose time limits for restoring the insurance company to actuarial balance. In Peru, the maximum time period is 3 months. The calculation of technical reserves is also subject to specific formulas, and in some cases, such as Peru and Bolivia, an official discount rate must be used in the calculations. In Peru, the discount rate is set at 3%, while in Bolivia there is a minimum rate of 4%.

Insurance company assets consist of real estate, credit and loans as well as financial securities. This contrasts with mandatory pension funds, which are only allowed to buy financial assets. The allocation among these different asset classes is not restricted, but supervisory agencies oversee the size of financial investments relative to insurance companies' liabilities to ensure their solvency. In most countries, however, no precise distinction is made between real estate and financial investments.

Insurance company investments are subject to similar regulations to those of pension funds. Most countries require monthly market valuation of financial assets and at least annual evaluation of real estate holdings by recognised experts. Most countries also require risk rating of investment assets, at least fixed-income securities. In Chile and Peru, fixed-income securities, both domestic and foreign, must be risk rated by at least two different rating agencies.

Insurance companies are also subject to minimum diversification requirements for individual securities, by issuer and by risk (see Table 30). The highest limits are in place in Peru. Securities issued by the same company or group cannot represent more than 20% of technical reserves and solvency margin. Bolivia, Chile, and Brazil have much tighter limits. Requirements in Bolivia include a maximum investment of 5% of the portfolio in securities of issuers linked to the insurance agency, 5% in equity of the same company, and 20% in bonds of the same issuer. There is also a limit of 20% on the on insurance-company holdings of the total capital of a company. In Chile, requirements include a limit of 10% of assets on bonds of the same issuer and 7% of the equity of the same company. The limit on the portion of a firm's equity that an insurance company can hold is lower than that in Bolivia, 8%. In Brazil, requirements include a maximum of 8% of the portfolio in corporate bonds from the same issuer, and a limit of 20% of the portfolio in equity of the same company. In addition, insurance companies cannot own more than 20% of the total issue of the same group, and no more than 15% of a company's stock with voting rights.

Table 30 **Insurance companies' minimum diversification requirements, December 1998**

	Bonds of same issuer	Shares of same company	Single mutual fund	Specific risks
Argentina	(i) 3% of assets (ii) 5% of same bond series.	(i) 3% of assets,. (ii) 5% of company's public capital.	3% of assets	Various rules by risk of assets including, e.g. minimum risk rating for fixed income securities BBB.
Bolivia	(i) 10% of assets (ii) 20% of same bond series.	(i) 5% of assets. (ii) 20% of company's public capital.		Various rules by risk of assets including, e.g. minimum risk rating of BBB for fixed-income securities.
Chile	(i) 10% of assets (ii) 20% of issue	Lower of: (i) 7% of assets (ii) 8% of firm's capital	Lower: of: (i) 5% of assets; (ii) 10% of mutual-fund quotas (lower limits applicable to specialised investment funds)	Various rules by risk of assets including, e.g. minimum risk rating of BBB for fixed-income securities.
Brazil	(i) 8% of assets (ii) 20% of issue	(i) 20% of assets (ii) 15% of firm's equity with voting rights	10% of assets	
Colombia	15% of issue	15% of firm's equity		Risk rating required for fixed income securities
Peru	20% of assets	20% of assets		No specific limits
Uruguay	Lower of: (i) 3% of assets; (ii) 20% of issue	Lower of: (i) % of assets; (ii) 10% of firm's equity	10% of assets	

Source: Insurance company regulators

Insurance companies are also subject to quantitative portfolio limits in most countries surveyed. The main exception is Bolivia, where the Superintedency is currently in the process of designing new limits. Unlike pension funds, portfolio limits of insurance companies are set only by regulation. In Peru, however, the limits are set by law. In other countries, the law gives the authority to the

Central Bank or the supervisory agency to define and alter them as it sees convenient. As shown in Table 31, most countries allow investment in all asset classes, including foreign securities. Limits are set as a percentage of the technical reserves in most countries. In Chile, however, the limits are set on the sum of technical reserves and the firm's capital.

Limits on all asset classes vary significantly across countries, but in general tend to be less onerous than those of pension funds in their respective country. In Chile, for example, the limit on foreign securities is set at 23% for general insurance reserves and 18% for life insurance reserves. This overall limit includes a sub-limit on foreign securities (20% for general, 15% for life) and a sub-limit on real estate (3% for both). There are also limits on two other sub-groups, foreign shares and corporate bonds (5% in general, 3.75% in life) and investment funds (10% in general, 7.5% in life).

In Brazil, portfolio limits are not homogeneous across insurance activities, but there are some common limits applied across all activities, which are shown in Table 31. The limits are quite liberal, except for foreign investment, which is not allowed. Additional limits include, for open funds, lending of up to an equivalent of 10% of their technical reserves to affiliates.

Table 31 **Insurance companies' portfolio limits (%), December 1998**

	Argentina	Chile (life / general)	Brazil	Peru	Colombia	Uruguay (life / general)
Government securities	100	50	100	30	100	85 / 70
Corporate bonds	60*	40		30	30	'25* / 40*
Deposits	60	40	80	20	40	30 / 50
Financial Institutions secs	60*	40		30		50
Shares	60*	40		30	60	25* / 40*
			50			
Mutual funds	30	10		30	30	0 / 10
Real estate	30	20	30	30	15	20 / 50
Foreign Securities	10	18 / 23	0	30	40	0 / 20

Note: * combined limit
Source: Insurance company regulators

In addition, some countries impose currency-matching requirements. In these countries, portfolio investment in securities denominated in foreign currencies may not be greater than the total liabilities issued in those currencies. There are, on the other hand, no maturity-matching requirements establishing the extent to which the duration of insurance company assets must coincide with their liabilities. The maturity matching assessment, however, is carried out on a regular basis as part of the wider process of solvency assessment. In Chile, the required minimum capital depends on the extent of matching.

Risk rating of insurers

In Chile, insurance companies must contract for continuous and uninterrupted ratings of the obligations they hold vis-à-vis their insured with at least two different and independent rating agencies registered in a special SVS registry. The ratings granted in range from Category A (for companies with the lowest risk) through D (the highest risk operations). Category E is reserved for insurers, which cannot be classified because the necessary information is not available.

Other countries apply similar requirements. In Peru, insurance companies are subject, at a minimum, to twice yearly evaluations. In September 1997, a new law was introduced which requires Peruvian insurance companies to be risk rated by at least two different and independent rating agencies registered with the Securities Commission, CONASEV. Risk categories are the same as in Chile, A to E.

Product regulation

There is compulsory insurance for third-party auto liability in various countries including Colombia, Venezuela, Argentina, Brazil, Bolivia, and Chile. Except in Venezuela, however, such insurance covers only bodily injury. In addition, many countries require mandatory purchase of specific insurance policies (*e.g..* residence fire insurance in Brazil). Table 32 contains a summary of the main types of compulsory insurance in some of the larger insurance markets of Latin America.

The process of liberalisation started by some Latin American countries in the 1990s has also involved the freeing of rates in most countries, Venezuela being an important exception. Similarly, commissions for intermediation are set jointly by the insurer and the broker and stipulated in the respective policy. The law in each country allows for partial or total transfer of business from one insurance company to another, subject to special authorisation by the supervisory agency.

Table 32 **Compulsory insurance in Latin American countries**

Argentina	Third-party auto liability; workmen's compensation; transport insurance; insurance for passengers on public transport
Bolivia	Third-party auto liability
Brazil	Residence fire insurance; RCTR-C (civil responsibility – compulsory for road freight); DPEM (personal damage caused by ships or their freight); DPVAT (personal damage caused by automobiles)
Chile	Personal accident cover; third party auto liability; workmen's compensation
Colombia	Third-party auto liability
Ecuador	Aviation insurance; common party insurance; fire insurance; public health insurance; renter's insurance; transport insurance
Mexico	Workmen's compensation.
Paraguay	Insurance for passengers; home insurance
Peru	Life insurance for employees working for over four years; liability insurance for oil and gas industry; insurance for public transport
Uruguay	Workmen's compensation; property ins. for apartments; ins. for passengers on public transport; third-party and passengers' liability for aircraft
Venezuela	Third-party auto liability; workmen's compensation

Source: International Insurance Council (1998)

Indexation is compulsory only in Chile. The law stipulates that the monetary value of premiums and indemnities must be stated in *Unidades de Fomento* (UFs), a measure of inflation, unless the contract has been agreed upon in a foreign currency in compliance with the law. Other systems of readjustment authorised by the supervisory agency may be contracted for.

Taxation

As shown in Table 33, taxation of insurance premiums varies significantly across countries. The highest sales taxes on premiums are imposed by Chile (18% VAT), the lowest in Venezuela, where only minimal city taxes on insurance policies are imposed.

Table 33 **Taxation of insurance premiums**

Colombia	16% VAT; 35% income tax
Mexico	15% VAT plus small-policy issuance fees (10% for cities bordering the US)
Venezuela	Minimal city taxes
Argentina	3% reinsurance; 11% premium tax; 21% VAT (on non-life policies)
Brazil	2% on life premiums; 4% on other premiums
Chile	18% VAT on premiums; 22% on premiums written abroad (exceptions: marine, aviation, and export credit)
Peru	18% VAT except for individual life policies; pension, and annuity

Source: International Insurance Council (1998)

Supervision

Regulation of the insurance sector is carried out by a variety of agencies. In Peru and Colombia, the banking supervisory authority is also in charge of controlling insurance companies. In Chile, the superintendency of insurance is also in charge of securities, while in Bolivia the supervisory agency is in charge of all institutional investors and securities markets.

However, not all-insurance companies are supervised by these agencies. In Chile, for example, private insurers such as ISAPRES and Mutualidades, which covers health risks and work-related accidents, respectively, are not under the supervision of the Superintendency of Securities and Insurance.

Supervisory activities include both off-site monitoring and on-site inspections. Monitoring takes place on a regular basis. Adherence to funding and investment rules is normally assessed on a monthly basis. On-site inspections occur without any notice, less than once a year in most countries. The agency's responsibilities, in addition to carrying out these supervisory tasks, include the reporting of relevant information to the government and Central Bank, and the imposition on insurance companies of sanctions if laws or regulations are breached.

5.   Investment companies

There are two main types of investment company in Latin America, those which cater for domestic investors and those which cater for foreign investors. Domestically oriented investment companies are organised as mutual funds.

Hedge funds are still an unfamiliar concept in these countries. Mutual funds can be either open-ended or closed. Closed-ended mutual funds (called unit trusts in the UK) issue securities whose value is equal to the net worth of the fund. Open-ended mutual funds (called investment funds in the UK), on the other hand, issue securities whose value is determined by market prices. Hence, at any time the price of an open-ended mutual fund need not reflect the net worth of the securities in the fund.

The establishment of mutual funds has sometimes been linked to a demand by investors for specialised investment products, but not always: in Mexico, mutual funds were used until around 1994 as a source of funding for banks, which were subject to very high reserve requirements. Hence, de facto, mutual fund assets were mainly illiquid loans.

5.1   Market overview

Market structure

Most mutual funds are owned and administered by private banks. Since, in most Latin American countries, a specific group of commercial banks (such as the *grupos financieros* in Mexico) dominate the financial sector, there is a high degree of integration, both functional and administrative, between the two institutions.

The mutual fund industry tends to be significantly less concentrated than the pension fund or insurance industries. Table 34 shows the level of concentration in Mexican mutual funds. The largest five funds account for 53% of industry assets, less than for the two other types of institutional investor.

Table 34 Mexico: mutual-fund industry: Concentration of assets (%), 1998

Bancomer	20
Inbursa	12
Inverlat	8
BBV	7
Santander	6
Banacci	6
Others	41

Source: CNSF

Brazil has the most developed mutual-fund industry in Latin America, accounting for over 70% of assets managed in the region. As shown in Table 35, assets have grown fast in recent years, by 123% between 1994 and 1998. This compares positively with growth rates in Mexico and Chile, but less so with those in Argentina, where mutual funds have become a very popular savings instruments since the stabilisation plan of the early 1990s. The worst performance was in Mexico, where the dual effect of the Tequila and Asian crises has caused mutual fund assets to stagnate: mutual fund assets fell from a high of US$ 26 billion in December 1993 to US$ 14 billion in December 1998, though part of this dramatic fall is due to the devaluation of the peso in 1994-5.

Table 35 Mutual funds, assets under management
million US$, 1994-98

	Brazil	Chile	Mexico	Argentina
1994	54 485	2 087	11 285	389
1995	50 520	2 523	7 579	643
1996	101 917	2 801	10 016	1 869
1997	104 298	4 233	13 469	5 347
1998	121 700	3 572	14 003	7 185
Growth (%) 1994-98	123.36	71.15	24.09	1 747.04

Source: Goldman Sachs

Unlike pension funds, the composition of mutual-fund investment portfolios by broad asset class is very similar across countries. As shown in Table 36, mutual fund investments are highly concentrated in fixed-income instruments, accounting for over 90% of assets in three of the largest mutual fund industries (Brazil, Chile, and Argentina) and 87% in Mexico.

Table 36 Mutual fund investment (%), May, 1998

	Equity	Fixed income and cash
Brazil	9.9	90.1
Chile	5.2	94.8
Argentina	4.2	95.8
Mexico	12.9	87.1

Source: Goldman Sachs

The investment allocation of mutual funds tends to be a lot more volatile than that of pension funds or insurance companies. There has been a marked shift away from equity towards fixed-income funds in recent years. In Chile, there was a dramatic fall in investment in equities, from 23.4% of total assets in 1994 to 5.5% in 1998 (see Table 37). In Mexico, investment in equities has dropped from 19.5% of total assets in 1994 to 12.5% in 1998 (see Table 38).

Table 37 **Chile: Asset allocation of mutual funds**

	1994	1995	1996	1997	1998
Total assets (US$ mill.)	2 087	2 523	2 801	4 233	3 572
Equities %	23.4	17.7	7.0	5.9	5.5
Fixed-income %	76.1	81.5	92.6	93.5	93.9
Other %	0.4	0.8	0.4	0.6	0.6

Source: Goldman Sachs

Table 38 **Mexico: Asset allocation of mutual funds**

	1994	1995	1996	1997	1998
Total assets (US$ mill.)	11 285	7 579	10 016	13 469	14 003
Equities %	19.5	20.0	14.1	15.8	12.5
Fixed-income %	75.4	74.8	81.9	78.0	80.0
Cash %	5.1	5.2	4.0	6.1	7.5

Source: Goldman Sachs

Performance

The performance of investment companies, like that of DC pension funds, must be evaluated by taking into account risk, return, and commissions. Mutual funds charge three types of commissions: entry commissions, exit commissions and commissions on assets managed. Information on returns and commissions is very limited. A recent study by Maturana and Walker (1999) has shown that Chilean mutual funds have performed adversely relative to standard equity and fixed-income benchmarks. As shown in Table 39, mutual funds have performed less well than benchmarks of similar risk characteristics on a gross basis, i.e. after adding back commissions to the net return actually obtained by the investor. Chilean mutual fund commissions have been as high as 6% for equity mutual funds, 3.1% for medium and long-term, fixed-income funds, and 2.4% for short-term fixed-income funds.

Table 39 Chile: real return on mutual funds (%), 1990-6

	Equity funds	Medium and long- term funds	Short-term funds
Annual net real return (%)	13.1	4.3	4.2
Commission fee (% assets)	6.0	3.1	2.4
VAT	1.1	0.6	0.4
Benchmark	21.7	9.0	6.5

Source: Maturana and Walker (1999)

The conclusion for Brazilian mutual funds is similar, though it must be noted that the time period (four years) permits only tentative conclusions and that returns are reported gross of fees. As shown in Table 40, each type of mutual fund performed less well on average than the respective benchmark (IBOVESPA for equity funds, yield on certificates of deposit for fixed-income funds) even before deducting commissions. For equity funds, no commissions data are available but, since most funds charge commissions above 4% of assets, these funds have performed even less well, relative to the benchmark, than fixed-income funds.

Table 40 Brazil: real return on mutual funds (%), 1995-98

	Equity Funds	60-day funds	90-day funds
Annual gross real return	20.4	26.5	26.1
Commission fee (% assets)	N.A.	1.9	2.3
Benchmark	23.4	27.0	27.0

Source: Central Bank

In general, these commission levels compare adversely with pension-fund fees or with mutual fund fees in OECD countries. Mitchell (1996) has reported commission levels in the US of the order of 1% for equity funds, and as low as 0.3% for funds based on a stock-market index like the Dow-Jones average. As pointed out by Valdes-Prieto (1998), mutual-fund fees also compare adversely with those of pension funds in other Latin American countries.[21]

5.2   *Regulation and supervision*

Market structure

Unlike those in the pension fund industry, and to some extent the insurance industry, mutual fund managers are not subject to any ownership rule in any Latin American country. Most Latin American countries, however, separate mutual funds oriented towards the domestic investor from those oriented towards foreign investors. The latter tend to be administered by foreign companies.

Investment management and rules

As shown in Table 41, the regulation of mutual fund investments establishes minimum diversification guidelines, portfolio floors, class-for-class funds, and portfolio limits on foreign securities. Minimum diversification guidelines tend to be more lax than those applied to pension funds. For example, in Argentina, the limit imposed on the funds' investments in bonds of the same issuer, or stocks of the same company, is 2.5% for pension funds but 12% for mutual funds. Similarly, in Argentina, the limit on the share of a bond issue, or a company's stock, that can be held by pension funds is 5% for pension funds but 10% for mutual funds. The limits are generally closer to those of insurance companies but still tend to be less strict. In Chile, for example, insurance companies can own up to 8% of a firm's equity, while mutual funds can own up to 10%.

Portfolio floors (not shown in the table) ensure definitional consistency between mutual funds of different types (equity funds, bond mutual funds, etc). The floors, however, vary significantly between countries, ranging from a minimum of 15% for equity-fund investment in equities in Colombia to a minimum of 80% for investment in any asset class, by funds in that asset class, in Argentina.

All countries impose limits on investment overseas by mutual funds. In most countries, in fact, mutual funds are banned from investing overseas at all. This is the case of Brazil, Colombia, Mexico, and Peru. Currently, the highest limit is Chile's, at 30% of the mutual fund's portfolio.

Table 41 Prudential investment guidelines in Latin American mutual-fund industries (maxima unless otherwise stated)

	Minimum and maximum by asset class	Foreign securities	Bonds of same issuer	Shares of same company	Conflict of interest
Argentina	Minimum 80% of asset class	25% in non-Mercosur securities	(i)12% of fund except government securities (30%) (ii)10% of issuers' debt	(i)12% of fund (ii)10% of issuers' capital (iii)May not exercise more than 5% of voting rights granted by single issuer.	2% of the equity or debt of the holding company
Brazil	Minimum 51% of respective asset class	0% outside Mercosur	(i) 20% of fund	(i) 20% of fund (ii) 10% of company's stock	
Chile		30% of fund in foreign securities	(i) Maximum 10% of fund in securities of same issuer and 25% in securities of same group. (ii) Fund can own maximum 10% of a debt issue	(i) Maximum 10% of fund and 25% in securities of same group. (ii) 10% of a firm's public capital and 40% of company's private capital	No investment in: (i)companies that control more than 20% of the fund administrator (ii) high-risk securities (D and E) (iii) other mutual funds or shares of mutual fund
Colombia	Minimum 15% and maximum 80% in equities for equity funds	0%	(i) 10% of fund, 25% in securities of same group (ii) 10% of issuer's debt	(i) 10% of fund, 25% in securities of same group (ii) 10% of issuer's capital	Investment prohibited in other mutual funds or shares of mutual fund
Mexico	Min 30% in equities for equity funds	0%	(i) 15% of fund, 40% in securities of same group (ii) 30% of issuer's debt	(i) 15% of fund, 40% in securities of same group (ii) 30% of company stock	Investment prohibited in other mutual funds or shares of mutual fund
Peru		0%	(i) 10% of fund, 20% in securities of same group (ii) 10% of issuer's debt	(i) 10% of fund, 20% in securities of same group (ii) 10% of issuer's capital	Investment prohibited in companies that control more than 20% of the fund administrator

Risk rating of mutual fund companies and portfolios

Not all Latin American countries require risk rating of mutual-fund managers or their investment portfolios. In Argentina, for example, there is no specific requirement for standard mutual funds to be rated although closed funds do require a rating from two accredited agencies. In Mexico, the regulator has recently introduced a mutual-fund rating system along the lines of those published by Morningstar in the US. These ratings are carried out by specialised rating agencies.

Commissions and performance evaluation

Some countries regulate commissions. In Mexico, the limit on the monthly fee is set at 0.4167% of the fund's average net assets over a month. Performance evaluation is not obligatory in any country.

6. Main regulatory and supervisory challenges

The ultimate goal of regulatory regimes in financial markets is to dampen or eliminate the effects of market failure as a result of systemic and agency risks and attendant problems of investment protection[22]. In the institutional investor sector, this goal is translated into two main objectives: first, to ensure the solvency and financial stability of institutional investors, and hence to contain systemic risks; second, to protect consumers from the consequences of asymmetric information between the sellers and consumers of financial services, and between these and the regulators. To achieve these objectives, specialised tools are needed. The most commonly used are so-called prudential and protective rules and regulations. These include standards for governance, fiduciary responsibility and disclosure; rules for funding, valuation and investment; and requirements for vesting and portability (the latter for pension funds only).

Latin American institutional investors are increasingly subject to such regulations. Indeed, prudential and protective regulations governing pension funds, especially for investment, are in some cases more stringent than those of OECD countries. In addition, new forms of regulation have been introduced. These include constraints on the industry structure, leading to a statutory separation of financial institutions dealing with mandatory, retirement savings (pension fund administrators) from those in the voluntary savings market (banks, mutual funds, etc). Pension funds are also subject to some controversial regulations, such as the requirement to charge the same front-loaded fees to all affiliates of a pension fund, and performance rules and guarantees. While these forms of government intervention may be justified on prudential or protective grounds, they can have undesirable side-effects. In particular, some of these rules may lessen competition, damage the efficiency of the industry (by raising the cost or/and lowering the quality of the financial services offered to consumers) and compromise the development of capital markets. Hence, "investor protection" may be obtained only at a heavy cost. For example, mandatory investment in individual pension fund accounts managed by specialised institutions may be necessary to ensure financial security but may expose affiliates to high commissions. Another example: regulations on asset allocation that limit investment in domestic equity and corporate bonds; while such regulations may be justified as a crude way to limit aggregate risk in an investment portfolio, they can constrain the extent of diversification possible and may also harm prospects for financial development. Moreover, limits on asset allocation may be less effective in reducing risk than other forms of risk management control.

Some of the new regulations may, at the outset, have had other objectives than those of a purely financial nature. For example, the requirement that pension funds fix front-loaded fees as a percentage of salaries or contributions may be justified as part of a government policy to limit adverse distributional effects of differential fee structures and to maximise coverage in private pension systems. Often the different objectives of government policy can come into conflict, and a trade off needs to be made. This section looks at some of the controversies that have arisen in the regulation and supervision of institutional investors in Latin America. Where necessary, a contrast with the experience of OECD countries is provided. OECD countries have a longer and more varied experience in the institutional investor market, and the greater development of their financial markets and institutional frameworks can provide a useful reference for Latin American countries. At the same time, the innovations of Latin American countries can provide an interesting example for study on the part of OECD countries.

6.1   Industry Structure and Competition

Restrictions on industry structure and on competition in the financial services industry are increasingly difficult to justify. Indeed, deregulation and liberalisation have been the key objectives, in order to ensure that barriers to entry are minimised and that services provided are competitively priced. In some countries, obstacles to competition in the insurance industry are still to be found while, in the mutual fund sector, barriers on entry into distribution channels still act as a powerful brake on competition. Meanwhile, the pension fund industry has been subject to new constraints. Not only is the provision of pension services limited to specialised financial institutions, but there are new restrictions on the interaction between pension funds and other institutional investors in four other areas: share ownership, investment management, asset allocation, and the annuities market. Unlike older restrictions on competition in the banking and insurance sectors, which reflected doubts as to the efficiency of the market in the economic system, the new forms of intervention have been justified on the grounds of providing "investor protection". However, these new constraints can also have negative repercussions on competition between institutional investors as well as on their integration.

Competition in the new mandatory pension systems of Latin America

In the new Latin American pension systems, there are restrictions on the structure of the institutional investor industry, as well as on the fees and commissions charged. The trend has been towards a more differentiated structure, with increasingly specialised institutional investors. This contrasts with the experience of many OECD countries where changes in the institutional sector have moved in the other direction, involving the fall of long-standing barriers between different types of financial intermediary: banks and non-bank financial intermediaries, pensions and insurance, banking and insurance, mutual funds and pension funds.

This contrasting experience in Latin America vis à vis the OECD countries would not have come about without government intervention which has precluded the integration of intermediaries so as to ensure that modern managerial and regulatory practices would take hold at the outset in these new industries. The differentiation has been most marked in the new mandatory, defined-contribution pension funds of eight Latin American countries.

The new industry structure, first adopted by Chile in 1981, limits the provision of DC pension plans to specialised financial institutions (pension fund administrators). Banks, mutual funds and insurance companies cannot administer these plans or sell their services, such as portfolio management, to the pension fund administrators. In some countries they cannot even own pension fund administrators directly. Brazil differs from these countries since mutual funds can manage pension fund assets. In fact, mutual funds are required to manage the investment portfolios of the latest innovations in personal pension plans (FAPI, PGBL). By restricting direct entry into the industry to specialised institutions the new industry structure has played an important role in simplifying supervision by the new agencies. Hence, one important objective of this policy has been to overcome the asymmetry of information between sellers of financial services and regulators.

The structure that has been imposed on the industry can also be understood in the light of the history of financial crises that have beset the region. While banks have usually been at the centre of rescue operations, other institutional investors have been undercapitalised as well: mutual funds (in Chile in 1981-2, and Mexico, 1995-6) and rudimentary pension funds (e.g. the *montepios* in Brazil in the 1980s). There has been growing public mistrust of existing financial intermediaries and regulators during this time. If one considers this historical background of institutional investors in Latin America, the need for a fresh start seems all the more necessary. At the same time, it is critical to continue evaluating the rationale for constraints that impinge on the competition of the industry as the regulatory framework of the financial system as a whole is strengthened.

Insurance companies and pension funds do however interact in the decumulation phase of pensions. By virtue of the early establishment of the system, Chile has one of the most developed annuities markets in Latin America, in which pension funds and insurance companies interact directly as, respectively, purchasers and providers of annuities. This trade in the institutional market, however, may not always be in the interest of the individual, since pension funds have little incentive to negotiate lower premiums with insurance companies. The situation is quite different in Brazil. There, closed pension funds offer DB plans, with no intervention of insurance companies. The new regulatory framework, however, is likely to permit the contracting of reinsurance of DB plan benefits with insurance companies. Brazil's open funds, on the other hand, are actually managed directly by insurance companies. This structure limits friction between insurance companies and pension funds, and ensures a direct access to insurance and pension products by individual investors.

Administrative costs of private pension systems

The artificial separation of pension fund administrators from other institutional investors must worry regulators in that it limits competition in the provision of retirement-income products. In particular, the prohibition on other financial institutions to provide some pension related services, such as asset management, to the pension fund administrators can have large costs in terms of efficiency. Some economies of scale in asset management may be lost. Pension funds also choose to invest in mutual funds via the retail market, rather than negotiating directly with professional asset managers, which can significantly cut administrative costs. The experience of OECD countries shows that increasing integration between financial institutions has been an important weapon in the drive towards reducing intermediation costs in financial markets. Banks have opened up to the pension and insurance businesses, while employer pension plans have increasingly contracted out the asset management function to institutional investors. In general, it is accepted that the high fixed costs of financial services can best be served via an integrated structure, with free access to the market for all financial intermediaries.

This argument has come into immediate conflict with the defined-contribution, pension-fund industries of Latin America, which are based on an isolationist model, involving specialised pension fund administrators. In particular, it has been argued (by *e.g.* Shah, 1997) that the specific structure of the pension-fund industry in countries with mandatory pension systems with limited or no interaction with existing financial institutions has led to a high level of concentration and high administrative costs.

While concentration is indeed high in the pension fund industry, an important policy question is whether this is due to entry restrictions and structural regulations or whether it is a natural consequence of the size of the market, the efficiency of capital markets, and the ability of workers to switch between fund managers. Moreover, there is no clear link between concentration and administrative costs.

With regard to administrative costs, the popular wisdom is that the fees charged by pension funds in the new Latin American pension systems are very high. While it is certainly true that the fees open a significant gap between gross and net returns, it is important to determine to what extent they are the result of fixed costs or other, additional expenses, such as sellers' commissions. To the extent that high commissions finance armies of sellers who encourage transfer of affiliates, there might be a cause for regulations that impinge on the degree of competition of the industry. Transferring pension fund accounts can add very little net value to an industry that produces near identical gross returns across pension funds. On the other hand, to the extent that economies of scale can be gained and administrative costs reduced by allowing sub-contracting of portfolio management and other pension services, entry into the pension business to other institutional investors and banks may be considered.

It is also important to realise that high administrative costs also affect the withdrawal period, though to a lesser extent. The Chilean evidence, for example, suggests an increase in annuity intermediation costs from 1.5% of the gross premium in 1988 to more than 5% today (Queisser, 1998). These costs include the marketing and administrative fees of the insurance companies as well as the commissions to brokers. Since, in the case of annuities, transfer between plans is not possible, high costs must be explained purely by structural factors. It has been argued that an important factor is the fact that all annuities are contracted on an individual basis and group contracts are not allowed.

Policies to reduce administrative costs

While the regulation of commissions has been used extensively in Latin America as a way to contain administrative costs in the system, it requires accurate knowledge of the operating costs of pension fund administrators and how these are likely to change over time. This problem is evident in the Bolivian system, where there is a controversy over whether the maximum level for fees (1% of assets), which was determined in a bidding process, is sufficiently high to ensure the profitability of the pension business. The opposite case can also arise, since fixing fees can lead to these levels becoming the benchmarks for setting prices, thereby reducing incentives for cost reduction.

Short of directly regulating commissions, the main policy option that has been discussed is to find institutional structures that tackle competition issues from different perspectives in order to achieve low operating expenses and hence low administrative costs. For the asset-withdrawal phase, policy proposals include group negotiation of annuities and the introduction of compulsory annuities, as in Uruguay. For the asset-accumulation phase, there are two well-differentiated schools. One argues that further restrictions on competition and greater centralisation are needed to reduce administrative costs, while the other argues that the solution is greater competition, indeed in the limiting case, a free market in pension provision.

The first school is the one that has been most widely accepted in Latin America. Competition between pension funds has been restricted by limiting the regularity of transfers between pension funds (e.g. in Mexico transfers are limited to one per year). Unfortunately there are drawbacks, because it can expose workers to a risk of under-performance, especially in those countries, like Mexico, that do not have minimum rate-of-return regulations. To the extent that transfers are the main culprit in raising administrative costs, alternative institutional arrangements that restrict individual choice even further may be proposed. James et al. (1998) consider a range of different restrictions applied to investment management, contribution collection and record keeping. They conclude that significant cost savings can be achieved through an individual account system with limited choice of investment managers, passive asset management, and centralised account keeping and collection. An example of this structure is an employer or non-profit pension fund, where the plan sponsor - a large institution - negotiates fees with asset managers for a contract lasting a specified period of time. The extreme case would be a centralised fund, such as the provident funds of some East Asian countries. Both of these structures, especially the latter, are also instrumental in ensuring a high level of centralisation of pension activities such as contribution collection and record keeping that are liable to efficiency gains from scale economies.

The opposing school (Shah, 1997) argues that the best way to reduce administrative costs would be to allow new entrants into the industry (insurance companies, banks, mutual funds) and allow free choice of pension provider; this would in principle increase the degree of competition and lead to economies of scale. While, indeed, this may help reduce fixed costs in the industry, it is unlikely that it would solve the problem of excessive switching between pension providers. The evidence on competition and commissions in the mutual fund industry in countries like Brazil, Chile or Mexico discussed below does in fact warrant much caution with this proposal. On the other hand, opening up certain pension related services such as portfolio management to other financial institutions can help reduce the operational costs of pension funds.

Mutual fund commissions and implication for the pension fund fees debate

The setting of commissions by mutual funds is deregulated in most countries, with some exceptions. One of the most important ones is Mexico, which fixes a maximum monthly fee of 0.4167% of the fund's average net assets during the previous month. Such restrictions are largely unwarranted in open, competitive markets, and the Mexican government is already considering overhauling them.

But, while it is a priori reasonable to argue that commissions charged by mutual funds should be set by the market and not by regulators, it is also to be expected that regulators will look into the relatively high fees charged by mutual funds in those countries which theoretically have competitive mutual fund industries. An example is equity-fund fees in Chile which have been around 6% of assets in the past years. Fees charged by equity mutual funds in Brazil are reportedly over 4% on average. While fees may not be high relative to operating expenses, they represent a very significant portion of the gross performance obtained. In the case of Chile, mutual fund commissions ate up nearly a third of the gross return in the 1990s.

Such commissions are very high by OECD standards and compare particularly adversely with levels in developed markets such as the United States. As reported by Mitchell (1998), equity mutual funds in the US charge an average of 1% of assets. Even among those funds charging the highest fees, the average is less than 2%. Amongst equity index mutual funds, the average is much lower, around 0.4%.

Most importantly, however, the comparable asset-based fees of pension funds are much lower than those of mutual funds in the same country. For example, the equivalent asset-based fee of pension funds is around 1% of assets over a forty-year contribution period, which is five percentage points lower than that charged by equity mutual funds. This sort of evidence raises significant qualms over the desirability of introducing competition in the provision of pension services, especially in the area of mutual funds. It is possible that greater competition would lead to more intense marketing and advertising activity by pension providers, and therefore even higher administrative costs.

To the extent that the high commissions charged by mutual funds in Latin American countries account for the high operating costs of mutual funds in these countries (and this remains to be proved), an argument may be made that the consolidation of the industry at the regional level should be encouraged. This will allow mutual funds to take advantage of economies of scale. The presence of regulations on cross-border investment flows and selling of financial services in some countries make such consolidation a difficult task.

In small countries, the limited size of the market may indeed be the main factor accounting for high fees. This cannot however be used as an explanation of the fees charged by equity mutual funds in Brazil, which has assets worth over US$ 120 billion. As yet, there has been no detailed study on commissions of mutual funds. In a recent study, Maturana and Walker (1999) argued that barriers to entry in distribution channels were an important factor in explaining the high fees charged by mutual funds in Chile. Banks can use their distribution channels and have access to a large investor base, gaining advantages in economies of scale, and constraining entry by non-bank competitors. Indeed, this may be an argument applicable to many Latin American countries since, in most cases, the banking sector controls the mutual fund industry. The opening up of new distribution channels can therefore be a way of increasing competition and reducing fees in the industry.

Competition in the insurance business

Apart from some remaining insurance monopolies in countries such as Uruguay and Costa Rica and the state monopoly of reinsurance in Brazil, domestic insurance markets are relatively liberalised in most of the larger Latin American countries (Mexico, Chile, Argentina, Paraguay, Colombia, Peru, and Bolivia). The remaining obstacles are those affecting the development of global competition in insurance markets in the region. These include:

- Regulations restricting foreign ownership of domestic insurance companies as in Brazil and Mexico.

- Corporate laws in Brazil, Paraguay, Uruguay and other countries that accommodate only "stock" insurance companies, and disallow mutual associations.

- Differences in insurance-premium taxes.

- Varying minimum capital requirements. For example, in Uruguay, a multi-line insurer is required to have a basic capital of US$1 200 000. In Brazil, on the other hand, minimum capital for an equivalent business would be US$7 300 000.

- Controls on capital flows, which limit the extent to which individuals can contract insurance services with foreign companies abroad. Only re-insurance services are free from these constraints.

While eliminating some of these constraints and harmonising regulations and taxation can lead to more cross-border insurance trade, there is also a need to ensure effective exit mechanisms for domestic companies affected by increased competition. Latin America has much to learn from the reciprocal agreements liberalising cross-border insurance services in OECD countries, most significantly within the EU, where in principle all classes of insurance are placed on a cross-border basis.

Not all countries have managed to achieve separation of life and non-life insurance companies. Specialisation along these lines ensures that assets are managed separately and that losses incurred, for instance, in the non life-insurance sector, will not affect life policyholders. Given their different management and funding requirements, clear barriers between the two activities should be required.

Restrictions on foreign investors

Foreign investors (both retail and institutional) are not treated in the same way in all industries or in all countries. While there are no restrictions on the ownership of pension fund administrators by foreign financial companies, foreign individual investors are not allowed to invest in domestic pension funds, except in countries like El Salvador, which have a large overseas population.

Such restrictions are less common in the insurance and mutual fund sectors, whose industries are increasingly open to foreign investors and whose products can be sold to foreign buyers. Some obstacles remain, however, such as the state monopoly of the reinsurance market in Brazil and Uruguay, and the presence of controls on capital flows in Chile and Colombia, which limit the extent to which foreign investors can bring capital into these countries.

The two forms of foreign investment - portfolio and direct investment - are not however seen in the same light. It has become commonly accepted that restrictions on portfolio flows are more justifiable than those on direct investment. The latter, it is argued, ensure that the country will have access to international best practice in managerial tasks as well as the latest technological advances. Direct ownership of domestic companies by foreign institutions can also encourage institutional change at home, since foreign companies demand similar fiscal and regulatory conditions to those pertaining in their home markets.

Portfolio flows, on the other hand, have become, at times, the villain of the process of globalisation and integration of financial markets. Most recently they have been in the spotlight as a result of the debacle that followed the Tequila, Asian and Russian currency crises of the mid and late 1990s. They have been blamed for causing contagion effects and bruising countries that had seemingly pursued appropriate macroeconomic policies, such as Argentina since 1991.

While the arguments that support such claims are far from being conclusive, there is little doubt that where countries can develop their own domestic savings base, this is preferable to a permanent dependency on volatile capital flows. Especially in Latin American countries, where investment requirements are so large, the development of an institutional investor base can be a long-term solution to the problem of savings deficiency in these countries. In the short term, however, it is likely that most of them will remain dependent on international capital flows.

6.2   Individual choice under compulsory savings and insurance

An issue closely related to industry competition is whether or not savings, savings allocation and insurance should be mandatory. The justification for mandatory treatment is based on a paternalistic view that individuals do not always make the right choices for themselves. There is a further argument that individuals expect the state to rescue them in the event of financial or personal distress and therefore have an incentive to take excessive risks (the moral hazard argument). Finally the difficulty of supervising a more complex industry (as a result of asymmetric information between the sellers of financial services and the regulators) is also sometimes used to justify restrictions on individual choice.

Mandatory pension-fund accounts

Mandatory savings have been justified by the argument that people are myopic, and that therefore the state must force them to save for old age. It has also been argued that, if savings were not mandatory, people would not save enough for old age in the knowledge that the state would bail them out. While these arguments are now generally accepted and constitute the basis of any social security system, the obligation to invest in a particular instrument (the pension fund account), administered by a specific institution, with a particular scheme (defined-contribution) without the possibility of opening up second accounts has been questioned.

The first restriction is that on choice of investment instruments. Currently, of all the eight Latin American countries with private pension systems, four countries have mandated systems with no diversification (Chile, Mexico, El Salvador, and Bolivia). Three countries (Peru, Colombia, and Argentina) offer an option between the public and private system, and two (Argentina and Uruguay) offer a combined public-private product. While an analysis of the desirability of diversification across public and private schemes lies outside the scope of this report (see Queisser, 1998 for a discussion), another very important issue is why the private component of the pension portfolio must necessarily be invested in a single financial instrument.

The diversification argument has been used to justify the Argentinean and Uruguayan mixed-pension systems (with a public DB pillar and a private DC one); one can also use it to question the rationale of compulsory investment of retirement contributions uniquely in specialised pension fund accounts. Risk diversification would theoretically be best achieved by diversifying the individual's savings portfolio across financial institutions and products.

This argument is hardly a trivial one in countries where people see their children and housing as important sources of retirement wealth. It might be asked why it would not be possible to organise a mandatory, funded, pension system that also required diversification of mandatory savings into housing finance and other financial instruments. This is a question that is being tackled in some countries, like Mexico, where there are currently mandatory contributions to the housing fund, run by INFONAVIT. This institution currently works as a housing-loans bank, but there are plans to turn it into an individual savings fund which would allow people to save enough to buy a home.

The question of why diversification is mandatorily restricted is not easy to answer; nor is it possible to determine whether mandatory diversification would have yielded better results. It is likely, however, that the complexity of a mandatorily diversified system has played a role. The lack of popularity of other financial institutions, such as banks and mutual funds, must also clearly have played a role in leading to the creation of an entirely new industry. In fact, even now, the evidence on the administrative costs and returns of what are theoretically competing products, such as mutual fund accounts, does not offer much support to the idea of mandatory diversification across financial institutions. On the other hand, mandatory diversification into term deposits could have been a reasonable option, since fees charged are generally much lower than for institutional investor products.

Unique pension plan administrator

The second restriction concerns plan administration. As the evidence from OECD countries (including Mexico) and some Latin American ones (such as Brazil) shows, financial institutions do not have a monopoly in the administration of pension plans. All the mandatory private pension systems of Latin America, however, are based on the individualised capitalisation model. This contrasts with the situation in most OECD countries and in Brazil, where employers are significant, if not the most important, providers of private pension plans. Employer pension plans can have some advantages over individual plans in terms of administrative costs, risk pooling, and oversight:

- Employers can exercise greater power in negotiating fees with asset managers and insurance companies, because they have a strong competitive position and benefit from economies of scale.

- Employers choose asset managers for the accumulated funds of their pension plans; hence, the problems caused by switching pension funds at the individual level do not arise.

- Employers can pool individual risks among many employees, allowing them to rely to some extent on pay-as-you-go financing when setting up defined-benefit schemes. Defined-benefit schemes are not possible in individual capitalisation regimes unless long-term, inflation-indexed financial products are offered.

- Employers can exert direct and effective oversight over fund managers and insurance companies. By pooling resources, they can obtain the services of professional advisors in controlling the financial institutions in charge of management of the pension plan.

At the same time, however, employer pension plans can expose individuals to some agency risks. In DB plans, there is the issue of ensuring adequate funding of the pension plan, while in DCs the problem that arises is choice of fund administrator, a decision that is typically left to the employer. However, these risks can be addressed through adequate regulations, such as funding rules, actuarial and accounting standards, effective disclosure to both regulators and affiliates, and proper governance requirements. Provided that employer-pension plans are subject to prudential and protective requirements as effective as those of individual pension plans, they can offer better and cheaper alternatives to individual account systems. However, making such plans compulsory in Latin America, as is currently the case in Australia and Switzerland, is more complicated because of the large number of self-employed workers and the small size of most companies.

Unique plan structure (defined-contribution)

All the new private pension systems are mandatorily designated as defined-contribution plans. Defined-benefit plans are not allowed in any country except in Brazil. Although often claimed to be the case, individual capitalisation does not necessarily imply defined-contribution plans. A relevant example is that of Chile's *seguro de vida con ahorro*, literally life insurance with saving. These plans offer a guaranteed real rate of return on savings and an annuity after death payable to the designated survivors. This retirement product offers attractive characteristics, such as flexibility and a defined-benefit structure, that appeal especially to the self-employed[23]. Another example is seen in the traditional open pension plans in Brazil, which offered a guaranteed 6% real rate of return as well as a portion of the excess return earned on the account.

Defined-benefit schemes can be offered on individual capitalisation accounts to the extent that there are suitable capital-market instruments that can be used by insurance companies to package such schemes. By far the most important such instrument is inflation-indexed government bonds with long maturities. Such assets allow an insurance company to offer guaranteed investment contracts with a fixed real interest rate over a long period; they also provide time-horizons long enough to permit the design of deferred annuities.

The presence of defined-benefit investment products is therefore not surprising in Chile and Brazil. Both countries have instruments which offer inflation-indexed returns. In the case of Chile, all government bonds are indexed to a measure of inflation (the *Unidad de Fomento*)[24], while in the case of Brazil the inflation-indexed return is only a short-term deposit rate. Hence, only Chilean insurance companies are able to offer long-term guaranteed rates of return at low levels of commission. Brazilian open funds, while offering similar guarantees, charge fees that often surpass the level of the guaranteed return, making these products very unattractive.

It may be argued that investment in inflation-indexed foreign securities (such as UK or US government bonds) may to some extent be used for designing defined-benefit schemes. However, such instruments are still exposed to long-term exchange rate risk[25], though it may be argued that there is little downside risk on the exchange rate for an investor in a developing country investing in securities of developed countries.

Single pension fund account per affiliate

Only one country, Brazil, permits more than one account per affiliate. In all the mandatory private pension schemes, only one account is allowed, though both

Colombia and Mexico have passed legislation permitting another account, while Chile introduced legislation in November 1999 that permits the establishment of a second account by pension fund administrators. This second account will be invested only in fixed-income instruments.

The restriction of one account per member severely limits the extent to which investor preferences can be met. Since, in most countries, pension funds are also subject to performance rules, all pension funds have similar portfolios, which may be adequate for a "representative" investor, but may not meet the risk and time preference of individual investors.

Since individuals can only contribute to one fund, and the fund's investment and performance are strictly regulated, it is clear that investors have no influence over the investment regime of the pension fund industry. This situation contrasts dramatically with that of the mutual fund industry, where consumers have a wide array of investment options, ranging from very low to very high risk.

Compulsory insurance.

The argument for compulsory insurance is less frequently invoked than that for mandatory retirement savings. With the exception of automobile liability, it is in fact very hard to suggest for which kind of risks insurance cover should be compulsory. The need for certain types of compulsory insurance will be appraised differently from one country to another. The OECD guidelines for insurance activities (OECD, 1997) include the following cases in which compulsory insurance may be advisable:

- In branches which are more closely related to the social sector than to private insurance.

- In specific areas where compulsory insurance is justified by the seriousness of risk exposure and/or by its generalised nature (automobile liability or occupational accidents for instance).

- In areas where premium payments are to be divided on an equitable basis among the policyholders.

A particularly controversial issue is that of compulsory annuities in mandatory private pension systems. Most workers in Latin American countries have two main ways of transforming their accumulated assets into retirement income: phased withdrawal and annuities. An exception is Uruguay, where the purchase of annuities is mandatory for all workers. The main problem with voluntary annuities is that they can be a source of adverse selection. This problem arises from an asymmetric distribution of information between the purchaser and the seller of the annuity. People who expect to live longer are more likely to purchase an annuity. Hence, providers of annuities will expect that any demand for annuities will come mainly from these "bad" risks and will therefore price the annuities accordingly (*i.e.*higher).

While mandatory annuities, as in Uruguay, can solve the adverse selection problem, they can also expose investors to timing risk, since the value of the annuity depends critically on the time at which they buy it. The riskier the portfolio, the more likely is this value likely to fluctuate over time, and hence it is desirable for workers to be able to take out partial annuities at different times before and after their retirement, and to have the option of switching to a more conservative portfolio when nearing retirement. In this way, they can diversify away from the risk of bad portfolio performance in any specific year.

6.3   *Prudential and protective regulations*

The financial security of the savings instruments and policies offered by institutional investors and the solvency of those companies are two other important objectives of regulations. In the case of defined- benefit pension plans and insurance companies, the security of the schemes is ensured by: i) requiring that the guaranteeing institution be adequately capitalised so that it can honour potential claims (prudential regulation); ii) defining certain basic rights of beneficiaries such as maximum vesting periods and portability of accrued pension rights (protective regulation). In defined-contribution plans and mutual funds, the main target is ensuring a high level of investor protection, via rules that control the financial security of the accumulated assets (prudential rules) and the dissemination of relevant information.

In general, however, it is difficult to clearly separate prudential and protective rules. Investment regulations, for example, have both prudential and protective characteristics. They can be used to ensure the financial solvency of financial institutions, as well as preventing misuse of information by sellers of financial services, and hence protecting consumers. Others, such as vesting and portability rules, have an exclusively protective nature.

Prudential and protective regulations have been most extensively used in the new mandatory pension systems. They are, on the other hand, most notable by their absence in employer pension plans (*e.g.* in Mexico). In Brazil, which also has a preponderance of employer pension plans, the industry has been historically subject to a regulatory regime that lacked the necessary breadth to ensure adequate supervision of pension funds. Mutual funds and insurance companies have in general been subject to more lax prudential rules, but there has recently been a strengthening of regulatory frameworks in countries like Peru, Bolivia, and El Salvador.

Fund governance

While governance regulations in some of the new pension industries have required a separation of banks and other financial intermediaries from direct administration of pension funds, mutual fund and insurance industries are highly integrated with the banking system in all countries. Indeed, this can represent one of the biggest obstacles to the development of these sectors, since it can lead to perverse incentives and promote conflict of interest. The linkage is particularly worrisome in countries that still have fragile banking systems, with high concentration of risk, relatively few borrowers and a low level of bank capital. It is also a problem for mutual funds, since there is the danger that, in situations of financial distress, banks will invest mutual fund assets in affiliate bank deposits at below-market rates, or in doubtful borrowers to help pay off bank loans.

The establishment of adequate governance and fiduciary standards, however, cannot be designed in isolation from that of other components of the regulatory framework. Investment rules, too, play an important role in ensuring that the similarity in the management objectives of institutional investors and private banks does not lead to increased risks to private investors.

Performance rules

Six Latin American countries impose performance regulations on pension funds. In Chile, Argentina, Peru, Colombia, and Uruguay, the rules consist of rate-of-return ceilings and floors, set relative to the average return of the industry. In Brazil the rate of return is only applicable on traditional open pension plans, and is set at 6% in real terms. In Peru a minimum absolute return of 0 per cent in real terms was introduced in 1997. Minimum absolute returns in defined contribution plans are rare in other countries. To our knowledge, they exist in only two other countries, Singapore and Switzerland. In these two cases, however, the rate of return is set in nominal terms (2.5 and 4% respectively).

Some observers have linked the presence of these performance regulations to the observed homogeneity of investment portfolios across pension funds, but hard evidence is still lacking. Ramirez Tomic (1997) found that herding by Chilean pension funds had actually decreased slightly after the fluctuation band around the minimum rate of return was narrowed. Absolute rates of return can have more distortionary effects. They force pension funds to invest in low risk securities and may not be feasibly reached unless adequate hedging instruments exist. Both in Brazil and Peru financial instruments exist which are indexed to inflation (deposits and leasing bonds, respectively) which may be suitable for risk management purposes under a minimum return rule. In the case of Peru, however, there is a limited supply of inflation indexed leasing bonds at 5 year maturities, which is the period over which the minimum return is calculated. So far, however, pension funds have only invested up to a tenth of their assets in these bonds and maintain the highest exposure to equities of all Latin American countries. It seems, therefore, that the rule has not imposed a significant constraint on pension fund asset allocation up to now. The distortionary effects of the rule, however, remain to be tested since the stock market had a very positive performance up to 1998.

Government return guarantees

Explicit government return guarantees are offered only in Uruguay, where the publicly owned República AFAP offers a guaranteed real rate of return of 2%, and in the Central Bank account for participants of the Mexican pension system who have not chosen a pension fund manager. While these guarantees can be a fiscal drain on the government, they can also be viewed as only an alternative risk-free security for pension fund investors. Indeed, to the extent that these countries do not have sufficiently diversified and deep capital markets, the offer of such investment accounts can be a transition solution to limit the volatility that characterises pension fund accounts.

At any rate, it is clearly more desirable for the government to offer such "products" than to require pension funds to offer an absolute return guarantee when the financial instruments required to hedge long-term risks are not available, as is the case in Brazil and Peru. It is also preferable to offering ad hoc guarantees on pension fund returns, which can have perverse incentive-effects on fund managers, since they can invest aggressively in the knowledge that this is a one-way bet. In essence, government accounts offering long term fixed rates of return behave like government bonds available exclusively to pension-fund investors, such as the recognition bonds issued in Chile and El Salvador. Indeed, they can be a temporary substitute for such bonds which require time to develop.

Funding rules

While all institutional investors need to be subject to fiduciary and governance standards to ensure that assets are only used for their established purpose, minimum funding rules are relevant only for defined- benefit pension funds and for insurance companies. Mutual funds and defined-contribution pension funds are by definition fully funded. The most significant funding problems, however, have arisen with the largely under-regulated defined-benefit plans in the region. Information on these plans is only available in Brazil, which is also the only country that has a regulatory system for them. The evidence shows that funding rules (70% funding of the PBO) have not been strictly enforced in the past, and that a lack of adequate valuation mechanisms has impeded regular monitoring of funding levels. In the past year, however, the regulator has embarked on a revision of the funding rules, and the new laws being discussed in Congress require full funding of the PBO and at least annual monitoring of funding levels.

Insurance companies are subject to funding rules in all countries, but some problems have arisen because of the lack of adequate information (*e.g* in Peru; Chile's mortality tables are used to calculate technical reserves) and the presence of some constraining forces. The use of fixed discount rates, as in Peru, is particularly controversial, because it does not permit an adequate adjustment of funding to structural changes in economic conditions (*e.g.* a fall in the inflation rate).

Other issues include solvency margins, which are calculated in very different ways throughout Latin America. Countries that have liberalised their insurance sectors (such as Chile, Peru, Colombia, Mexico, and Argentina) have also simultaneously introduced solvency rules. In general, EU standards have been followed, though some countries (like Mexico) have imposed more complex rules. Solvency margins vary according to the line of business, premium volume and other industry characteristics. Some noteworthy rules include the 40% solvency requirement on Argentinean life insurance companies.

Asset Valuation

In general, Latin American pension fund regulators have effectively established valuation. The only country where problems remain is Brazil, where there is no requirement for daily market valuation as in other Latin American countries. It is expected, however that this year the regulatory agency will issue new guidelines.

Argentina, too, has slightly departed from standard practice, by permitting pension funds to invest up to 30% of their portfolio in government securities that are held to maturity in an investment account. Government securities are calculated according to a book value rather than their market value. This decision was taken soon after the start of the system, in 1995, at a time of very high bond volatility following the Tequila crisis. Then the limit was set at 25%, but with the renewed upheaval in bond markets in 1997, the government decided to introduce legislation which raised the limit to 30% and permitted further rises to 50%.

The Argentine valuation method clearly has its advantages, since the general public can over-react to excessive short-term volatility in their pension fund balances, which may not adequately reflect the long-term risk of their future income. Moreover, by limiting fluctuations in returns, differences between pension funds can be further reduced, decreasing the incentive for switching pension funds when there is very little gain in performance to be obtained. However, differences in returns do not appear to be an important factor in explaining switching, and so there may be very little gain from further reducing differences between pension fund returns. At the same time, however, the failure to report market rates can distort risk management by pension funds since it may create the illusion that the assets in the investment account are risk free. Indeed, pension fund administrators may manage their portfolios ignoring those assets that are not market-linked. These problems are clearly most relevant for workers near retirement, who can be severely affected by short-term changes in government bond prices.

Risk management and investment rules

By their nature, the products offered by institutional investors are subject to financial risk. Risk management therefore is a basic concern of regulators. Regulatory policies aim to achieve two basic goals:

- Control conflicts of interest in the investment of institutional investor assets.

- Ensure that institutional investors can meet their liabilities by adequate diversification of their asset portfolios.

The first main goal of regulation is to limit conflicts of interest that arise when pension funds, insurance companies, and mutual funds invest their assets in companies controlled by the owners of those institutional investors. This problem has been addressed in the pension fund industry by regulations that limit or ban completely investment by institutional investors in companies that own some of the stock of the institutional investor. These rules are well designed, but effectively enforcing them has become an arduous task, because it is difficult to establish ownership in financial systems that have a high degree of cross-shareholding, such as the financial groups of Mexico and Peru. Regulations also significantly limit investment by pension funds in mutual funds in all countries except Brazil. Pension funds are subject to limits ranging from 0 to 7 per cent of the portfolio on investment in mutual funds. In Brazil there are no such limits, and pension funds and insurance companies invest over a third of their assets in mutual fund accounts. Such limits have been justified by the fact that large banks often own both pension and mutual funds and may try to direct investment from the former to the latter. However, these conflicts of interest could be solved in principle by limits similar to those applied on investment in other private sector institutions. A more relevant reason for this rule seems to have been concerns over the performance of the mutual fund industry in some Latin American countries.

The second of these goals is particularly relevant for insurance companies and defined benefit pension plans. In the case of mutual funds and defined contribution pension systems this objective is translated into ensuring that fund managers maximise returns for the given level of risk chosen by individuals. This goal becomes critical in mandatory funded pension systems, where the government implicitly bears the ultimate responsibility for ensuring adequate risk management of society's savings, and often explicitly guarantees the performance of the private pension system.

In Latin America, despite having relatively conservative portfolios, pension fund returns have shown a high volatility (see Table 13). In countries with the highest investment in equity (Chile, Peru, and Argentina) there have been worries that the public's confidence in the new pension systems may be thwarted as returns could turn negative. This is indeed what happened in 1998 in Peru, Chile, Argentina, and Colombia, when for the first time pension funds had a negative annual return to their portfolios. Since the new systems are designed to be highly transparent, workers have been very disturbed by their latest pension account statements, which showed a fall in their accumulated balance.

While, clearly, a high degree of volatility is inevitable in countries with capital markets that lack breadth and depth, regulations can play a role in reducing the exposure of pension funds to specific risks. This is indeed the objective of prudential rules, such as minimum diversification requirements, limits by risk level and liquidity, and quantitative portfolio limits. In Latin America, industry regulators have made use of all these rules to limit excessive exposure to individual securities, individual issuers, and high-risk or low-liquidity securities. However, no effort has been made at limiting the concentration of risk in specific sectors.

In Chile, for example, the electricity sector accounts for over 50% of the stocks held by pension funds. Such overexposure to an individual sector seems to go against basic notions of portfolio diversification. Overexposure to a specific sector has also been observed in Peru, where pension funds' portfolios are heavily concentrated in financial institutions. While the long-term solution to this problem must lie in an expansion of the range of investible instruments (in Chile, for example, until 1997, only 30 stocks out of a total of 300 were eligible for pension fund investment), regulations can also play an important role. Regulations should ensure that prudential principles of investment are followed, and that there is a high degree of diversification, not just across asset classes but also across securities and industry sectors with low levels of correlation.

No effort has been made either to control the aggregate risk of pension fund portfolios; this has been left to the pension fund administrators. Though in principle portfolio limits by asset class limit the exposure to risk of the aggregate portfolio, they can in fact, if set at too stringent levels, have the effect of raising the overall level of risk of the pension fund portfolios by precluding a sufficient degree of diversification. Chile and Peru exemplify the complexity of setting portfolio limits. These two countries that have had to modify their respective investment regime over time. This is not surprising, since the evolution of capital markets will necessitate an evolving investment regime. However, this flexibility is difficult to achieve when portfolio limits are set by law (as in Mexico or El Salvador) rather than by regulation (as in Brazil).

Portfolio limits are also used in Brazil, though they are by far the least constraining of all Latin American countries surveyed. In fact, problems have arisen from an excessively lenient attitude towards some forms of investment. In particular, pension funds are allowed to invest a significant part of their portfolio (20%) in assets whose risk is difficult to diversify away, like loans to the sponsoring company or to affiliates. Pension funds can also invest up to 19% of their portfolio in real estate, an illiquid asset that cannot be market-linked like securities traded on an exchange. Overall, investment in real estate and direct lending represented 25% of the closed funds' portfolios in August 1998.

Perhaps the most controversial limit is that which constrains investment in foreign securities. While it is generally accepted that all standard asset classes (such as corporate bonds, and equities) should be allowed as investment instruments, there is an on-going dispute on the extent to which investment in foreign securities should be liberalised. The complication arises from the potentially negative impact of capital outflows on macroeconomic stability and domestic capital markets. There is also a fear that they could lead to an institutionalisation of capital flight. In Latin America, only three countries (Chile, Argentina, and Peru) currently permit investment in foreign securities, and the limits were far from being binding up to 1998. Pension funds in these countries had shown a very strong home bias. Since 1998, however, Chilean pension funds have started to increase rapidly their portfolio invested abroad. As shown in Table 42, by December 1998 nearly 6 per cent of their portfolio was invested abroad. By August 1999 the level was close to the ceiling of 12 per cent. Hence, it is likely that the limit will be increased once again in the near future.

Table 42 Chile: Investment in foreign securities by pension funds
1991-98

Year	Foreign Investment		Limit	Difference
	Amount (US$million)	% of portfolio	% of portfolio	% of portfolio
1991	0	0	0	0
1992	0	0.0	3	3.0
1993	95.7	0.6	9	8.4
1994	200.7	0.9	9	8.1
1995	50.3	0.2	12	11.8
1996	146.9	0.5	12	11.5
1997	368.7	1.1	13	11.9
1998	1753.6	5.6	13	7.4

Source: Superintendencia de Fondos de Pensiones de Chile.

The limits are particularly controversial, because they have been set at much lower levels than for insurance companies. For example, Peruvian insurance companies can invest up to 30% of their portfolio in foreign securities, while pension funds can only invest up to 5% abroad. Similarly, Chilean pension funds can invest 13% abroad, while the limit on insurance companies is slightly higher, at 18-23%. To the extent that governments worry about the possibility of excessive capital outflows and their potential side-effects, it can be understood that they would want to impose tighter controls on mandatory pension funds, which are likely to accumulate assets more rapidly than the (largely voluntary) insurance companies. At the same time, however, the tighter limits impose a greater constraint on diversification in pension-fund portfolios. Since private savings in such instruments are mandatory, the government faces a great responsibility in ensuring that such investments are adequately diversified.

This difference between pension funds and insurance companies in strictness of the limit on investment in foreign securities is diametrically opposed to what prevails in most OECD countries. In countries like Germany, Canada, Switzerland and Finland, which impose quantitative portfolio limits, the levels tend to be set higher for pension funds than for insurance companies. For example, the limit on investment in foreign securities for pension funds in Germany is set at 60%, whereas the limit for insurance companies is 5% of the portfolio. In Canada, the limit for pension funds is 20% and 0% for all insurance lines except life insurance.

The limits on investment in foreign securities for pension funds in Latin America, however, tend to be higher than those for mutual funds, with the important exceptions of Chile and Argentina. In fact, except for these two countries, investment in foreign securities by mutual funds is not permitted at all. This decision may be justified because, to the extent that mutual fund investment is voluntary, the additional benefit from diversification of a mutual fund portfolio is marginal and tends to benefit the richer segments of the population. In practice, the decision on whether or not to permit investment abroad by mutual funds and pension funds seems to have little to do with a specific preoccupation with risk diversification or income redistribution. The two large Latin American countries that do permit investment in foreign securities by mutual funds also allow such investment by pension funds. Furthermore, the limit on mutual funds is much higher than for pension funds, despite what may seem to be a more socially desirable outcome. In Chile, mutual funds may invest up to 30% of their portfolio in foreign securities, more than twice as much as pension funds. In Argentina, mutual funds can invest up to 25% of their portfolio in non-Mercosur countries, which compares rather generously with the 10% limit on pension funds.

The tighter restrictions on pension funds in these two countries can be linked to the structure of the market and governments' concern with institutionalised capital outflows. However, it is certainly inequitable to permit investment overseas via instruments (mutual funds) that are accessible only to the richer segments of the population, while the majority (including the poorer households), who are mandatorily affiliated to the pension system, have to invest in products (pension fund accounts) that are not as diversified internationally. Furthermore, investing in foreign securities can bring important externalities. For example, the exposure of local fund managers to foreign markets can, by helping them learn about investment and regulatory practices in these markets, be a source of technology transfer for Latin American countries.

The controversies regarding portfolio limits are generally not as relevant to insurance companies as to pension funds: first, because the limits are generally less strict than those for pension funds; second, because they are specified in regulations and not in the law, as is the case with pension funds in many Latin American countries (*e.g.* Chile, Peru, Mexico, and El Salvador). Hence, there is in general a much greater degree of flexibility in the investment regime of insurance companies than in that of pension funds. Even in Peru, where the limits are set by law, insurance-company limits tend to be higher than those for pension funds. The only exception is investment in corporate bonds, which is subject to a 30% limit for insurance companies, but 35% for pension funds. All other limits are higher for insurance companies; for example, insurance companies can invest up to 30% in foreign securities, and another 30% in mutual funds, while pension funds can only invest 5 and 10% respectively.

Rules on admissible investments and adequate definitions of capital are widely established in Latin America. Currency matching is also guaranteed, since most countries do not allow investment in established foreign assets, and there is limited cross-border trading in insurance activities. On the other hand, progress is still needed in ensuring maturity matching. Imposing limits on deviations in the maturity of assets relative to those of liabilities can be an effective tool in minimising the effects of changes in asset prices and interest rates. At the same time, however, too stringent requirements that are too frequently assessed can inhibit investment in riskier assets, such as company stocks.

Even if such requirements are introduced, it may be difficult to ensure adequate maturity matching because of the lack of financial products with sufficiently long maturities. In most Latin American countries, Chile being an important exception, the average maturity of fixed-income securities is less than 10 years. Even in Chile, life insurance companies find it difficult to cover pension flows with investments having a maturity of more than 17 years. The lengthening of maturities and the creation of new financial instruments, such as infrastructure bonds, will be critical in ensuring adequate currency matching in the life insurance sector.

Of all institutional investors, mutual funds enjoy the most liberal investment rules, having only minimum diversification requirements and limits on portfolio investment in foreign securities. This is perhaps understandable, since investment in mutual funds is voluntary and there is no risk of insolvency arising from under-funding as may happen with insurance companies. As a result, governments are under less pressure to increase returns by investing overseas and can leave the investment regime under prudent-person management.

Here, too, there are controversies. The limit on corporate ownership can be higher for mutual funds, because the higher turnover of their portfolios restricts their corporate governance interests. On the other hand, there is no a priori reason to impose less stringent limits on mutual funds' investment in a particular security or the securities of a specific issuer, inasmuch as diversification should be the primary objective of their investment strategy. This is however the case in most Latin American countries.

Performance evaluation and indexing

Rates of return on pension fund portfolios in the Latin American DC pension systems are reported on a gross basis, while fees tend to be reported separately. Two exceptions are Colombia and Uruguay, where pension funds must report both gross and net returns. The failure to report net fees directly can easily lead to investors being misinformed. Since commissions are front-loaded, there is no standard way of transforming them into asset-based fees. Regulatory frameworks should ideally consider both requiring a standard calculation method and reporting net returns. Information could also be provided on expected replacement rates, though in this case the margin of error can be very large, and could lead to unwarranted expectations regarding pensions that could have undesirable effects on labour market and savings behaviour.

In addition to reporting net fees, investors need a way to compare them against market benchmarks. The extent to which performance evaluation can be carried out in Latin American countries, however, is limited by the lack of suitable indices of fixed-income markets. While the short term nature of most fixed income securities means that yields tend to show less variation across maturities than in OECD countries, there is a need to standardise some suitable rates for usage in performance evaluation. So far, only the securities exchange in Chile has developed a bond market index that includes government securities as well as corporate bonds and mortgage bonds.

Meanwhile, the use of stock market indices is widespread, but there is a lack of agreement as to what the relevant indices are, and whether or not there are useful indicators of passive performance in capital markets which are constantly expanding and adding new securities. The first problem relates to the confusion caused by the multiplicity of stock market indices. Domestic fund managers tend to prefer indices constructed by local stock markets (e.g. Merval of Buenos Aires, IBOVESPA of Sao Paulo), while foreign fund managers prefer those constructed by international organisations (International Finance Corporation) and financial institutions. Since markets in Latin America are highly volatile, small differences in the composition of the different indices can lead to large differences in their value.

The second problem arises because new issues in Latin American markets tend to be a significant portion of total capitalisation. In some of the recently established, smaller stock markets (such as Bolivia's and most Central American markets), new issues can sometimes be as large as the aggregate market value of all securities traded. Establishing a correct benchmark under such circumstances is a highly complicated task, requiring constant updating of its composition. This, however, would defeat the purpose of the benchmark, which should reflect a stable, passive-investment strategy. Since in practice benchmarks are not constantly updated, actual pension fund performance often diverges significantly from the index. In such circumstances, the index may lose much of its usefulness as a measure of absolute performance, but could still be used to measure relative performance between pension funds. For the time being, the likelihood is that the industry average return will continue to be used as the relevant benchmark, especially in countries that actually require pension funds to obtain returns within a certain band of the industry average.

Information disclosure of mutual funds and other investment companies covers the same aspects as DC pension funds, namely investment regime, returns and fees. In practice, however, reporting to investors is less developed in the mutual fund industry than in the mandatory pension fund industry, except, perhaps, in Brazil, where the Central Bank, through the financial press, is a source of regular information on these issues.

The lack of understanding as to the risk involved of some of these instruments is widespread, even in the richer countries, like Mexico and Argentina. In some cases, however, it has been the mutual funds' sponsors, the banks that have pursued a strategy of misinformation using their mutual-fund products to attract customers towards more profitable investments for the bank, like deposits.

Vesting and portability in private pension systems

Vesting and portability rules have a clearly protective nature. They are also only mainly relevant to defined-benefit schemes, though company-based defined-contribution schemes may also require vesting rules. The country in most dire need of such rules is Brazil, where affiliates of employer pension plans only have rights to their own contributions and often lose accumulated pension rights from employer contributions when they leave their jobs.

Portability has also become an issue in the new mandatory pension systems of Latin America, where it has come into conflict with the objective of minimising administrative costs. Clearly, a balance needs to be struck between allowing sufficient mobility between pension funds and limiting costs to consumers. Alternatively, as shown above, other ways to limit administrative costs may be found.

Supervisory functions

A proper regulatory framework requires a body that is autonomous (both functionally and financially), professionally trained and able to exert both on-site and off-site supervision. While most of the new individual capitalisation regimes of Latin America have new supervisory agencies[26], the largest private system, the Brazilian closed-fund system, still has a supervisory agency that depends both financially and operationally on the Ministry of Social Security. The agency can impose only minimal sanctions, and its capacity to hire professional staff independently is limited. The government, however, has recently sent a proposal to Congress for the establishment of a new regulatory agency, encompassing both closed and open funds that would be largely self-financed, independent, and staffed with professionals.

An important issue in supervision is whether separate supervisory authorities are necessary for each institutional investor, or whether one centralised authority could be created to regulate and supervise all classes of institutional investors. This is the case in the UK, where in June 1998, the responsibility for supervising all financial institutions was centralised in the newly established Financial Services Authority.

In the Latin American countries surveyed, except in Bolivia and Colombia, decentralised supervisory structures are in place, with at least two types of institutional investors supervised by different agencies. The case of Bolivia is quite recent, the unification of the three supervisory agencies (securities, pensions, and insurance) dating from 1998. Colombia too has a centralised structure, with the Superintendency of Banks also having responsibility for supervising pension funds and insurance companies.

Introducing some degree of centralisation may lead to gains in efficiency, especially in the smaller and poorer countries that have a very limited supply of qualified professionals and where it is more difficult to guarantee the independence of the agencies. In some cases, there is also a clear duplication of functions. This is the case in Brazil, where the closed and open funds are supervised by different agencies, despite the fact that pension plans in Brazil, irrespective of whether they are open or not, are mainly of a defined- benefit nature.

The rationale for a centralised structure may be even stronger when there is a high level of integration between different institutional investors. In fact, the country with the most integrated pensions and insurance industries, Chile, has separate supervisory agencies (see Table 43). Similarly, the country with the most integrated pensions and mutual fund industries, Brazil, also has separate agencies.

Table 43 **Supervisory authorities**

	Pensions	Insurance	Mutual Funds
Argentina	Superintendencia de AFJPs	Superintendencia de Seguros de la Nacion	Comisión Nacional de Valores
Bolivia	Superintendencia de Pensiones, Valores, y Seguros	Same	Same
Brazil	Secretaria de previdencia Complementar / SUSEP	SUSEP	Banco Central
Chile	Superintendencia de AFPs	Superintendencia de Valores y Seguros	Same
Colombia	Superintendencia Bancaria	Same	Superint. De Valores y Superint. Bancaria
Mexico	CONSAR	Comisión Nacional de Seguros	Comisión Bancaria y de Valores
Peru	Superintendencia de AFPs	Superintendencia de Banca y Seguros	CONASEV
Uruguay	Banco Central	Superintendencia de Seguros y reaseguros	
Venezuela	None	Superintendencia de Seguros	

Source: OECD

102

7.   The role of institutional investors as holders of financial assets

Institutional investors pool the funds of market participants and use these funds to buy a portfolio of financial assets. The symbiotic relationship that can develop between institutional investors and capital markets consists in reducing risk through diversification and pooling, and lowering the costs of contracting and information processing (Blommestein, 1998). Capital-market development can be beneficial both to investors, by offering new investment instruments, and to borrowers, by offering cheaper and more flexible sources of finance.

Of all institutional investors in Latin America, pension funds are the best placed to have a significant impact on capital markets. Pension funds tend to hold long-term assets to match their long-term liabilities. This is also true for the life insurance sector, but in Latin America the new DC pension systems are mandatory, while life insurance is voluntary. Hence, coverage of pension funds is much broader that that of life insurance companies. Meanwhile, mutual funds have a very unstable investor base and are increasingly dependent on retail investors, who tend to have shorter investment horizons and carry out more conservative investment strategies than institutional investors with investment strategies independent of their investor base (such as mandatory pension funds and life insurance companies).

Already pension funds hold the largest share of financial assets of institutional investors in Chile, Argentina, Bolivia, Peru, Colombia, Uruguay and El Salvador. Pension funds are also set to overtake mutual funds in Mexico in the coming years. In Brazil, assets held by closed and open pension funds will get a significant boost with the planned expansion of the complementary pension system to government workers and with the passing of the new laws and regulations, planned for this year. Pension funds, more than any of the other two institutional investors will therefore be the critical players in the development of capital markets.

The increasing importance of pension funds is most patent in the case of Chile. As shown in Figure 2, pension fund assets overtook those of insurance companies and mutual funds within a year of being established, despite the fact that the latter had been running for many years. Over the period 1982 to 1997 pension fund asset growth was 26%, against 17% for insurance companies and 13% for mutual funds. In December 1997, the assets of all other institutional investors combined (including foreign mutual funds) were approximately half of those of the pension funds.

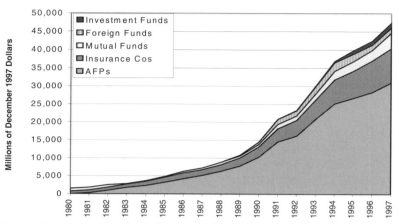

Figure 2: Chile, Total Assets of Institutional Investors, Millions of December 1997 Dollars

Source: Superintendencia de Valores y Seguros

7.1 The development of the financial infrastructure

The relationship between institutional investors and capital markets is conditioned by the existence of liquid and transparent markets, where insider trading and other illegal practices are eradicated. Institutional investors can contribute to the development of capital markets through the need they create for efficient trading, custodianship, risk rating and corporate governance. A controversial issue, however, is whether such practices will arise as a result of self-regulation or whether they need to be imposed via statutory, external rules.

In Latin America, significant improvements in the financial infrastructure have been intrinsically linked to the establishment of mandatory pension fund accounts. Indeed, in many instances there is a direct causal link as in the creation of risk-rating companies. The experience from Latin America has shown that critical elements of the financial infrastructure, like risk rating companies, adequate custodial services, and valuation methods do not develop of their own accord, even in the presence of institutional investors. For example, a country like Mexico has continued for many decades with a mutual fund industry and at the same time a deficient financial infrastructure.

The critical determining factor has been the establishment of a modern regulatory framework for pension funds that has made it necessary to develop this infrastructure as a *sine qua non* for the running of the system. Hence, for example, in Bolivia, pension funds have by law been allowed to invest by in shares and corporate bonds, subject to risk rating of these securities. Pension funds have had to wait until June 1999 for licensing of the first risk-rating company, which will in due course allow pension funds to invest in these asset classes.

Another clear example of financial innovation is the price vector developed by the national securities commission in Mexico to permit a standard valuation method for thinly traded securities. Such a method was originally designed with a view to ensuring the comparability of pension fund portfolios and permit adequate monitoring by the regulator, CONSAR. It is now expected that insurance companies and mutual funds will be required to use the same valuation method.

7.2   The deepening and broadening of capital markets

By virtue of their role as financial intermediaries, institutional investors play a central function in the development of capital markets. Their effects, however, vary significantly. Pension funds have a greater impact on long-term instruments such as stocks and fixed-income instruments with long maturities, which match their long-term liabilities. The investment regime of insurance companies varies according to the type of risk insured. Life insurance tends to require investment regimes similar to those of pension funds, while non-life activities require portfolios with much shorter maturities and greater levels of liquidity. Mutual funds, finally, can suit any investment horizon and degree of risk aversion, depending on the preferences of individual investors.

In Latin America, individual investors play little if any role in shaping the portfolios of pension funds and insurance companies, while they have full freedom to choose mutual funds according to their risk preferences. Hence, the industry aggregate portfolio of pension funds and insurance companies is largely determined by the time and risk preferences of the administrators of these institutional investors, while the industry aggregate portfolio of mutual funds is largely determined by the time and risk preferences of individual investors.

The effect is illustrated in Table 44, which compares the aggregate portfolio of institutional investors for Argentina, Brazil and Chile. Pension funds invest more in equities than the other two types of instutional investors, despite being subject to the lowest portfolio ceiling. Hence, it appears that there is a significantly greater preference for equity on the part of pension fund managers than on the part of the general public. To the extent that individual investors are given greater say in the choice of portfolio in pension funds in the future, it is likely that there will be a move towards more conservative portfolios.

Table 44 **Investment in stocks by institutional investors
in selected Latin American countries**
percentage of portfolio, December 1998

	Chile	Argentina	Brazil
Pension Funds	15.0	18.0	31.0
Insurance Companies	3.6	10.3	7.1
Mutual Funds	5.5	4.0	9.5
All institutions	11.6	12.2	23.8

Source: National securities commissions, pension fund regulators
and insurance supervisory agencies, Goldman Sachs,
ASSAL.

In addition, the volume of inflows into stock markets will be limited by the
existence of portfolio limits in most Latin American countries. Some countries
like Mexico and Uruguay even prohibit investment in equities. Portfolio limits
alone, however, cannot explain why it is that investment in stocks by
institutional investors is so low compared to such OECD countries as the United
States or the United Kingdom. Even in countries like Chile or Argentina, which
have a liberal investment regime, overall investment in stocks by institutional
investors is less than 15% of the total investment portfolio.

While it is difficult to establish a causal link between institutional investor
activity and capital market development, it is certainly the case that the
countries with the most developed institutional sector are also the ones with the
highest level of market capitalisation relative to GDP. As shown in Table 45,
Chile had the highest ratio, at nearly 100% of GDP, a level similar to those of
the US and the UK.

Moreover, there is a high degree of correlation between the growth of equities
held by pension funds (the largest holders of equities in Chile) and market
capitalisation. As shown in Figure 3, the growth path of equities held by
pension fund assets has closely matched the increase in the ratio of stock market
capitalisation to GDP.

Table 45 Stock market profile, December 1997

	Argentina	Chile	Bolivia	Peru	Colombia	Mexico	Uruguay
Number of listed companies	136	295	11	248	189	198	16
Market cap. (US$ million)	59 252	72 046	344	17 586	19 529	156 595	212
Market cap. (%GDP)	18.5%	97.7%	4.9%	28.0%	18.8%	37.3%	1.1%
Trading value (US$ million)	25 702	7 445	1	4 033	1 894	52 646	3
Turnover ratio (annual)	43.4%	10.3%	0.2%	22.9%	9.7%	33.6%	1.4%

Source: Pension Fund Regulators, Central Banks, National Securities Commissions, Queisser (1998)

Figure 3: Chile, pension fund equity portfolio and stock market capitalization, 1981-1997

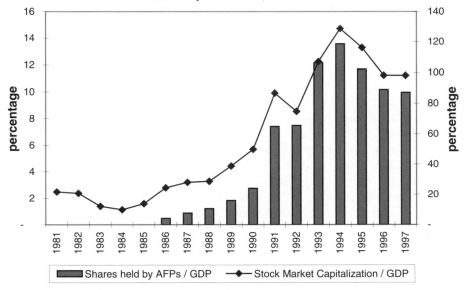

Source: Superintedencia de AFPs, Superintendencia de Valores y Seguros

107

7.3   Stability of financial markets

Volatility in financial markets has sometimes been linked to increased activity by institutional investors at the international level. The argument put forward is that herd behaviour causes these institutions to invest euphorically in markets and to flee in a panic when fundamentals do not apparently justify such actions. While herding can accelerate the market's adjustment to a new equilibrium price, it has been argued that it can also be a source of instability in markets when asymmetric information abounds and - even worse -   cause disruption in the fundamentals.

So far, however, studies have failed to find clear evidence of a long-term link between institutional investors and volatility. However, short periods of heightened price volatility seem to have become more common, especially in the smaller and less liquid segment of capital markets (Blommestein, 1998). In Latin America, capital market volatility, both long-term and short-term, has generally been higher than that of OECD countries. The impact of institutional investors on the turnover and volatility of domestic capital markets is, however, limited by the investment regulations to which they are subjects. In Chile, for example, the limitations on equity investment in force until 1985 led pension funds to invest heavily in private sector fixed-income securities such as corporate bonds and mortgage securities. As a result, pension funds quickly became the largest holders of such assets. By 1997, they held over half the capitalisation of these two asset classes (see Figure 4). The growth of equities has been much slower, but by 1998 pension funds held over 10% of the capitalisation of the stock market. Moreover, their presence in the stock market is highly concentrated. At the end of 1998, over 50% of the stocks held by pension funds were in the electricity sector.

Since pension funds in Chile (and indeed in all other Latin American countries) invest in practically identical portfolios, the extent of ownership in some markets reduces their ability to trade without affecting prices. Paradoxically, therefore, there has been little active trading in securities in Latin America. Indeed, pension funds have behaved largely as passive investors, with a buy-and-hold strategy (Reisen, 1998). In addition, since investment in pension funds is mandatory, there is no possibility of a run on pension funds. The lack of significant impact of pension funds on stock market liquidity can be seen in Figure 5, which charts market liquidity (measured as the turnover rate) and pension assets as a percentage of GDP. While there seems to be have been a jump in the turnover rate after 1985, when pension funds were first allowed to invest in equities, there is little sign that increased asset holdings and, in particular, the increase in the equity portfolio held by pension funds, has had any impact on stock market liquidity.

Figure 4: Chile, market presence of pension funds

Source: Superintedencia de AFPs, Superintendencia de Valores y Seguros

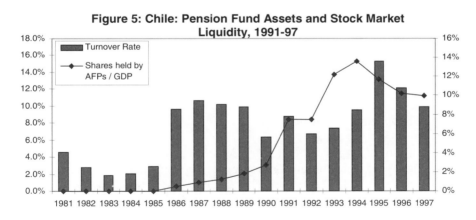

Figure 5: Chile: Pension Fund Assets and Stock Market Liquidity, 1991-97

Source: Superintedencia de AFPs, Superintendencia de Valores y Seguros

The situation is quite different for mutual funds which, unlike pension funds, have no restrictions on investment, the number of accounts or performance, and are moreover voluntary. Hence, it is likely that increased activity by mutual funds would to some extent counteract the increased stability brought about by pension funds. To the extent that mandatory pension funds dominate financial markets, therefore, it is unlikely that volatility will increase. The greater presence of pension funds in the institutional market may indeed explain why there has been very little sign of an increase in volatility in the Chilean stock market. As shown in Figure 6, apart from a rise in 1992, the trend has been towards a significant drop in volatility since the mid 1980s.

Figure 6: Chile, stock market volatility, 1985-98

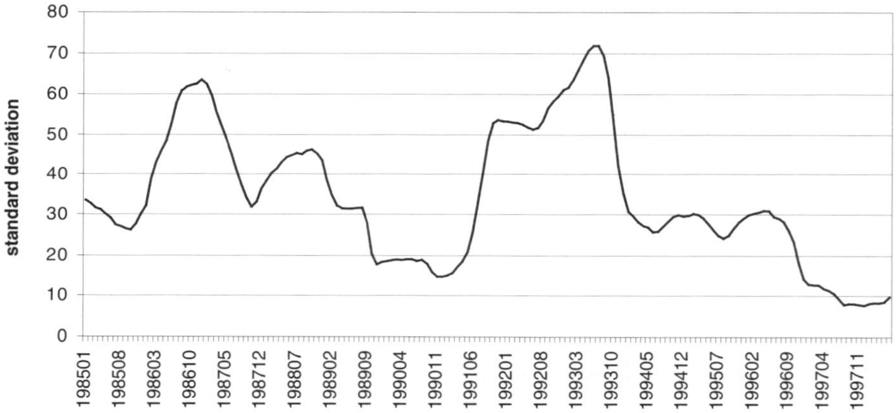

Source: Superintendencia de Valores y Seguros

7.4   Corporate governance

Despite restrictions on investment in stocks by pension funds, these institutional investors are quickly becoming on aggregate significant shareholders of some private companies in Latin America (see Table 46). In fact, to the extent that there are no limits on the aggregate ownership of a company's equity by these institutional investors, their market presence is likely to go on increasing rapidly. Mutual fund and insurance company share ownership is, by comparison, much lower, despite the lack of restrictions on investment in stocks.

The main limit to institutional investors' presence in equity markets arises from portfolio limits. Some countries prohibit such investment altogether, at least for the time being (pension funds in Bolivia, Uruguay, and Mexico). Ownership concentration rules by individual institutional investors are also applied in all the countries surveyed, the only exception being the capitalisation funds in Bolivia[27]. In Chile, for example, pension funds cannot hold more than 7% of a firm's public capital, mutual funds cannot hold more than 10%, while insurance companies cannot hold more than 10%. Brazil has a much higher ceiling for pension funds, 25%, but similar limits for insurance companies and mutual funds (10%).

Table 46 **Portfolio invested in stocks by Institutional Investors in Latin America, as a percentage of stock market capitalisation**
December 1997

	Pension Funds	Insurance companies	Mutual Funds	Total
Brazil	12.2	0.3	4.6	17.0
Chile	10.0	0.8	0.3	11.2
Argentina	3.9	0.6	0.7	5.2
Mexico	0.0	0.6	1.4	2.0
Average	6.5	0.6	1.8	8.8

Source: Pension funds, insurance and securities market regulators

As long as these constraints remain and the holdings of stocks remain low, institutional investors will probably play a passive role in corporate governance. But when institutional investors become a dominant group of shareholders, they will demand a more active role in corporate management than is presently allowed. This is most likely to apply to pension funds and insurance companies which, by the long-term nature of their liabilities, are well suited to develop a long-term interest in the companies whose equity they hold. For mutual funds, on the other hand, restrictions on their role in corporate control are likely to be less painful, because of the high volatility and liquidity of their liabilities.

7.5   The supply of risk capital

In a region where small businesses account for the bulk of sales and employment, and where there is such need for massive infrastructural investment, it may be wondered to what extent institutional investors can play a central role as providers of finance. The experience from OECD countries shows that pension funds and insurance companies tend to avoid direct investment in these infrastructure, largely because of high monitoring costs and a lack of liquidity in the investment. Instead, these institutions have opted to invest via specialised mutual funds.

In Latin America, only specialised investment funds are authorised in these markets. Pension funds and insurance companies are allowed to participate indirectly by investing in such funds in just a few countries (Argentina, Brazil, Chile, Colombia, and Peru). As with other securities, investments in these instruments are subject to portfolio limits. None of these limits are currently being exercised, though there has been an increase in activity in this area by pension funds, especially in Chile, and Argentina.

In Chile, for example, investment in private equity was less than 3%, compared to a maximum of 5%, while in Argentina investment was less than 0.1%, against a limit of 10%. In Peru and Colombia there is still no significant investment in such instruments, despite their high limits (15% in Colombia and 10% in Peru). While the uncertainty about these novel products, and their low liquidity may partly explain the limited activity in this area, it is possible also that lack of expertise in setting up these funds may be an important factor. Indeed, the creation of these funds has been mainly led by foreign institutional investors and financial companies. To the extent that more professionals enter this area, and greater involvement by foreign investors is achieved, it is likely that the supply of profitable private capital instruments will increase, and that, in consequence, institutional investors will gradually turn towards them.

Conclusion

Latin America provides an interesting showcase of how the evolution of the institutional investor sector is determined by government policies. Historically, Latin America has suffered from financial systems that lacked solidity and transparency and regulatory systems that paid little attention to prudential objectives or investor protection. In addition, decades of unstable macroeconomic conditions in many Latin American countries have limited the attractiveness of capital markets and diverted investors' attention towards short-term assets.

The 1990s have witnessed dramatic changes in many countries, from the largest, such as Brazil or Argentina, to the smallest, such as El Salvador. During this decade, inflation has been brought under control in a number of countries, while new regulations and supervisory frameworks have been established, in a short but intense experience of institutional change. Most dramatically, decades-old models of social security have been overhauled in the space of an electoral calendar, and innovative concepts for mandatory, funded pension systems have been implemented.

As reform processes throughout the region have taken hold, governments have proceeded by overhauling obsolete or ineffective regulations, and creating new supervisory agencies capable of carrying out regular, independent, and effective control of financial institutions. This trend manifests itself most clearly in the newly established pension fund industries. Mandatory pension funds in Latin America operate under modern regulatory guidelines, which are effectively enforced by new supervisory agencies. The insurance and mutual fund industries too are increasingly subject to adequate regulatory and supervisory frameworks. Remaining problems include state presence in the insurance industries of some countries (Brazil, Uruguay, Costa Rica) and the lack of effective regulations designed to prevent conflicts of interest between banking and mutual fund products. Meanwhile, much work remains to be done in the sectors of employer pension funds in Brazil, Mexico and most of Central America and the Caribbean. Employer pension funds in these countries remain relatively underregulated, especially in the areas of funding, investment, and portability rules.

While generally perceived as effective, the new regulatory frameworks have led to some controversy as to whether they are too stringent. The new regulations may help ensure the solvency of financial institutions and contain fragility in financial markets. They may also offer consumers and investors protection from institutions that are inherently better informed about the quality of financial products than either they - or the regulatory agencies - can possibly be. However, such "investor protection" may have been achieved at a high cost. Constraints on competition and interaction between the different institutional investors can raise operating costs, and these can be passed on to consumers in the form of higher commission fees. Quantitative portfolio limits may fail to permit a sufficient degree of diversification across asset classes, may hamper performance, and may even raise aggregate portfolio risk if they are set at very low levels. Mandatory savings in specific financial instruments can prevent workers from achieving better performance on their retirement savings elsewhere. Finally, organising mandatory funded pension plans at the individual level reduces incentives for establishing employer pension plans, which have lower operating expenses.

The Latin American experience shows that, although institutional investors are dependent on a strong and transparent regulatory framework and effective supervision, the specific rules to be applied are by no means free of controversy. While, in the past, draconian measures may have been necessary to limit the exposure of mandatory investments to certain markets and institutions, it is important to realise that overly stringent regulations can lead to excessive concentration of risk in too few asset classes, markets, or institutions. Modern regulatory practices that rely on risk management at the aggregate portfolio level may be better suited to ensuring an adequate degree of portfolio diversification, while the spreading of risks by investing in a range of retirement instruments may offer better performance at lower cost.

Finally, the actual development of the institutional-investor sector depends not only on finding the right balance between different goals through specific rules and regulations, but on such factors as fiscal incentives, economic growth, demographic trends, the degree of income inequality, and the process of public-sector reform. As the experience of OECD countries has shown, institutional investors thrive in economies that are ageing yet growing, that provide favourable tax treatment for long-term savings and that give an increased role to the private sector in the provision of physical and social infrastructures.

NOTES

1. Recent work on the relationship between institutional investors and financial markets include Blommestein (1998), Fischer (1998), and Vittas (1998).

2. The assets held in these funds are not trivial. In Bolivia the capitalisation fund holds approximately US$ 800 million in assets, or 12.5% of GDP. The Guatemalan social security fund has assets equivalent to 5% of GDP. These figures are higher than those of the new private pension systems except Chile and Brazil.

3. The only exception, apart from Brazil, is Mexico, where it was estimated that in the late 80s there were over 2 000 private pension plans covering up to 4 million people (Skully and Vittas, 1991). Little information is available on the size and operation of these funds, and on their regulatory and supervisory framework.

4. Assets considered are only financial, except for those of insurance companies, which also include real estate.

5. *Administradoras de Fondos de Pensiones* (AFPs) in Chile, Peru, Bolivia, Colombia and El Salvador, *Administradoras de Fondos de Jubilaciones y Pensiones* (AFJPs) in Argentina, *Administradoras de Fondos de Ahorro Previsional* (AFAPs) in Uruguay, and *Administradoras de Fondos para el Retiro* (AFOREs) in Mexico.

6. See Queisser (1998), chapter 4.

7. The first pillar consists of programs under the *Regime Geral da Previdencia (RGPS)*, which covers workers in private firms and public sector employees who were hired under the Consolidated Labor Code and the Federal, state and municipal *Regimes Juridico Unico (RJUs)*, which covers tenured government employees in the executive, legislative, and judicial branches and the military. A Constitutional Amendment in November 1998 allowed the establishment of complementary funds for the RJUs.

8. The actual amount varies between funds. Normally, the maximum that can be transferred is only achieved after a few years in the plan (about 5 on average).

The excess return accumulated in a year can be retrieved or allowed to accumulate in the fund.

9. Each exclusive fund may receive contributions from more than one PGBL plan, as long as they have similar characteristics. The funds, however, are only open to investment from PGBLs.

10. Figures for financial institution securities/time deposits include mortgage bonds, which are insignificant in most cases except in Chile, where they represent about 15% of the total portfolio (1998 figures).

11. One would expect internally managed funds to rely more on mutual funds. The largest public funds, however, are able to hire professionals to manage their funds internally.

12. The only exception is Colombia, where pension funds are also in charge of administering severance funds.

13. Contributions are themselves fixed as a percentage of salaries.

14. This situation was expected to change in 1999, when the first risk-rating company was given a license to operate in Bolivia.

15. The Mexican pensions law also requires that funds must invest in securities that encourage national productive activity, create infrastructure, generate employment, housing investment, and regional development (article 43).

16. Chile is considering changing the application of the rule to a 36-month rolling basis.

17. From 1 July 1995, the composition of the market portfolio is: (percentage of total pension-industry assets invested in shares x 90% of the average rate of return of the three stock exchanges in the country) + (percentage of total pension-industry assets not invested in shares x 95% of rate of return of a fixed-income index). As of June 1998, only 5% of industry assets were invested in equities, so the market portfolio is mainly a fixed-income index.

18. The legislation does not specify whether the calculated benefits should be indexed or not.

19 The investment regime in place before 1994 was draconian; it included investment floors.

20 Colombia (1990), Mexico (1990-9), Peru (1991), Argentina (1992), Panama (1996), Paraguay (1996), Brazil (1996-9), El Salvador (1996), and Bolivia (1998).

21. The fees are not directly comparable because, except in Mexico, pension funds charge only front-load fees. The equivalent annual asset-based fee for a Chilean pension fund over a forty-year horizon has been estimated at 1% (Srinivas and Yermo, 1999).

22. See Davis (1998), Laboul (1998), and Vittas (1998a) for a more detailed discussion on the role of regulatory regimes.

23. Cuesta, Holzman, and Packard (1999), based on fieldwork interviews in Santiago de Chile in June 1999.

24. In fact, over 80% of fixed-income products are indexed to the UF.

25. Hedging products are only available over short time periods, of less than one year. The time horizon of investors can be as long as forty years.

26. The only exceptions are Colombia and Uruguay.

27. In Bolivia, half the assets of privatised companies were transferred to the two pension funds as part of the capitalisation process.

BIBLIOGRAPHY

Blommestein, H. (1998), "Impact of Financial Investors on Financial Markets", in *Institutional Investors in the New Financial Landscape*, OECD, Paris.

Cuesta, J., Holzmann R., and Packard, T. (1999), "Extending Coverage in Multi-Pillar Pension Systems: Constraints and Hypothesis, Preliminary Evidence and Future Research Agenda, paper prepared for The World Bank Conference *New Ideas about Old-Age Security*, September 14-15, 1999.

Davis, E. P. (1998), "Regulation of Pension Fund Assets", in *Institutional Investors in the New Financial Landscape*, OECD, Paris.

FIDES (1999), *El Seguro Iberoamericano en Cifras*, Federación Interamericana de Empresas de Seguros, Mexico, D.F., January 1999.

Fischer, B. (1998), "The Role of Contractual Savings Institutions in Emerging Markets", in *Institutional Investors in the New Financial Landscape*, OECD, Paris.

Holzmann, R. (1997), "Pension Reform, Financial Market Development, and Economic Growth: preliminary Evidence from Chile", *IMF Working Paper WP/96/*34, Washington, D.C.

International Insurance Council (1998), *Latin America: An Insurance Reference Guide*, Washington, D.C.

James, E., Ferrier, G., Smalhout, J., and Vittas, D. (1998), *Mutual Funds and Institutional Investments: What is the Most Efficient Way to Set Up Individual Accounts in a Social Security System?*, paper presented at NBER Conference on Social Security, December 1998.

Laboul, A. (1998), *Private Pension Systems: Regulatory Policies*, Ageing Working Paper 2.2, OECD: Paris.

118

OECD (1997), *Insurance Guidelines for Economies in Transition*, Centre for Co-operation with the Economies in Transition, OECD, Paris.

OECD (1998), *Maintaining Prosperity in an Ageing Society*, OECD, Paris.

OECD (1999), *Institutional Investors' Statistical Yearbook 1998*, OECD, Paris.

Queisser, M. (1998), *The Second Generation Pension Reforms in Latin America*, OECD Development Centre Study, OECD, Paris.

Queisser, M. (1999), *Pension Reform: Lessons from Latin America*, OECD Development Centre, Policy Brief No. 15, OECD, Paris.

Reisen, H. (1997), *Liberalising Foreign Investments by Pensions Funds: Positive and Normative Aspects*, OECD Development Centre Technical Paper, No. 120, Paris

Salomon Smith Barney (1998), *Private Pension Funds in Latin America*, Salomon Smith Barney Latin America Equity Research, December 1998.

Shah, H. (1997), *Towards Better Regulation of Private Pension Funds*, PRE Working Paper No. 1791, Wormd Bank, Washington, D.C.

Skully, M. and Vittas, D. (1991), *Overview of Contractual Savings Institutions*, World Bank, WPS, No. 605, Washington, D.C.

Srinivas, P.S. and Yermo, J. (1999), *Do Investment Regulations Compromise Pension Fund Performance?: Evidence from Latin America*, Latin America and Caribbean Region Viewpoint Series, World Bank, Washington, D.C.

Srinivas, P.S. and Yermo, J., *International Diversification by Latin American Private Pension Funds: Issues and Prospects*, World Bank, Washington,D.C., forthcoming.

Vittas, D. (1998a), *Regulatory Controversies of Private Pension Funds*, PRE Working Paper, No. 1893, March. Washington, D.C.: World Bank

Vittas, D. (1998b), *Institutional Investors and Securities Markets: Which Comes First?*, paper presented at the ABCD LAC Conference, June 28-30, 1998, San Salvador, El Salvador

INDIVIDUAL SAVINGS AND CAPITALISATION REGIMES. THE LATIN AMERICAN EXPERIENCE

by
Pedro Corona Bozzo[*]

The crisis faced by the public pay-as-you-go (PAYG) systems around the world

The crisis currently faced by public PAYG systems is characterised by two main factors, both of them of a demographic nature: the decrease in the fertility rate and the increase in life expectancy. Since these two factors, in combination, produce a rise in the rate of dependency, it must be said that all the public PAYG systems are entering a period of profound and terminal crisis.

If we examine the fertility rate over a series of five-year periods, it can be seen that between 1950 and 1955 the average figure world-wide was 5.0 children per woman, while by 1990/1995 it had fallen to 3.0. Current projections suggest a figure of around 2.4 children per woman between 2020 and 2025.

In Latin America, the drop in the fertility rate has been particularly dramatic in Brazil, where it has fallen from 6.2 to 2.4, and in Mexico, where it has fallen from 6.9 to 3.1, in the 40 years in question (see Graph 1).

On the other hand, the increase in life expectancy which has resulted from, among other things, scientific advances, improved living conditions, a higher level of education and so on, means that pension systems find themselves obliged to provide pensions over longer and longer periods. While there is no doubt that it is the responsibility of governments to seek, and to provide a better quality of life for their populations, by improving nutrition, education and access to healthcare and providing better environmental and working conditions, there is of course an impact on the funding of pensions and health services.

---

*   President of the International Federation of Pension Fund Managers.

In short, we have a continuing decrease in the population of working age, who must take responsibility for an ever-increasing number of pensioners or people of retirement age.

As a result of the fall in the rate of fertility and the increase in life expectancy, the rate of old age dependency in the world has started to rise: this has gone from 9.2% in 1960 to 10.5% in 1995, and current trends suggest it is likely to reach 15.2% by 2025. The incongruity of having a smaller population of working age obliged to take care of an ever-increasing number of people of retirement age is now in view, and this will mean that public pension schemes are subjected to strong economic and social tensions.

Graph 1

FALL IN THE FERTILITY RATE
Number of children by region (South America/USA)

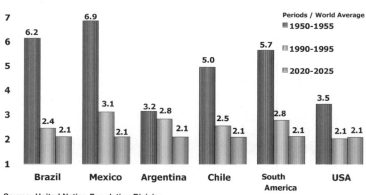

Source: United Nation Population Division

Effects of the crisis

The crisis in the public PAYG system has been highlighted by a series of negative results for the countries involved and their populations: growing deficits (the state incurs higher costs); a decrease in benefits; a permanent increase in contribution rates; and poverty and social unrest.

In South American countries, which have had rather unstable currencies, the benefits paid by the public PAYG pension system have not been inflation linked, and this has resulted in a double burden for the active population, who have had to bear higher costs and, at the same time, contribute to the intergenerational funding of pensions.

By way of illustration, the shortfall in pension funding (that is to say, the gap between contributions and the cost of pensions in real terms) recently reached 60% in Uruguay. The impact on the labour market is a negative one, since if contributions to pension systems are effectively a tax on work, they lead to a rise in labour costs, and countries and jobs become less competitive.

The situation was becoming untenable, and resulted in the changes which I shall be examining shortly.

Pension systems in Latin America

The different countries that make up Latin America may be divided into four main groups according to the type of pension system they have adopted:

Some countries have set up single systems, replacing public PAYG systems by privately managed, fully-funded pension schemes. Bolivia, Chile, El Salvador and Mexico are in this group.

There are also countries with a multi-pillar system, in which distributive public systems and private individual fully-funded schemes coexist; both are obligatory and fully integrated, and the two do not compete with one another. Argentina, Uruguay and Venezuela fall into this category.

The third group is made up of those countries in which the public PAYG system and the privately managed, fully-funded system coexist but are mutually exclusive; that is to say, they compete with one another. Colombia and Peru belong in this category.

Lastly, there are countries with complementary systems, in which a mandatory PAYG system exists alongside a privately managed, fully-funded scheme, which is voluntary and complementary. These include Brazil, Costa Rica, Ecuador, Guatemala, Honduras and the Dominican Republic.

According to data from the International Federation of Pension Funds (FIAP), 39.7 million people were affiliated to private pension systems in Latin America in June 1999. Mexico, Argentina and Chile registered the highest number of affiliates.

As regards the total assets held by pension funds, this amounted to US $ 117 307 million in June 1999. The funds are mainly concentrated in Brazil, Chile and Argentina.

Assets managed by the pension funds are expected to continue to increase significantly over the next few years; capital owned by employees is therefore being converted into valuable resources which can consolidate and sustain development and growth in our region.

From a macroeconomic perspective, we can see that in 1997, pension fund assets represented 7.9% of the gross domestic product of the countries concerned; in the year 2000 pension assets will account for 10.2% of GDP; and it is expected that by 2015, when the figure of one trillion dollars is reached in pension savings, they will represent 26.8% of GDP.

The contribution pension funds have made to national savings can therefore be recognised as particularly important in Latin America, given the serious difficulties we experienced in the past when the lack of domestic savings hampered our attempts to sustain economic development.

Pension fund investment

In Latin America, more than 60% of the portfolio is invested in fixed income instruments.

The countries in which there is higher investment in shares are those in which the system has been in operation longer, such as Argentina, Chile and Peru. In Colombia, investment in shares is negligible, while in Bolivia, El Salvador, Mexico and Uruguay it does not take place at all.

In spite of recent advances, Latin America has been slow to invest pension assets abroad since, of all the countries examined, only Argentina and Chile have so far authorised such investments. That is why looking at the way other systems operate around the world is an essential exercise which highlights the importance of diversification in investment portfolios.

Graph 2 **Latin America: Number of Affiliates to the Private Pension System**

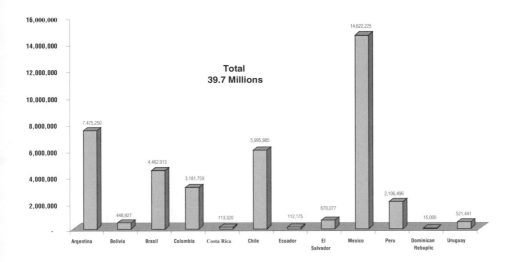

Graph 3 **Latin America: Pension Funds, June 1999**

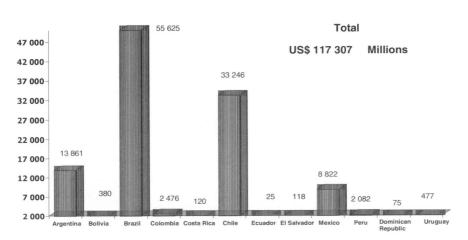

**Bolivia: Data quoted for March 1999

**Brazil: ABRAPP (March 1999) ANAPP (December 1998)

Table 1

Latin American Pension Funds
Macroeconomic Context
Assets as a percentage of GDP

	1997	2000*	2015*
Argentina	2.8%	6.0%	26.1%
Bolivia	39.80%	43.8%	32.0%
Brazil	10.0%	11.5%	24.4%
Colombia	1.5%	3.6%	26.3%
Chile	41.8%	44.3%	52.9%
Mexico	0.2%	6.2%	28.5%
Peru	2.3%	4.1%	18.5%
Uruguay	0.7%	2.3%	7.8%
Total	**7.9%**	**10.2%**	**26.8%**

Estimated
Source: Salomón Smith Barney

Table 2
Distribution of Pension Fund Investments in latin America
(in percentage terms - June 1999)

	Bonds	Shares	Foreign Investment	Others	Total
Argentina	73.58	17.33	0.23	8.86	100
Bolivia	100.00	0.00	0.00	0.00	100
Columbia	85.52	3.03	0.00	11.45	100
Chile	72.15	12.72	12.41	2.72	100
El Salvador	100	0.00	0.00	0.00	100
Mexico	97.40	0.00	0.00	2.60	100
Peru	61.86	36.84	0.00	1.30	100
Uruguay	93.20	0.00	0.00	6.80	100

Bonds include government promissory notes, term deposits, corporate donds and mortgage drafts.

The International Federation of Pension Fund Managers

To coincide with the International Congress held in Santiago, Chile, to mark the 15th anniversary of the setting-up of the Chilean system, the International Federation of Pension Fund Managers (FIAP) came into existence on 3rd May 1996.

On that occasion, 11 countries entered an agreement to establish the Federation, which now comprises 17 separate nations. Its members are associations and organisations in countries where the Pension Fund Management System is legally established or where social security systems are undergoing reform.

The aim of the Federation is to promote, co-ordinate, protect, streamline and unify the efforts and practices of members within the sphere of each country's private pension fund system.

The FIAP is a technical and professional body which aims to promote the discussion, study and analysis of individual savings and capitalisation systems.

We believe that we must face up to the new century with a different pension strategy, so that we may guarantee our employees a more secure future which does not depend exclusively on the ability of governments to face up to an obligation to pay pensions.

Challenges

Looking to the future, we need first to take up the following challenges:

- Promoting change from public to private individual capitalisation systems.

- Favouring the establishment of new rules which facilitate the transfer of pension savings for affiliated employees whose country of residence changes.

- Creating a new set of regulations which will make it easier to invest pension assets in other Latin American countries, aiding the development of capital markets in those countries.

- Emphasising the need to diversify into international portfolios. There is no sense in concentrating all of one's resources in one country.

On the other hand, we believe it is important to generate long-term funding for such purposes as helping people to purchase a home, reducing housing deficits and improving the quality of life.

A further challenge is making investment regulation more homogeneous, so that resources may be more easily channelled into projects linked to countries' basic infrastructures.

The formation of pension fund syndicates, which can play a part in the privatisation of companies, or other large-scale investment projects, is also important.

As regards the possible benefits, we are convinced that promoting regulations and requirements for old age, disability and survival pensions, and removing differences between state guarantees in the various individual capitalisation and saving systems, will be a great victory for employees.

We also need to extend pension cover, bringing independent employees into the system. We should stress that the majority of dependent employees belong to pension schemes; there are, however, a great many people who work independently, such as agricultural labourers, seasonal workers and others in various trades and occupations, who have no pension protection at all. Illiteracy and administrative difficulties are other factors preventing cover from being extended to the rural population.

Another important challenge is to offer employees a genuine pension culture, which will provide them with the tools needed to cope satisfactorily with today's world.

We are seeking to foster a change in outlook which will enable employees to understand the reasons for the crisis currently affecting the PAYG pension systems and the change in direction that pension provision is now taking.

We need all employees to recognise the advantages of the combined pension and individual savings system. An exercise on this subject should, in our view, be included in the standard syllabus in all schools, so that students are made aware of the basic features of the new system and develop a concept of pension provision which is different from that of their parents.

PENSION FUNDS IN LATIN AMERICA: FEATURES AND LIMITS

by
Aldo Simonetti[*]

Features of pension funds

General features

Following the reform of the Chilean pension system in 1981, its benefits began to attract the interest of many other countries in the region. These benefits may be summarised as the fall in the cost of pensions for employees, the sound returns on investments and the system's ability to deliver improved pensions and also its positive impact on the reform of the nation's economy.

Today almost the entire region has adopted, with varying degrees of fidelity, systems based on the Chilean model: that is to say, privately managed individual capitalisation regimes. All the countries that have not yet incorporated the model in their legislation – and these are the exception – are currently undertaking surveys, initiatives or projects on the subject. Table 1 illustrates the situation in those countries in the region, which conform to the model.

The process of accumulating funds

If we examine the features of the individual capitalisation regime, as shown in Graph 1, we can see that pension funds are currently in the process of accumulation and thus contributing significant resources to the national economies in question. It is estimated that in 2015 pension funds will represent on average 30 per cent of these countries' GDP, as shown in Graph 2.

---

*   General Manager, AFP Sta. María, AETNA International, Chile

Table 1

Country	Start of reform	Type	Number of Affiliates	Funds (millions US$)
Chile	1981	Mandatory	5 995 996	33 246
Peru	1993	Optional	2 106 496	2 076
Argentina	1994	Optional	7 475 250	13 861
Colombia	1994	Optional	2 908 633	2 110
Uruguay	1996	Optional	506 517	374
Bolivia	1997	Mandatory	461 214	333
Mexico	1997	Mandatory	14 622	8 405
El Salvador	1998	Mandatory	569 972	57
Venezuela	2000	Mandatory	--	--

Graph 1

EVOLUTION OF THE ASSETS OF LATIN AMERICAN PENSION FUNDS (figures in millions of dollars)

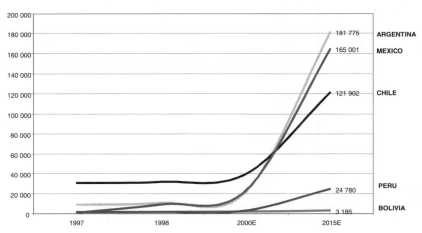

Source: Salomon Smith Barney.

130

Graph 2

EVOLUTION OF ASSETS OF LATIN AMERICAN PENSION FUNDS AS A PERCENTAGE

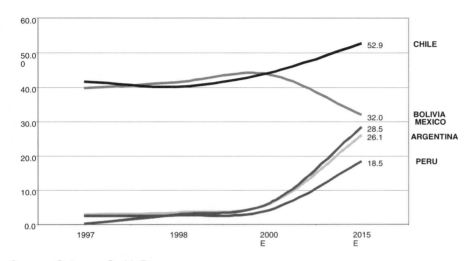

Source: Salomon Smith Barney

Chart 1

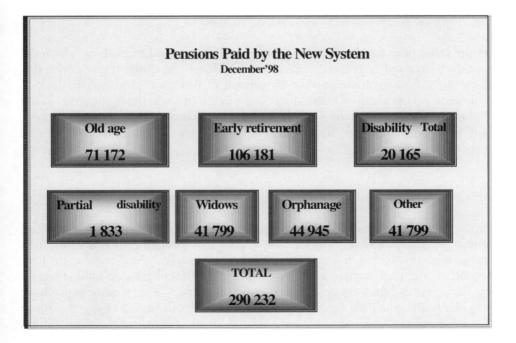

Deferred benefits

Given the particular features of this type of system and its recent implementation, its large-scale benefits are necessarily deferred and can be properly assessed only in Chile, where it has been in operation for more than 18 years.

Specific features

Since the type of systems we are dealing with have generally been in operation for only a few years, and for other reasons which we will be looking at, the resources of Latin American pension funds are characterised by the following:

Concentration in domestic markets

First of all, investment of pension funds has been concentrated in domestic markets. Eighty-five per cent of funds in Chile are, effectively, invested in instruments issued by Chilean enterprises (in both the private and state sectors), while 98% of funds in Argentina are held in Argentinean investments. Funds in Mexico and Peru are invested only in the respective national markets.

The low level of development of domestic markets

At the same time the development of the domestic capital markets in which the funds are invested is generally at a rather low level. In Chile, for example, this is due to various restraints on the movement of foreign capital and the lack of technological updating of instruments in general. In some other countries in the region, long-term financial instruments have not been sufficiently developed, and in others, the only instruments available are securities issued by the respective governments.

Inflexible requirements and the high level of regulation and control

From another perspective, the specific regulations governing investment do appear to be excessively rigid. In Chile, for example, the pension fund managers are obliged to maintain a special "reserve" fund with their own resources, and to guarantee a minimum rate of profitability based on that shown by the pension funds on a yearly average. In Chile these requirements have resulted in the so-called "*efecto manada*" (herd effect); that is to say, the funds have maintained very similar investment portfolios in order to avoid falling

132

below the minimum rate of profitability and finding themselves having to use their own resources to cover the shortfall.

At the same time, the pension fund managers generally have to comply with a series of strict rules requiring information on their investment portfolios to be made available on a daily basis, and to remain within rather rigid investment limits; all of this increases the cost of managing the funds, which must ultimately be borne by affiliates in the form of the commission paid to fund managers.

Volatility of results

Finally, a high level of volatility in results may be seen as a product of all of the above. The Chilean system has been capable of generating an average rate of profitability of more than 11% per annum in real terms, but performance has been very mixed over the years, as can be seen in Graph 3, in which standard deviation, also shown, amounts to 9.2%. The lower part of the graph shows the average figure invested in foreign instruments from 1993 onwards, expressed as a percentage of pension funds as a whole. Attention is drawn to the very significant increase experienced during the last two years as a result of modifications to the regulations in force and the arrival of genuine, and attractive, foreign investment alternatives.

Graph 3

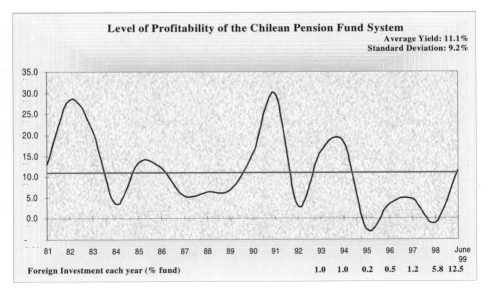

133

For their part, funds in Argentina have shown an overall return of 16.7% in real terms between September 1995 and September 1998, but with the figures for different months showing a wide variation.

The recent opening-up of investments to international instruments and markets has helped to contribute, especially in Chile, to a fall in the volatility of returns from the funds' investment portfolio, which only a few years ago was made up almost exclusively of national instruments.

Graph 4 shows not only the increase in the Chilean pension fund's level of investment abroad, but also the evolution of this type of investment from its beginnings in 1993 – which were timid in terms of scale as well as risk, with only 0.6% of funds invested outside the country (and that only in instruments offering fixed income) – to its position in mid-1999, with 12.5% of the funds invested abroad. This time, the 12.5% includes a significant percentage of variable-interest investments composed essentially of mutual funds quotas.

Graph 4

THE CHILEAN PENSION FUND'S DIVERSIFICATION INTO INVESTMENT ABROAD
(US$ millions)

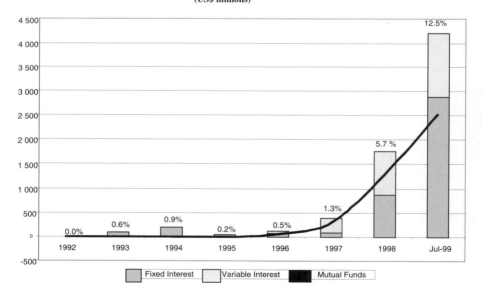

Factors limiting the development of pension funds in Latin America, and some suggested solutions

The following are some factors which limit the development of pension funds in the region, and indicate some possible alternatives which could, in our opinion, represent a solution to the problem.

Coverage

It is certainly a fact that the systems' coverage is not as wide as it should be. In Chile, for example, only slightly over 50% of affiliates regularly contribute to their scheme. Solutions to this problem may lie in greater regularisation of the labour markets of the region, especially in those countries which are less developed. Measures could include a higher level of state supervision of employers who either do not pay contributions or isolate their employees from pension cover; and introducing tax incentives to encourage independent and informal employees to contribute to the system. In the case of the last of these, it should be borne in mind that the state will often recover any money it invests in such incentives – and more – in the long term, since it will have fewer obligations in terms of minimum pensions and welfare benefits.

Commercial costs

Commercial costs have until now been a major problem for pension fund systems, particularly in Chile. There are a number of possible solutions, focusing on changing incentives for sales performance by rewarding fund managers not only for gaining affiliates but also for maintaining clients' portfolios. They could involve: legislating for the possibility of negotiating predetermined membership periods with affiliates and/or charging special commission for early switching of pension fund managers; offering other incentives to encourage the loyalty of affiliates, such as (for example) reduced commission for effective membership periods; and introducing the possibility of charging specific commission for additional special services not required by the majority of affiliates, as a way of cutting guaranteed subsidies and reducing the pressure to attract people on high incomes.

Operational costs

It has to be said that the pension systems of the region which have gone through the reform process have generally shown the ability to operate at low cost, and even to bring down operational costs on a permanent basis, albeit gradually.

However, it is possible to make further progress in this area by easing the very stringent rules (we have already referred to some of these, particularly in the area of guarantees and investments), by continuing to introduce state-of-the-art technology, and by allowing the contracting-out of many of the services offered to affiliates by pension fund managers. In the case of the last of these, we should like to draw attention to initiatives such as the Second Pension Fund bill shortly to be passed by the Chilean National Congress, which will allow the function of portfolio management to be handed over to special *sociedades anónimas* (public limited companies) with that exclusive purpose. All these initiatives are part of the search for economies of scale.

Unique product

This is a major constraint. Not only do the features of the product in question make it a form of mandatory saving, the benefits of which will not be obtained for many years, but the fact of having a unique product discourages affiliates from remaining with the same pension fund manager, and thus results in an inordinate increase in the number of transfers taking place, with the resulting cost to the system.

It would seem then, that the solution is likely to lie in measures which allow different pension fund managers to adopt different approaches without exceeding their role as administrators of pension resources. These could include allowing pension fund managers: *i)* to administer different funds (with different portfolios) – provision is already being made for this by Mexico's pension law and Chile's forthcoming 'second fund' law; *ii)* to manage voluntary pension schemes (current legislation in Chile includes various elements which operate on the basis of voluntary contributions and deposits agreed with employers – tax incentives exist in both cases and *iii)* to administer additional pension products, such as unemployment insurance accounts, savings accounts and new types of pension, such as the variable annuities already taken into account by Bolivian law.

Volatility of investments

We have already referred to the problem of volatility and the resulting high fluctuations in returns, which we noted when discussing the features of Latin American pension funds (see Graph 3). Now that operators are showing signs of increased responsibility and efficiency in their management of funds, gradual deregulation, through a more proactive outlook on the part of the respective authorities, more flexible limits for investments and an increase in international investment alternatives, should in our opinion be seen as a possible solution.

Direction of restrictions

Finally, there are currently a variety of regulations which limit the development of pension funds in that they represent burdens or risks for operators or act as a constraint or disincentive in terms of investment options. We refer specifically to the requirements imposed on pension fund managers to guarantee a minimum profitability and, to that end, maintain a reserve of shareholders' charges. In practice these regulations have generated in Chile a "herd effect".

Considering the accumulated experience and the technology available, progress in solving these difficulties cannot be made without eliminating, or at least limiting, the requirement to guarantee a minimum profitability and maintain a reserve, continuing to create new investment alternatives, and significantly increasing the limits on investment abroad.

THE REGULATION OF INVESTMENTS IN LATIN AMERICAN DEFINED-CONTRIBUTION PUBLIC PENSION SCHEMES

by
Fernando Solís-Soberón[*]

Introduction

A number of countries provide income security to the elderly through public pension systems. The way in which these schemes are structured varies considerably from country to country. Some have adopted Defined-Benefit (DB) schemes, others have adopted Defined- Contribution (DC) schemes, and others a combination of the two.

Since 1981, several countries in Latin America have carried out major pension system reform. In all of these countries, a multi-pillar approach has been followed to replace pay-as-you-go (PAYG), defined-benefit schemes. The common features of the new systems are a defined-benefit first pillar (either maintaining a pay-as-you-go scheme or providing a minimum pension guarantee) and a defined-contribution second pillar. Some have also introduced a third pillar for voluntary savings. For the second pillar, specialised pension fund managers have been licensed, and workers have been given the possibility of choosing among them. Pension funds are strictly regulated: fund managers can offer workers only one fund, for example, and investments are subject to quantitative restrictions.

The regulation of investments in these countries is inefficient. Fund managers are not allowed to diversify risks appropriately and, by restricting product

---

[*]   President of the National Commission for the Retirement Savings Systems (Comision Nacional del Sistema de Ahorro para el Retiro, CONSAR) and Professor of Economics at the Instituto Tecnológico Autónomo de México (ITAM). The opinions presented in this paper are solely those of the author and do not necessarily coincide with those of CONSAR. I would like to thank Jaime Villaseñor for his comments and Maylin Ulacia for her assistance.

diversity, the system gives workers less choice in selecting portfolios according to their risk-return preferences.

The inefficient regulation of investments has substantial costs for workers, firms and governments. Workers are obtaining smaller returns for a given level of risk or are facing greater risk for a given expected return. This means that the accumulated balance at retirement will be lower as will the replacement rate (the ratio of the pension amount to the final wage). For firms, there are costs due to the requirement that capital be invested in the same way as workers' assets. If management fees are based on net asset value, managers will also realise lower returns. The fiscal cost to government varies inversely with investment returns because there is a minimum pension guarantee (MPG). The lower the returns, the more likely it is that workers will have recourse to the guarantee.

In this paper, we analyse the regulation of investments in the defined-contribution public pension schemes in Latin America and highlight the inefficiencies mentioned above.

The first section of the paper presents a conceptual framework for pension systems. In the second, the main features of the Latin American model are discussed. The third section presents an analytical framework for different approaches to investment regulation. The fourth examines how Latin American countries with defined-contribution systems regulate pension fund investments, while the fifth assesses the costs of current regulations in Mexico. The last section summarises the main conclusions.

1.   Pension systems

The objective of public pension schemes is to provide income security to the elderly. For individuals, public pension plans are a way of smoothing out consumption over time on a compulsory basis. When a pension plan is designed, the government (the plan sponsor) must determine for plan members the target replacement rate: the target pension with respect to the last wage. The plan is usually structured so as to minimise society's contributions in achieving its goals.

The pension plan can be structured as a DC, a DB, or a combination of both. In any case, the pension scheme consists of two stages: the accumulation stage and the decumulation stage. During the accumulation stage the worker, the plan sponsor or both, contribute to the system, generally a fixed percentage of the wage, for a certain number of years or until the plan member reaches a certain age. At retirement, during the decumulation stage, the member is entitled to a pension, to a lump sum payment, or both.

Figure 1 illustrates the functioning of a pension plan. The accumulation and decumulation stages are shown on the horizontal axis. The vertical axis represents monetary units. The plan objective is to guarantee the plan member a pension equal to BD until he dies. The worker enters the labour force at point A, works for AB years, retires at point B, and receives a pension for a period of time equal to BC years.

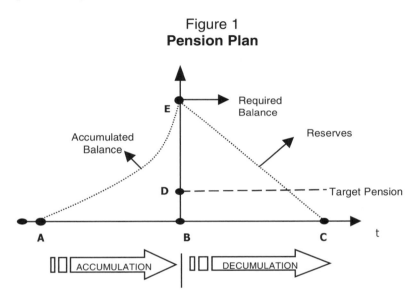

Figure 1
Pension Plan

The plan may stipulate a retirement age with a minimum number of years of contributions, or may provide a pension after a defined number of years of service. In any case, ex ante, the contribution period is a random variable. The retirement period is also a random variable, since the worker may die at any time after retirement or may live longer than expected.

The balance required to finance the pension is equal to BE. It is determined according to the joint probability of survivorship of the worker and his beneficiaries and to the expected real rate of return on the assets that constitute the reserves. The longer (or shorter) the period that the worker is expected to live as pensioner and the lower (or higher) the expected real rate of return on reserves, the higher (or lower) must be the balance required to finance the pension.

141

Given the expected number of years of contributions, the expected path of real wages, and the expected real rate of return on assets during the accumulation stage, the contribution rate, as a percentage of the wage, is determined so as to meet the target balance. The higher (lower) the expected number of years of contribution, the growth rate of wages and the expected return on assets, the lower (higher) the necessary contribution rate.

Under a DC scheme, the worker may be entitled to withdraw the balance as a lump sum upon retirement or may be required to follow a programmed withdrawal or to purchase an annuity. If the worker withdraws the balance or follows a programmed withdrawal, the annuitant will bear the investment risks and the risk of living longer than expected. If the worker purchases an annuity, the investment risk and the survivorship risk are transferred to an insurance carrier. In this case, given the accumulated balance, the pension level will depend on the price of the annuity.

Figure 2
Pension plan with lower rate of return

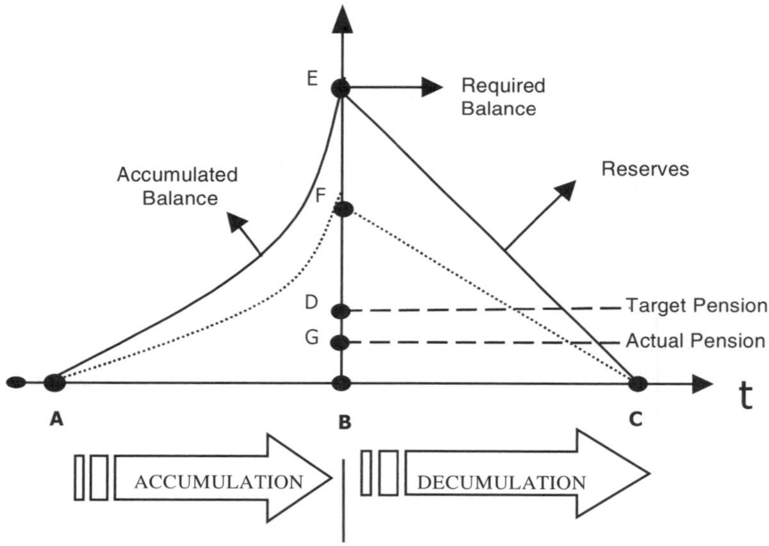

The plan sponsor and/or its member may find, ex post, that the realisation of the random variables is different from what was expected. For example, Figure 2 shows the case in which the observed real rate of return on the accumulated assets is lower than expected, everything else being equal. The accumulated balance is equal at retirement to BF instead of the expected BE. Under a defined-contribution plan, the worker ends with a lower pension, BG instead of BD. Under a defined-benefit plan, the sponsor guarantees the pension BD and therefore must meet an unexpected liability equal to EF.

As must be clear from the example, illustrated in Figure 3, under a DC plan, at retirement, assets (A) are equal to liabilities (L) whereas under a DB plan, assets may be greater than, lower than or equal to liabilities. If we define the pension plan surplus (S) as the difference between assets and liabilities (A-L), S is always equal to zero for DC plans.

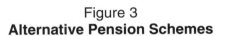

Figure 3
Alternative Pension Schemes

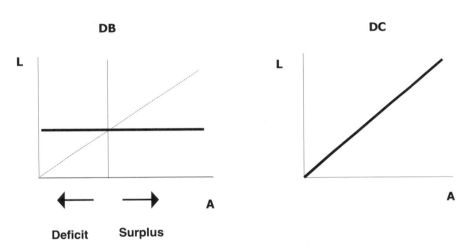

Under a DC plan, the equilibrium between contributions and payments is always achieved individually by each plan member. On the other hand, DB plans are fully funded only if the surplus is equal to zero, *i.e.* if the ratio of assets to liabilities is equal to one. If S is negative, (if there is a deficit), the plan is under-funded and, to achieve the collective equilibrium, contributions must be raised and/or benefits reduced.[1]

As has been shown by Blake (1998), there is a relationship between DC and DB pension schemes. A DB plan is equal to a DC plan plus a put option, written by the sponsor and purchased by the worker, and a call option, written by the member and purchased by the sponsor. The options are exercised at retirement with an exercise price equal to the level of assets required to finance the compromised liabilities.

In a number of countries, there are DB public pension schemes whose assets are either non- existent or lower than what would be required if promised benefits were to be financed from current contributions. Some of these plans have already accumulated substantial liabilities (measured in terms of implicit debt to GNP) that sooner or later will have to be met in some way by the governments (plan sponsors) and/or workers.

2.   Public pension schemes in Latin America

Several countries have recently reformed their public pension schemes, and many others will follow in the years to come. The reason is that these plans were simply not financially viable. Latin America is in the vanguard of pension reform. After the Chilean reform of 1981, seven countries in the region have implemented multi-pillar models for their public pension systems: Peru, Colombia, Argentina, Uruguay, Bolivia, Mexico and El Salvador.[2]

In most of these countries, a DB first pillar has been established, either by maintaining a pay-as-you-go scheme or instituting a minimum pension guarantee (MPG). A second, DC, scheme has been introduced, with private pension fund managers and individual choice. A third pillar - also DC - has been put in place for voluntary savings.

Figure 4 shows the relationship between assets and liabilities for the Latin American pension schemes with a MPG. The DB pillar is equivalent to a put option, written by the government that is given at no cost to plan members. This option may be exercised upon retirement at an exercise price equal to M. If the accumulated assets in the individual account are less than M, the option is a good one and will be exercised by the worker.

The government (taxpayers) will therefore assume a cost equal to M-A.[3]

As can be seen in Table 1, for the seven countries that have reformed their pension schemes in Latin America, there are some important differences in the rate of contribution to the new DC pillar. In some countries workers can choose between a pay-as-you-go scheme and the new system. The size of the markets, in terms of affiliated workers, varies considerably as well, as shown in Table 2.

Figure 4
Basic Design of Latin American Pension Plans

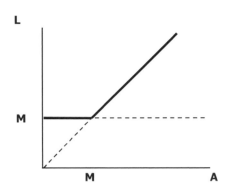

Table 1
Basic Structure of New Pension Schemes

Country	Reform year	Affiliation to the NPS	Contributions (% of wage)	Previous Scheme
Chile	1981	Mandatory	10	Gradual close
Peru	1993	Voluntary	8	Remains
Argentina	1994	Voluntary	11	Remains
Colombia	1994	Voluntary	13.50	N.A.
Uruguay	1995	Voluntary	15	Remains
Bolivia	1997	Mandatory	12.50	Close
Mexico	1997	Mandatory	13.3*	Gradual close

* calculated using average wage
N.A.: Not available
NPS: National Pension Scheme

Table 3 shows the accumulated resources at the end of 1998 and a projection for 2015. As can be seen, in Chile the accumulated balance is equal to 40% of GDP, and in Bolivia 17.8%; for the others, it is still below 4%.

Table 4 shows the number of firms in each market and the concentration ratio of the three largest firms with respect to the number of affiliates and funds under management.

Table 2
Affiliates and Contributors

Country	Affiliates	Contributors	Contributors / Affiliates
Chile	5 993 206	3 174 475	53.0%
Peru	2 106 496	896 039	42.5%
Argentina	7 475 250	3 366 206	45.0%
Colombia	3 144 824	1 639 461	52.1%
Uruguay	521 441	N.A.	N.A.
Bolivia	448 927	N.A.	N.A.
Mexico	14 750 729	9 076 345	61.5%
El Salvador	670 077	328973	49.1%

Notes: July 1999 for Mexico; June 1999 for Argentina, Peru, Uruguay and El Salvador; May 1999 for Chile and Colombia March 1999 Bolivia
          N.A.:   Not available
Sources: Information provide by PrimaAmérica, Chile; CONSAR, Reporte Estadístico Semanal, (26-30 julio)

Table 3
Accumulated Resources

Country	Accumulated Resources (millions of USD)	Accumulated Resources 1998 (%GNP)	Accumulated Resources 2015 (%GNP) (Estimate)
Chile	33 142.7	40.3	52.9
Peru	2 082.5	2.5	18.5
Argentina	13 861.2	3.3	26.1
Uruguay	476.9	1.3	7.8
Bolivia	395.1	17.8	32.0
Mexico	17 947.2	2.7	28.5
El Salvador	118.2	N.A.	N.A.

Notes: Dates at July 1999 for Mexico; June 1999 for Argentina, Peru, Uruguay and I Salvador; May 1999 for Chile and Colombia March 1999 Bolivia
          N.A.: Not available
Sources: Salomon, Smith, Barney. (1998) "Private Pension Funds in Latin America: 1998 Update."; Queisser, Monika(1998). "The Second-Generation Pension Reforms in Latin America."; CONSAR, Reporte Estadístico Semanal. (26-39 julio)

Table 4
Market Structure

	Number of Managers	CR3* (Assets)	CR3 (Affiliation)
Chile	8	70.5	70.5
Peru	5	76.2	75.2
Argentina	15	52.1	52.1
Uruguay	6	77	69.1
Bolivia	2	100	100
Colombia	8	62.5	75.8
Mexico	14	49.5	43.1
El Salvador	5	97.4	81.5

Notes: Dates at July 1999 for Mexico; June 1999 for Argentina, Peru, Uruguay and I Salvador; May 1999 for Chile and Colombia March 1999 Bolivia

Source: Information provide by PrimaAmérica, Chile. CONSAR, Reporte Estadístico Semanal. (26-30 julio)

3.   Investment regulations for pension funds

The manager of a pension fund must invest the assets in a prudent way, avoid conflicts of interest and use his professional expertise to achieve the objectives of the plan.

As mentioned above, for DB systems, plan members generally have a guaranteed replacement rate regardless of the performance of the fund's investments. In this situation, the plan sponsor bears the investment risks alone. Therefore, the fund manager must focus on proper management of assets and liabilities and must follow investment practices corresponding to the risk-return profile preferred by the plan sponsor.

Under DC schemes, the worker bears the entire investment risk during the accumulation stage. At retirement, he may transfer these risks to an insurance carrier by purchasing an annuity. Therefore, the fund manager must invest the funds according to the risk preferences of the workers in order to maximise return for his acceptable level of risk.

In the world at large, three approaches have been followed with regard to regulation of investments in public pension schemes and in the mutual fund industry[4]: (1) quantitative restrictions, (2) the prudent-person rule, and (3) the prudent-investor rule.

With the quantitative approach, the objective is to preserve the principal by limiting market- risk exposure according to the risk preference of regulators. For this purpose some assets that are considered too risky, in terms of market or credit risks, are excluded from the portfolio. Usually there is an approved list of securities which, for example, may or may not include equity or foreign securities. The approved securities are subject to minimum and maximum investment limits.

The prudent-person rule means acting as an intelligent and prudent person would in making investments. It may also have as an objective to preserve the value of the principal. Under this rule, some asset classes considered too risky are deemed unsuitable for investment, but there are neither minimum nor maximum investment limits as there are in the quantitative approach. The prudent-investor rule focuses on the risk-return profile of a portfolio, not on the risk of a particular asset, and therefore does not prohibit the fund manager from purchasing any asset class.

To illustrate the effects of imposing quantitative restrictions rather than the prudent-person rule or the prudent-investor rule, consider three assets with different expected returns and risk (measured as the standard deviation of returns), as shown in Figure 5.[5] The most risky asset is A; A is also the one with the highest expected return. Figure 6 shows all possible combinations for these assets. The efficient frontier shows those combinations with the highest return for a given level of risk.

Figure 5

Return and Risk for three assets

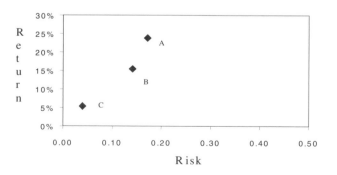

Now consider that the following investment limits are imposed on these assets: a maximum of 35% in asset A and a minimum of 30% in asset B. These limits restrict the possible combinations as shown in Figure 6, and have the effect of shifting inward the efficient frontier. As can be seen, the restrictions have the effect of limiting the risk of the portfolio. However, the quantitative restrictions also have the effect of reducing the expected return on the different portfolios for the same level of risk.

Figure 6

Markowitz´s Efficent Frontier

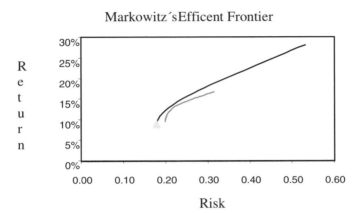

Figure 7
Efficient Frontiers

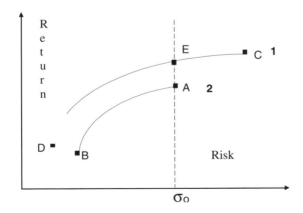

It should be clear from the previous example that the imposition of quantitative restrictions is inefficient. If a regulator wishes to limit the maximum level of risk, it would be advisable to allow the fund managers to invest in all asset classes with no restriction, and to limit risk by requiring the funds to invest in portfolios with a risk level equal to or below a given benchmark.

To illustrate the point, consider Figure 7, where two efficient frontiers are shown: 1 is the one that would be obtained without quantitative restrictions and 2 with them. As can be observed in 2, A is the riskier portfolio, and the less risky is B. In 2 the riskier portfolio is C and the less risky is D. For the same level of risk, all portfolios in 1 have higher expected returns than those in 2.

Suppose that a regulator's objective is to limit the risk of the pension funds to σ_0. This objective can be achieved with both efficient frontiers. With quantitative restrictions, the most risky possible portfolio is A, with standard deviation equal to σ_0. Alternatively, without imposing quantitative restrictions, the regulator may prohibit the pension fund managers from choosing portfolios to the left of E. This regulation will, in expected value, lead to higher returns than the one that imposes quantitative restrictions.

4.   Investment regulations of pension funds in Latin America

In Latin American countries that have adopted DC pillars, new pension fund managers have been licensed to manage the workers' accounts. These firms are tightly regulated with respect to the services that can be offered and the fees that can be charged. Besides, among other things, in most countries fund managers are able to offer only one fund, subject to quantitative restrictions, and are obliged to guarantee a minimum relative rate of return. [6]

Table 5 shows the different fee structures across the region. As can be seen, most of the countries only allow the fund managers to charge front-end fees. In some countries, it is possible to charge a management fee equal to a specific percentage of the fund assets. The country with the greatest flexibility regarding fees is Mexico.

Table 6 shows the quantitative restrictions that are imposed in six Latin American countries with DC public pension schemes. Clearly, some countries impose more restrictions in their investment guidelines than others. For example, in Mexico pension funds are not allowed to invest either in equity or in securities of foreign firms or governments. The country with the most flexible investment regime is Bolivia. Figure 8 shows the composition of investments in the region and the observed returns for the period June 1998-June 1999.

Table 5
Fee Structure

Country	NAV	Fixed	Front -end	Mixed	Average
Chile		✓	✓	✓	1.97%
Peru	✓		✓	✓	2.35%
Argentina	✓		✓	✓	3.42%
Colombia		✓			1.63%
Uruguay	✓	✓	✓	✓	2.05%
Bolivia	✓	N.A.	✓	✓	0.50%
Mexico	✓	✓ *	✓	✓	1.83%

*Only for certain services
N.A.: Not available
N.A.V.: Net Asset Value
Sources: Salomon Smith Barney (1998) "Private Pension Funds in Latin America: 1998 Update."   Queisser, Monika (1998). "The second Generation Pension Reforms in Latin America." CONSAR, Reporte Estadístico Semanal. (26-30 July)

Table 6
Limits on Instruments

	Private Firms	Privatized Firms	Public Firms	Investment Funds
Argentina	50%	20%		
Bolivia	20-40%			5-15%
Brasil	50%	10%	50%	50%
Chile*				5%
México				
Peru	20%			3%

Source: Salomon, Smith, Barney. (1998) "Private Pension Funds in Latin America: 1998 Update."

Limits to Debt Instruments

	Federal Government	Local Government	Investment Funds	Foreign Instruments	Mortgages
Argentina	50%	30%	20%	10%	40%
Bolivia	100%	10%	20%	50%	50%
Brasil	100%	50%	50%	10%	80%
Chile*	50%	40%	5%	12%	50%
México	100%				
Peru	30%		3%	5%	40%

Source: Salomon, Smith, Barney. (1998) "Private Pension Funds in Latin America: 1998 Update."

Figure 8

Composition and Return of Portfolio

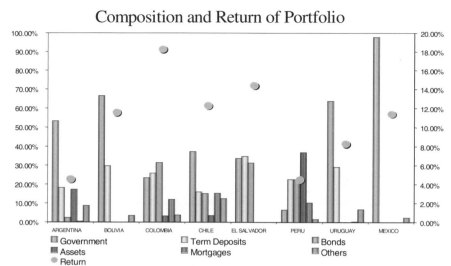

Source: Information provided by PrimaAmérica , Chile.and CONSAR, Reporte Estadístico Semanal

The rationale for not allowing a family of funds to be offered by the pension fund managers is not clear. For instance, a worker may be attracted to a fund manager because of the low fees charged for fund management but may not like the portfolio that is being offered. Besides, the more variety he is offered, the more likely it is that the worker will seek to optimise his position by selecting the portfolios according to his liquidity needs and risk-return preferences. Allowing the fund managers to offer a family of funds would enhance competition through product differentiation.

The purpose of establishing a minimum relative rate of return is to protect workers against the possibility of a badly managed pension fund. If the observed rate of return of a fund, for a predetermined period of time, falls below the average market rate minus a certain percentage, the manager is required to pay the difference to the affiliates. Managers tend to respond by closely following the investment portfolios of their peers in order to avoid losses. This phenomenon has been called the "herd effect".

The minimum relative rate of return may, contrary to its supposed objective, inhibit proper risk management and deter product differentiation, since fund managers will be more concerned not to fall below the artificial benchmark than to follow the best investment strategy for their affiliates[7].

For public pension systems like the ones recently adopted in Latin America, the investment performance of the pension funds is important not only for workers and fund managers, but also for governments. It is important for workers because, the higher the returns, the higher will be the balance at retirement and the higher the replacement rate. For fund managers with management fees based on accumulated assets, the higher the return, the higher their profits. The government guarantees an implicit real rate of return to workers through the MPG. This implicit return is higher, the higher the level of the minimum pension and the shorter the period of time that a worker must contribute to be eligible for it. Accordingly, the lower the observed real rates of return on the pension funds, the more likely it will be that a worker will exercise the put option at retirement. Therefore, for the government, the return on assets determines the fiscal cost of the pension system. As more workers exercise the option, the fiscal cost increases.

Unfortunately regulation of pension funds in Latin America imposes quantitative restrictions and restricts workers' and firms' choice. In the following section we review the investment guidelines of Mexico in order to determine the cost of the present regulations as compared to prudent-investor practices.

5.   An Assessment of the costs of quantitative restrictions in Mexico[8]

In Mexico, by law, fund managers can offer several funds but at least one must be invested primarily in securities that protect workers' savings against unexpected changes in the Consumer Price Index (CPI). Pension funds are forbidden by law to invest in foreign securities. The regulatory body of the pension funds is named National Retirement Savings System Commission (Comisión Nacional del Sistema de Ahorro para el Retiro, CONSAR). This Commission is responsible, among other things, for licensing pension funds and fund managers and for issuing the investment guidelines that must be followed by the funds.

The new pension system started operations on July 1st 1997. To facilitate workers' choice, it was decided that, during the first year, fund managers would be authorised to offer only one fund. Accordingly, the investment guidelines issued by CONSAR require the funds to invest at least 51% in securities to protect accumulated savings against unexpected changes in the CPI. It was also decided that the funds could only invest in fixed-income securities, that securities issued by private corporations must be rated and that only those with investment grade would be allowed; quantitative restrictions were imposed on the list of approved securities[9].

Table 7
Mexico's Pension Funds Investment Guidelines

		% of Total Asset Value
I.	Inflation Linked Bonds	51% Min.
II.		
	a) Bonds issued by either the Federal Government or the Central Bank (not including development Banks)	100% Max. 10% Max.
	b) Bonds issued by either the Federal Government or the Central Bank in US dollars	35% Max.
	c) Corporate bonds , bonds issued by Banks and other Financial Intermediaries and checking accounts	10% Max. 5% Max.
	d) Bonds issued by Banks and other Financial Intermediaries	$250,000.00 Max
	e) Repurchase Agreements	
	f) Checking accounts	
III.		
	a) Bonds issued by a single issuer (excluding the Federal Government and the Central Bank)	10%Max.
	b) Bonds issued by a company or Financial Intermediary in which the Fund manager has beneficial interest.	5% Max.
	c) Bonds issued by companies part of single Holding company	15% Max.
	d) Percentage of single issue that can be bought (excluding the Federal Government, the Central Bank and Financial intermediaries).	10% Max (% of the issue)
IV.		
	a) Either Fixed Rate Bonds with maturity shorter than 183 days or Fixed Rate Notes with a coupon Maturity less than 183 days.	65% Min. %Min established by the fund.
	b) Bonds either issued by the Federal Government or the Central bank with a maturity less than 90 days, checking accounts and repurchase agreements.	

The investment regime is summarised in Table 7. The funds are also required to invest at least 65% in securities issued by the Federal Government, 65% in bonds with a maturity less than or equal to 183 days or with a coupon having an interest rate that is adjusted within that period of time.

In Mexico, unlike in other Latin American countries, pension fund managers are not required to guarantee a relative rate of return. However, fund managers are obliged to establish a reserve equal to 1% of the value of the pension fund, which must be invested in the same way as workers' assets.[10]

Table 8
Asset Allocation

Manager	Market Value (millions of Mexican pesos)	Cetes	Bondes	Bonde 91	PIC	Udibonos	UMS	DEPBMX	Private	Banks
Bancomer	22 498.49	6.63	-	78.33	-	12.54	-	0.00	2.51	-
Banamex Aegon	16 737.44	8.98	-	76.21	-	12.30	-	0.00	2.52	-
Profuturo GNP	9 382.72	18.01	5.99	74.85	-	-	-	0.00	1.15	
Garante	8 437.57	9.67	-	76.05	1.61	10.63	-	0.00	1.43	0.61
Santander Mexicano	8 393.31	7.95	1.57	76.46	-	11.93	-	0.00	2.09	-
Bital	8 212.59	12.11	3.68	63.72	-	18.86	-	0.00	1.63	-
Inbursa	8 204.33	15.83	0.10	74.04	-	8.69	1.08	0.00	0.27	-
XXI	5 512.38	7.18	-	81.62	-	2.63	4.28	0.00	4.30	-
Sólida Banorte	4 868.34	4.18	6.61	75.68	0.25	11.00	0.01	0.00	1.76	0.51
Bancrecer Dresdner	3 404.58	10.88	-	82.40	-	5.48	-	0.00	1.25	-
Principal	1 899.80	35.92	-	50.17	-	10.69	1.84	0.00	0.87	0.52
Tepeyac	579.73	13.20	-	77.12	6.09	2.81	-	0.00	0.79	-
Zurich	412.59	11.14	4.76	75.93	-	7.68	-	0.00	0.49	-
TOTAL	98 543.9	9.17	1.23	76.12	0.50	10.29	0.44	0.00	2.15	0.10

October 1999
Source: CONSAR, Reporte Estadístico Semanal. (25-29 October)

Table 8 shows how fund managers are investing the pension funds according to the investment guidelines. Table 9 shows the size of each fund, the duration and the weighted average maturity (WAM). Figure 9 shows the risk/return profile of each fund.

Table 9
Value of Funds

Manager	Market Share	Duration	WAM
Bancomer	22.7%	192	209
Banamex	17.0%	185	201
Profuturo	9.6%	127	132
Garante	8.6%	224	250
Santander	8.5%	188	210
Bital	8.2%	186	202
Inbursa	8.1%	260	289
Xxi	5.6%	176	193
Banorte	5.2%	118	128
Bancrecer	3.5%	69	73
Principal	1.9%	148	174
Tepeyac	0.6%	133	137
Zurich	0.4%	126	136
Total	100.0%	182	199

November , 1999
Source: CONSAR, Reporte Estadístico Semanal.(25-29 octubre)

Figure 9

Performance Risk / Return

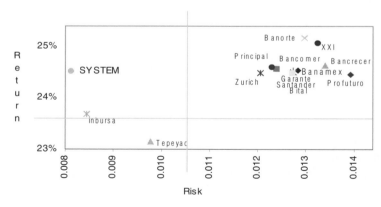

November , 1999
Source : CONSAR, Reporte Estadístico Semanal

As can be observed, even with the current guidelines, there is significant heterogeneity in the portfolios of different pension funds. Accordingly, even with the current regulations, it would make sense to allow fund managers to offer more funds.

In order to determine the cost of the quantitative approach as compared to the prudent- investor rule, three efficient frontiers for the Mexican case are shown in figure 10.[11] Efficient frontier A is the one obtained with the current regulations, B if there were no quantitative restrictions (except that funds would not be allowed to buy securities of foreign issuers) and C if no asset classes were excluded.

Figure 10
Efficient Frontiers for Mexican Case

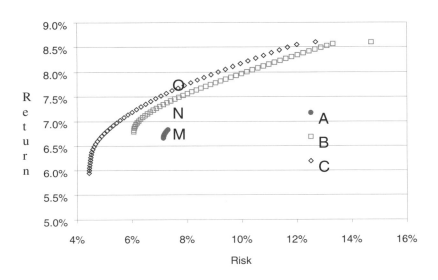

For every risk level, the expected return with quantitative restrictions is lower than with the other efficient frontiers. The quantitative approach, for every risk level, will lead to lower accumulated balances. Therefore workers will end with lower pensions, firms will earn fewer profits and the fiscal cost will be higher than it would be under the prudent-investor rule.

Portfolio M in efficient frontier A is the most risky portfolio and presumably that risk level is the maximum that the regulator is willing to bear. As can be seen in figure 10, portfolios N and O in efficient frontiers B and C have the same risk as portfolio M, but have higher expected returns: 55 basis points more with N and 75 basis points more with O.

Table 10 shows the cost of the regulation for a Mexican worker earning three times the minimum wage after 25 years of contributions, the foregone earnings of fund managers, and the fiscal cost to the government for minimum wage earners likely to exercise the put option. For the worker, the accumulated balance would be 10.8% lower with portfolio M than with N and 15.01% than with O. Fund managers would have 4.3% lower profits (net present value) with M than with N and 6.1% than with O. The fiscal cost to the government would be lower in N and O, -7.95% and –11.04% respectively.

Table 10 Cost of Investment Regulation

	% change in accumulated balance	% change in profits	% change in fiscal cost
	Workers	Fund Managers	Government
Domestic asset classes	10.8	4.3	-7.95
All asset classes	15.01	6.1	-11.04

Source: CONSAR

6.   Conclusions

This paper has analysed the regulation of pension funds' investments in DC schemes in Latin America and discussed the importance of proper regulation. Three approaches have been adopted: quantitative restrictions, prudent-person rule and prudent- investor rule. The first imposes maximum and/or minimum investment limits. The second restricts the possibility of investing in certain asset classes considered too risky. The third relies on portfolio theory, and without investment restrictions, allows fund managers to engage in proper risk management practices according to the risk-return preferences of investors.

In all Latin American countries, pension funds are tightly regulated, following the quantitative restriction approach. Some countries impose more restrictions than others in the region. The objective is to limit portfolio risk.

It has been shown that the quantitative restriction regulation on investments is inefficient. Since fund managers cannot diversify risks as they would like to, the available portfolios show lower returns for the same risk level than those that would be available with the prudent-investor rule. If a regulator wishes to limit portfolio risk for pension funds, it would be advisable not to impose quantitative restrictions. A better solution would be to regulate the risk level by preventing fund managers from purchasing those portfolios in the efficient frontier that are considered too risky by the regulators.

The regulation that has been used in Latin America has important costs for workers, firms and governments (pension plan sponsors), due to lower expected returns for every risk level. For workers, lower returns lead to lower accumulated balances at retirement and lower replacement rates. For firms, the opportunity cost of capital requirements is higher and future expected profits lower. For governments, a lower return on assets entails a higher fiscal cost because of the minimum pension guarantee.

Regulation also restricts product differentiation by not allowing fund managers to offer several products, *i.e.* several funds under different price structures. Workers have different preferences, but this restriction prevents them from choosing among different portfolios even within the same firm and hence leads to a lower level of welfare.

An assessment of the costs of the regulation of pension fund investments in Mexico has been provided. It has been shown that, for the maximum risk portfolio that pension funds are allowed, expected returns are 75 basis points lower than with the prudent-investor rule. This will lead, in terms of expected value, to accumulated balances 13.75% lower, to firms' profits 6.72% lower and a fiscal cost 12.41% higher than would be needed to achieve regulators' goals.

NOTES

1.   It is possible to find DB plans where assets are not properly managed. In this situation, it may be possible to close the gap between assets and liabilities by improving expected returns on assets.

2.   Venezuela, Panama, Costa Rica and Nicaragua are in the process of replacing their pension systems.

3.   It may be that, for the established level of MPG, low-income workers will always accumulate fewer assets than M for the expected rates of return on assets, expected contribution period and expected wage path. In this situation the MPG is not only a shelter for poor performance of the variables that determine the accumulated balance, but also an instrument for redistributing income.

4.   See Davis (1995).

5.   The discussion that follows has been familiar since Markowitz (1952).

6.   In Mexico, there is no guaranteed minimum relative rate of return and, by law, the fund managers can offer several funds. However, only one fund is currently authorised. Recently, Chile reformed the pension law to allow the fund managers to offer a new fixed-income fund.

7.   The only country in the region without the minimum relative rate of return guarantee is Mexico.

8.   This section will discuss only the investment guidelines for the pension fund managers and therefore the analysis is limited to the accumulation stage. It should be mentioned, however, that in our opinion there are also significant inefficiencies in the regulation of investments for the insurance companies that supply annuities during the decumulation stage.

9.   Suitability for purchase by the pension funds is assessed according to the following criteria (Standard &Poor's): short-term securities (maturity less than or equal to one year) mxA-1, mxA-1; mxA-2; mxA-3; long-term secutities mxAAA, mxAA and mxAA.

10.   Fund managers are also required to have 25 million pesos as capital, plus the maximum between 25 million pesos or 1% of the assets under management as a special reserve, plus 4 million pesos as a minimum capital for the fund. The fund managers' capital must be invested in the pension fund.

11.   The technical details can be found in Villaseñor (1999).

REFERENCES

CONSAR, Impacto del Régimen de Inversión en los Participantes del Sistema de Pensiones. Working Paper, 1999.

Blake, David, Financial System Requirements for Successful Pension Reform, presented at Pension Systems in Asia, Manila, 1998.

Davis, E. Philip, Pension Funds: Retirement Income Security and Capital Markets, Clarendon Press, Oxford, 1995.

Markowitz, H. M., Portfolio Selection, Journal of finance, 1952.

Pozen, Robert C. The Mutual Fund Business. The MIT Press, Cambridge, Massachusetts 1998.

Queisser, Monika. The Second-Generation Pension Reforms in Latin America. Development Centre Studies, OECD 1998.

Salomon Smith Barney, Private Pension Funds in Latin America 1998 Update, Industry Report, 1998.

Shah, Hemant, Towards Better Regulation of Private Pension Funds, in Promoting Pension Reform: A critical Assessment of the Policy Agenda, Asian Development Bank, Manila, 1998.

Villaseñor, Jaime, Effects of Pension Fund Guidelines on Investment Returns. CONSAR Working Paper, 1999.

REGULATION AND CURRENT SITUATION OF PENSION FUND INVESTMENTS IN PERU

by
Augusto Mouchard[*]

This paper begins with a brief overview of the private pension system in Peru. It then outlines how the industry is regulated and describes the role of pension fund managers. After examining the overall situation regarding investments, it looks at some of future challenges and concludes with some general considerations and recommendations for future action.

1. Features of the private pension system

The principal characteristics of the Peruvian pension system may be summarised as follows:

- Symmetry between contributions made and benefits obtained

- The value of the pension secured at the end of an affiliate's working life will depend on the amount accumulated during the period he or she has spent within the system, so that increased length of service will be rewarded by a higher level of pension.

- Participation of the private sector in welfare management

- The private sector participates directly in the private pension system through the pension fund managers. It administers the pension funds and, through the insurance companies, manages the risks of disability and death during active service, as well as granting annuities to those pensioners who opt for them.

---

*   Superintendent, Superintendency of Pension Funds Administrators, Peru.

– Openness and accountability

– There is an ongoing process of informing affiliates on how the system is evolving in regard to the destination of investments, the profitability achieved by the pension fund managers, the contribution records of affiliates and other factors which are likely to be of interest. The aim is to improve the flow of information within the system, and so provide those involved with an environment that enables affiliates to make more informed decisions.

– Government supervision

– The participation of the private sector in the administration of any mandatory saving on the part of affiliates requires the assurance of an adequate level of regulation by the government through the Superintendency of Pension Fund Managers, whose aim is to supervise and monitor the system and its sound functioning.

2. Regulation of the industry

When pension funds are of a long-term nature, it is important to ensure that the regulations introduced are both a) maintained on a solid basis and b) flexible enough to provide an adequate response to the challenges and innovations of the capital and social insurance markets as a result of increasing globalisation and specialisation in world business.

Likewise, it should be ensured that any regulation introduced does not significantly impede the free development of participating agencies so they can generate the climate of competition necessary to obtain improved standards of quality that are in the interest of the pension system in general.

A dilemma inevitably arises here: how far should the industry be regulated? What level of intervention is necessary, and how can it be achieved? There are, no doubt, a number of possible responses. These depend on the type of system in question, which will vary according to the degree of development and maturity shown by the industry.

The specific regulation of investments in the private pension system, as well as being designed to encourage maximum profitability in real terms, and the highest level of security, needs to focus on the following points:

- The instruments available to the funds should be offered within a limited framework.

- Investments should be in classified instruments.

- Maximum limits should be established for instruments, groups of instruments, issuer and amounts issued.

- There should be a guaranteed minimum return in relation to the average within the private pension system; the yield should be non-negative in real terms for a period of five years.

- Guarantees, in the form of a legal reserve should be established.

- The practice of investment instruments being kept by custodian institutions should be mandatory.

- Information should be provided daily on the status of investments

It should be emphasised that regulation in Peru came about within a context of wide-ranging structural reforms carried out by the government in a number of sectors, which included, inter alia, parliamentary reform, the pensions system, capital markets and the financial system in general. It should also be pointed out that a series of measures were introduced to tighten up the running of the private pension system in order to improve its ability to adapt to their development, in particular in the financial system.

3.　　Pension fund managers

During the first stage of consolidation of the system, which took place between 1993 and 1996, three mergers of pension fund managers took place, bringing the total number down from eight to five. In each case, the stated aim was to consolidate the system by strengthening the capital backing of the fund managers and by improving efficiency in the provision of services to affiliates.

It is interesting to note that significant differences exist between the portfolios administered by the pension funds. Some have aimed at gaining a large share of the market, while others have targeted markets selectively, favouring aspects relating to deposits, depending on employers' expansion and growth policies. It is interesting to illustrate the differences between the various pension fund managers in terms of the contributions affiliates are able to make and the size of the funds administered, as seen below:

165

Graph 1

Differential between affiliates' portfolios by pension fund manager (000s of nuevos soles** per affiliate) (1)

Distribution of affiliates by pension fund manager(1)

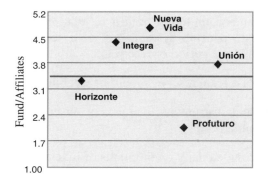

(1) at 13 August 1999
** The *nuevo sol* is the Peruvian unit of currency

Regarding the structure of commission charges made by pension fund managers, it will be noted that in 1997 the right to charge a fixed commission on salaries, or to charge commission on balances administered, was abolished. This means that the only commission that can now be charged is the variable fee on salaries which, in line with existing rules, allows varying rates to be charged depending on the period of time affiliates have spent within a given fund.

4.   The situation regarding investments

4.1   Peruvian capital markets

In 1993 the Peruvian capital market was small in scale. Its liquidity levels were low, due in part to the limited number of investment instruments available, notably short-term bank deposits and a stock market which was relatively undeveloped.

Nevertheless, from 1994 onwards a number of new instruments have been issued, in order to satisfy the pension funds' demand for investment. A medium and long-term fixed-income market in which a growing number of more substantial and more sophisticated fixed income securities are being issued has thus started to come into existence.

166

Graph 2 **Investment Instruments in the Managed Portfolio**
(1993-1999) [1]

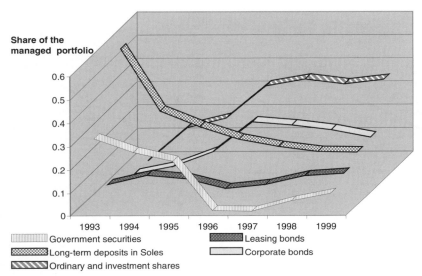

Share of the managed portfolio

- Government securities
- Long-term deposits in Soles
- Ordinary and investment shares
- Leasing bonds
- Corporate bonds

1.   13 August 1999

As part of the economic programme, the government no longer issues debt locally, and it is therefore the number of fixed-income securities issued by private firms which stands out in this graph; while financial institutions issue bank leasing bonds and subordinate debt, non-financial companies – most of them industrial – issue corporate bonds and structured bonds, which offer features designed to satisfy pension funds' investment needs.

Likewise, the mortgage securities market, which issues securities on terms of up to 15 years, is beginning to gain importance. Also, in the short-term market, commercial bonds are now being issued for the first time, and investment in certificates of deposit is also experiencing significant growth, since in the absence of other investment instruments these securities have become a natural source of investment for pension funds.

It should be noted that many of the above-mentioned issues have taken place in CAV *soles* (instruments issued at constant actual value). The pension funds, which held no long-term fixed-income investment instruments in 1993, had placed 62.8% of their investment portfolio in this type of instrument by the end of July 1999.

4.2   The share of the pension fund in capital markets

Graph 3

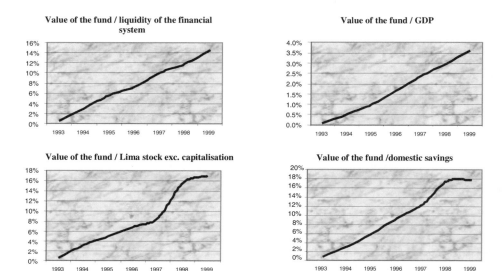

Value of the fund / liquidity of the financial system

Value of the fund / GDP

Value of the fund / Lima stock exc. capitalisation

Value of the fund /domestic savings

(1)July 1999

As can be seen clearly from these graphs, the volume of funds has shown consistent growth since the system was first set up. In July 1999, six years after the pension fund system was started, the resources accumulated reached US$ 2.1 billion, or 3.6% of GDP, 14.5% of the liquidity of the financial system as a whole, 17% of the capitalisation of the Lima stock exchange and 18% of domestic savings.

Attention should be drawn to the fact that the pension funds are gaining a significant share of the domestic savings market; this situation helps to strengthen the domestic position as far as the financing of the real sector in Peru is concerned.

Likewise, the impact of the pension funds on capital markets is shown by their very active participation in the secondary securities market dealing in stocks and shares. They now account for about 38% of the volume of share dealing and 60% of the dealing in bonds on the Lima stock exchange. The effect that this share in the market has had on the volume of dealing currently taking place on the Lima stock exchange is considerable.

In short, the pension funds have become the country's main institutional investors, with total assets exceeding the total of the mutual funds currently operating within the Peruvian market. They have made a sizeable contribution to the growth of the national capital market in both quantitative and qualitative terms by broadening the range of instruments available, extending investment horizons to longer terms and enabling private risk to be shouldered by the risk-rating industry, in which pension fund managers have been the main driving force.

4.3 *Profitability of investments*

Graph 4
Collection vs. profitability in the private pension system
(August 1993 – July 1999)

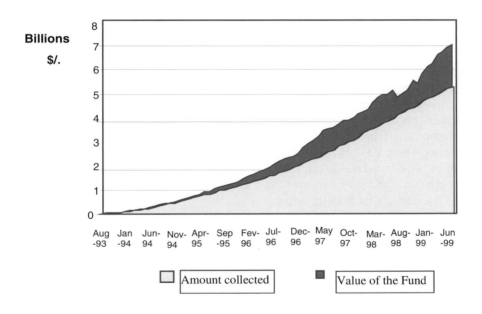

This graph shows that, of the total value of pension funds in July 1999, 75.4% (US$ 1.5 billion) represented employees' contributions and 24.6% (US$ 514 million) the accumulated return.

Investments are gradually being diversified in line with the development of the local assets market. For instance, in 1993 the ten main issuers secured 96.4% of investments, while in July 1999 the ten main issuers succeeded in attracting only 51.2% of the total. Likewise, the investment in shares issued by financial institutions as a percentage of total funds fell from 86.5% in 1993 to 45.6% in July 1999.

For its part, the profitability of pension funds (as measured over the last 60 months) is now showing an annual average return of 5.9% in real terms. This figure suggests an optimistic outlook for the system in terms of its ability to provide affiliates with adequate pensions at retirement, achieving replacement rates that are satisfactory in social terms.

4.4 The contribution made by pension funds to the country's development

The process of collection started in July 1993, resulting in a relative shortage of investment alternatives for pension funds, both in terms of level of stock and of adequacy to the conditions of maturity and currency matching.

Thus, although the system is designed to contribute to the strengthening of social security in the area of pensions, it also generates positive side effects, especially in terms of the growth of the capital markets. In this respect, the implementation of a scheme of mandatory risk rating for investments has gradually encouraged improved handling of information on the part of those issuing securities, and an improved process of evaluation of the qualities of securities on the part of investors. At the same time, the increasing accumulation of investment resources, and the stability and macroeconomic growth experienced during the early years of the system have created conditions which have allowed the greater demand for investment instruments on the part of the pension funds to be met by the gradual appearance of new alternatives for the investment of funds in the market.

We would also stress the importance of social insurance as regards the management of risk of disability and death on the basis of premiums collected by the insurance companies during employees' active service, and the still limited annuities market represented by retired pensioners.

5. Challenges for the future

The Peruvian system has been in operation for six years. During this time the profitability across pension funds has been very close to the average of the system as a whole, with minor variations between the different fund managers. This situation seems to be due partly to the requirement to achieve a minimum level of return calculated in relation to the system average.

This requirement appears to create incentives for pension fund managers to keep the average return of the system as a whole as their benchmark. Their central aim then is no longer merely to obtain the highest potential return for affiliates but rather to ensure that returns do not fall below the minimum level.

One way of encouraging competition between pension fund managers, on the basis of profitability, and thus avoiding the situation in which different investments perform at a similar level, would be to set up management portfolios graded according to risk level and requirements for minimum growth. Pension fund managers could then compete amongst themselves to obtain increased returns. This would provide the general public with an improved perception of the services offered by pension funds.

In this way, portfolios categorised by level of risk would allow the different degrees of risk aversion experienced by affiliates during the course of their lives (they are likely to be more conservative as they get older) to be taken into account. An affiliate who has recently entered the labour market thinks in terms of a retirement still some way off, and may prefer to invest in a portfolio more exposed to risk but offering potentially higher returns, basically through a high level of participation in instruments with variable yields. On the other hand, an affiliate who is close to retirement would be well advised to hold a portfolio which is less volatile over time and which is generally concentrated in instruments offering established returns.

This so-called multipolarity of funds could contribute significantly towards overcoming some of the limitations of the pension systems in Peru by promoting more effective competition between the different fund managers and improving the service offered to affiliates in terms of better potential yields and a wider choice of alternatives.

6. Final considerations

We need to be aware that the reform of the pension system in our country was designed to achieve increased efficiency and fairness in the granting of pension rights. This was a matter of providing the affiliate with security for the future, enabling him or her to face up to economic contingencies and ensuring that Peruvian families can rely on a higher degree of protection.

To achieve this end, specialised strategies have been put into practice, such as regulations governing pension fund investments. These have the flexibility necessary to adapt to the country's economic progress and cycles of activity.

Nevertheless, we must not forget that the fluctuations of the world market are transmitted with ever-increasing intensity and speed due to the disappearance of political and economic boundaries; large-scale flows of capital accelerate the globalisation process and technological innovation, the impact of which will increasingly be felt in the fields of education and employment.

It is here that those of us who are responsible for the supervision and regulation of the pension schemes should concentrate our greatest efforts, so as to encourage and formulate a creative and effective approach to the restrictions and the challenges which will surely be imposed upon us over the coming years by new labour market conditions and recruitment patterns.

THE REGULATION OF LIFE INSURANCE POLICIES IN CHILE

by
Mónica Cáceres[*]

This presentation gives a brief overview of the position of the insurance sector as an institutional investor in Chile; it highlights some aspects of regulation, which seem to warrant attention and examines how life insurance policies have evolved over the past decade.

I.   A brief overview of institutional investors

The major institutional investors in Chile are pension fund managers and the insurance companies, in particular life insurance companies.

Managers of non-pension related funds, of which three types exist in Chile –mutual funds, foreign capital investment funds and investment funds– also play an important role as institutional investors.

The figures in the following table give an idea of how these institutional investors have evolved in recent years.

It may be noted from their total assets that insurance companies are the second largest category of institutional investor in Chile, their growth being closely linked to that of the pension system. At the end of 1998, the investment portfolio held by the pension fund managers and insurance companies as a group represented 54% of GDP.

There seems to be little need to go into an in-depth analysis of the impact of institutional investors on the nation's economy, since this has been widely commented on. However, I should like to stress two factors related to the insurance industry, which seem to me particularly relevant:

---

[*]   Intendant of Insurance, Superintendency of Securities and Insurance of Chile (SVS).

a) Housing construction

The insurance companies and pension fund managers have financed thousands of private homes through the purchase of mortgage securities, issued by the banks and also, in the case of the life insurance companies, through the granting of endorsable mortgage bonds. The investment in mortgage securities by insurance companies and pension fund managers is now almost eight times higher than it was ten years ago, while the life insurance companies have invested heavily in endorsable mortgage bonds; according to estimates by the SVS (Superintendencia de Valores y Seguros de Chile), insurance companies have financed the purchase or construction by private individuals of more than 20 000 homes since this instrument was first introduced in 1988.

b) Infrastructure

Insurance companies have participated in the financing of infrastructure projects by acquiring "infrastructure bonds". Although this tool has not been fully developed, it plays an important role in the nation's development, insurance companies being the main purchasers of these bonds.

Institutional Investors' Total Assets
(in millions of dollars in december of each year

	Pension Funds Managers	Insurance Companies	Mutual Funds	Foreign Investment Funds	Investment Funds
1990	6 679	2 080	435	455	-
1991	10 088	2 811	849	954	22
1992	12 416	3 726	944	1 091	60
1993	15 972	4 620	1 240	1 563	107
1994	22 332	6 458	2 087	2 097	304
1995	25 433	7 760	2 549	1 949	901
1996	27 523	9 136	2 812	1 408	1 073
1997	30 863	10 757	4 241	1 386	1 273
1998	31 145	11 281	2 739	852	1 254

Source: S.V.S. / S.A.F.P.

The importance of investment in projects which are considered to have a social dimension can be seen clearly in the profile and growth of insurance companies' investments. At present, these are concentrated in government securities, which represent 37% of the total, and in housing finance, such as mortgage securities and endorsable mortgage bonds, which together account for some 33% of the portfolio as a whole, or almost twice the level of investment they represented nine years ago (17.5% in 1989).

Total Investments held by Insurance Companies
(in millions of dollars in December of each year)

	1989	1990	1991	1992	1993	1994	1995	1996	1997	1998	% 1998
Shares	89	101	231	318	369	675	737	612	576	357	3.4
Term deposits	178	119	151	171	194	222	200	280	181	252	2.4
Mortgage securities	202	259	329	418	612	934	1288	1757	2241	2502	23.9
Mortage mutuals	17	42	70	121	187	291	397	569	776	939	9.0
Corporate bonds	259	391	534	633	667	872	874	1030	1139	1245	11.9
Government securities	407	714	941	1321	1718	2283	2796	3262	3769	3866	36.8
Foreign investments	0	0	0	0	0	6	8	27	73	104	1.0
Other investments [1]	157	227	286	360	406	585	820	954	1105	1219	11.6
Total	1309	1853	2541	3342	4155	5869	7120	8490	9859	10483	

(1) Includes investments in property, mutual funds, saving banks and banks (and other investments held).

Souce: S.V.S.

II.   Regulation

If the growth of the insurance industry is to be sustained, it is important to have a suitable legal and regulatory framework – one allowing freedom to manage investments as well as providing the necessary safeguards. The search for a balance between profitability and risk, within an adequate set of rules governing diversification, will mean that profits can be secured with a limited level of risk without jeopardising the inherent strength of the system.

In this context, it falls to the supervisory bodies to fulfil their responsibilities in a professional manner. The approach adopted should allow a degree of self-regulation and give priority to an appropriate level of technological support.

1. Investments

The insurance companies can invest their technical reserves (TR) and risk capital (RC) in any legally authorised instruments and assets; they may choose freely within authorised portfolios and are not tied to a minimum investment in each type of instrument. There are maximum investment limits, however, as well as limits to diversification in terms of issuers, relations with economic groups, risk rating and so on. The companies can also deal in derivatives, but only in order to hedge against financial risk.

Eligible investments	Maximum **Limits** % TR & RC
- Government Securities	50%
- Securities issued by the banking system *	40%
- Mortgage securities *	40%
- Endorsable mortgage bonds	40%
- Corporate bonds *	40%
- Shares in public limited companies (PLCs)	40%
- Investment fund quotas	10%
- Investments abroad **	20%

(*) :   These securities must carry obligatory risk rating; by private classifying agents, equal to or higher than BBB.

(**):   Fixed income instruments abroad must carry an 'investment grade' risk rating.

2. Relationships between insurance companies and the finance industry

The interrelationship between different sectors of the financial world is now very much a reality: in Latin America, the insurance, banking and securities sectors were brought together some time ago, and the 1990s have seen the social security sector become very much a part of this world, particularly in Chile where the private pension system came into existence in the early 1980s. It is also true to say that these sectors have developed in a sphere in which there is significant participation on the part of financial conglomerates.

The link between insurance and other financial sectors is particularly strong in two areas:

– **Investments**

  – The insurance companies invest large quantities of their resources in securities issued by companies which may have business relations with the same financial conglomerate; for its part, the insurance company which itself invests in that conglomerate may or may not have formal links with it. This connection between different economic groups brings with it the problem of conflicts of interest.

– Commercialisation

- Insurance companies can sell insurance policies through banking brokerage subsidiaries; certain safeguards are in place to protect those insured from improper pressure on the part of the banks. This means that the banks cannot sell insurance policies directly.

- If the interrelationship between the different financial sectors is to make a significant contribution to the development of a solid assets market and also to the progress of the insurance sector, it is essential to have in place appropriate regulation ensuring efficient supervision so as to minimise any conflicts of interest that may arise.

- In the sphere of investments, regulation has been put in place to limit investment in instruments issued by companies which have business relations with the insurance firm. Laws governing the securities market also ensure that the regulator also supervises individuals who, because of their position, are aware of decisions to buy, maintain or sell investments.

- As far as the marketing of insurance through banks is concerned, the intention is to protect those insured from improper pressure to take out insurance policies through a bank brokerage subsidiary. This will be a matter for the insurance ombudsman. With the aim of safeguarding the rights of those insured to decide freely whether or not to take out a particular policy, it is prohibited to make the purchase conditional upon the provision of other benefits, products or services provided by the parent company, in this case the bank.

3. *Requirement on the part of life insurance companies to hedge financial risks*

In Chile, life insurance companies have to date sold 215 000-annuity policies. As these are long-term policies (payment is made over 20 to 25 years on average), the level of the financial liability carried by the insurers is high.

177

Insurers are facing up to the challenge of having to place funds received in the form of a lump sum in investments which offer a term profile roughly equivalent to the liabilities held; that is, maturity matching is sought between the payment of pensions from pension annuities and the dividends from investments in which these funds are placed. Where this matching is high the life insurance companies will be less exposed to reinvestment risk.

Liability flows are covered in full by asset flows only up to year 16 in Chile; from year 17 onwards, matching is partial since few long-term financial instruments, which would enable final pension payments to be covered, are available locally. Those instruments on the Chilean market in which insurance companies do invest mature on average over a period of less than 20 years.

The types of fixed income financial instruments in which life insurance companies invest pension assets are as follows:

CHILE	% of total fixed income
Government securities Maturing on average over less than 20 years	42%
Corporate bonds Maturing on average over less than 15 years	14%
Mortgage securities Maturing on average over less than 15 years	28%
Mortgage mutuals Maturing on average over less than 20 years	10%
Real estate leasing contracts Maturing on average over less than 24 years	3%
Fixed term deposits	3%

Source: SVS, December 1998

We may infer from the above that, as in Chile, there will be a strong demand for long-term investments in the other Latin American countries where social security reforms have been introduced.

Turning now to the composition of the fixed-income investments of "Retirement Insurance Companies" in Argentina and pension-related insurance investments in Mexico, we note that, in both of these countries, the government instruments in which insurance companies invest do not have a term profile well suited to effective 'matching'. This reflects the shortage of long-term investments of the type in which life insurance policies linked to the pension system are currently placed.

178

ARGENTINA		MEXICO	
Government instruments (public securities) Maturing on average over less than 8 years	42.9%	Government securities Maturing on average over less than 3 years	67.1%
Corporate (negotiable) bonds Maturing on average over less than 5 years	5.6%	Corporate bonds Maturing on average over less than 3 years	12.6%
Fixed term bank deposits	40.6%	Bank deposits	20.3%
Fixed income investment funds	7.6%	Fixed-term investment funds	-
Loans (mortgages, sureties, other)	3.3%	Loans (mortgages, sureties, other)	-

Source: SSN Argentina, December 1998   *Source:* CNSF Mexico, December 1998

The challenge therefore is to set up fixed income instruments with a long-term profile. A united effort on the part of the insurance sector, the supervisory bodies and the government would allow securities of this type to be issued, thus favouring the financing of long-term projects. An example of is the creation in Chile of the infrastructure bond and of securitised bonds, designed to satisfy life insurance companies' matching requirements. If successful, this type of instrument could also benefit capital markets.

III.   Development of the life-insurance market

The life insurance market is made up of two main types of insurance: those, which are linked to the pension system, representing 72% of sales, and those that are not (28%).

The composition of the life insurance market in December 1998 is as shown in the following diagram:

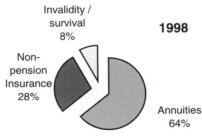

The life annuity is currently the main form of insurance in the life insurance industry. Sales of annuities are closely linked to decisions made by people at the time of retirement, the profitability of pension funds at this time being one of the principal deciding factors.

Annuities have evolved rapidly over the last ten years, having multiplied by a factor of 15. They currently represent 64% of the life insurance market.

Year	Premium (*)
1988	74
1989	160
1990	299
1991	431
1992	525
1993	598
1994	723
1995	928
1996	1 128
1997	1 270
1998	1 101

(*) in millions of dollars per year .

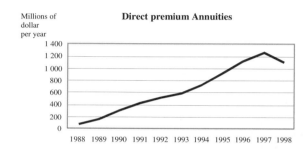

In 1998 there was a fall in the sale of annuities: the low profitability of pension fund investments that year led many affiliates to postpone the decision to take up their pensions until the situation improved. To ensure that future pensioners did not find themselves faced with fluctuations in profits at the time of retirement, the pension fund managers approved introduction of a second fund made up of fixed income investments.

The other form of pension insurance on the market is disability and survivor's insurance. The contracting out of these policies is mandatory for pension fund managers, who must cover the risk of the disability or death of affiliates. This type of insurance represents some 8% of the life insurance market as a whole.

The importance of insurance policies not linked to the pension system should not be overlooked. Although the figures for these policies are not strictly relevant, the growth they have sustained over recent years certainly is. This growth is shown in the following chart:

Direct Premium (Non-Pension Related) Insurance Policies
(millions of US$ per year)

	1988	1989	1990	1991	1992	1993	1994	1995	1996	1997	1998
Life	25	32	40	49	58	64	74	103	122	157	180
Individual	(12)	(14)	(17)	(24)	(31)	(35)	(42)	(57)	(74)	(101)	(123)
Group	(13)	(18)	(23)	(24)	(27)	(29)	(32)	(46)	(48)	(55)	(57)
Income	2	2	2	1	1	1	1	2	2	7	5
Mixed	10	13	18	23	31	37	45	62	73	86	82
Health	4	6	8	11	15	20	29	45	61	75	83
Tax Relief	15	17	18	21	25	33	41	58	78	100	108
Other	3	3	4	7	8	16	13	15	17	22	22
Total	58	73	90	111	139	171	204	286	353	447	480

There has been a significant increase in the cost of these policies; premiums are now more than eight times as high as they were ten years ago. In terms of actual policies, there are 3.5 times as many life insurance policies as there were ten years ago, and 23 times as many health insurance policies as there were seven years ago. This growth is due to various factors, which include:

—   The number of new policies taken out, in particular universal insurance policies and others having a strong savings component, as well as health policies complementing mandatory insurance; the latter now forms part of Chile's health system.

—   The growth of policies on which tax relief is available; this trend is linked to a strong increase in mortgage and consumer credit in Chile.

—   The strong element of competition in the Chilean market which has generated a significant increase in the number of people insured; this is due in large part to the development of new products and services and intensive marketing campaigns.

—   The introduction of new ways to market and sell insurance:

—   Direct marketing of insurance policies via mail shots or other means providing direct access to customers, the distribution of policies through banks or '*Bancaseguros*' – an insurance bank, which first operated in Chile in mid-1998 – and distribution through businesses.

IV.   Challenges and final comments

There is no doubt that life insurance represents one of the main channels of domestic saving, which in Chile most notably takes the form of annuity policies linked to the pension system. The new millennium brings us the challenge of continuing to increase the habit of saving; encouraging the growth of individual life insurance policies is an important way of achieving this. Over the next few years, these policies are expected to grow at an annual rate of around 20%, a truly impressive figure.

This trend can already be seen in the widespread distribution of insurance products through insurance banks and other businesses, while a growth in products complementing health coverage (Isapres, Fonasa) and life insurance policies with a savings element is also expected. The latter fit in well with annuities, since they are an addition to mandatory saving, thereby enhancing any pension paid from the annuity (which forms part of the pension system) and protecting families of insured persons in the event of premature death.

Since life insurance policies offering tax advantages are more attractive than other financial products, we have recently seen an increase in the availability of insurance with a high savings element. Life insurance policies of this type, which allow the purchaser to decide how the money should be invested and thus to assume completely the financial risk associated with it (if this is laid down in the contract), are now on the market.

Since individual life insurance policies are taken out by the majority of the active population, they are likely to become an additional pillar of the country's pension system; they will contribute to the growth of national savings, thus reinforcing the virtuous circle of savings and investment.

Notwithstanding the above, I should like to point out that this potential growth of life insurance (whether in the form of annuities which form part of the pension system or life insurance policies which do not) will depend not only on the growth of the country's economy but also on an effective policy for educating the insured.

A healthy growth in the life insurance sector will be closely linked to the insurance culture, particularly where sophisticated products such as annuities are concerned. People's ignorance of the type of pension best suited to their situation at the moment of retirement can lead them to make the wrong decisions, sometimes under the influence of brokers who behave in an unprofessional manner. It is essential that future pensioners are aware of the importance of obtaining a "good pension", as opposed to its alternative, instant consumption.

We will only be able to see insurance really flourish when we can count on insured persons being satisfied with the products they have purchased (in terms of adequate coverage), when after-sale service is truly efficient, and when brokers carry out their duties in a fully professional manner while charging a fair commission.

The Chilean insurance market has now reached a second stage: we can offer the insured person the protection of openness and accountability in terms of the supply, brokering and structure of products, without neglecting the very delicate task of ensuring solvency.

Finally, I believe that today's great challenge is to have a market of "educated" insured persons in Chile, both now and in the future. Increased confidence in the insurance industry will enable it to participate effectively in setting up the second mainstay in the pension system: financially sound companies which have at their disposal enough capital, properly invested, to meet any crisis that might occur.

BRAZIL : EMERGING ECONOMY, SUBMERGING SOCIAL SECURITY

by
Eduardo Bom Angelo[*]

Brazil is a country of contradictions. It is one of the world's top ten economies, with a productive and widely diversified industrial base and the most developed financial system in Latin America. On the other hand, the country has one of the worst income distributions and one of the most ineffective social security systems among emerging economies.

Compounding the problem, and in line with the international trend, its demographic pyramid shows an increase in the elderly population, a result of decreasing birth and mortality rates. This shift is putting chronic pressure on the social security system, the private savings rate and the public deficit. As in many other countries, the social security imbalance is the product of a pay-as-you-go system, aggravated by a number of specific factors, including:

1. A long inflationary process

2. Distorted benefits

3. Evasion of contributions

4. Fraud in the system

5. Misuse and/or poor allocation of resources

6. New labour relationships (outsourcing, more women in the labour market)

7. Growth of the informal economy.

---

[*] Economist, President of Cigna Brazil Retirement and Investments, Professor at FAAP Business School

In the last few years, the social security deficit has been the single most important factor bloating the country's fiscal deficit, adding in 1999 alone an estimated R$ 45 billion, more than half of the total deficit. This imbalance of the public accounts reduces the government's capacity to invest in important areas, such as education, law enforcement, health, sanitation and transport, and obviously limits the country's economic growth. Yet this is only the visible part of the problem.

Less apparent are the tremendous inequities in the way citizens are treated by the system. The graphs and tables below help illustrate this problem. Brazil's social security system pays benefits to some 21.7 million people. While private-sector employees comprise 86% of the beneficiaries, they receive only 57% of the benefits, generating only 24% of the total deficit.

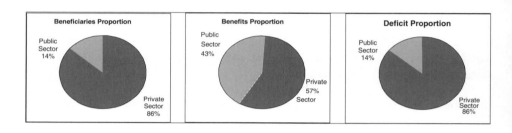

	Expenses (R$ billion)	Contributions (R$ billion)	Deficit (R$ billion)	No. Beneficiaries (thousands)	Contribution per capita
Union	23.3	4.8	18.5	918	R$ 5 229
States	17.9	4.7	13.2	1 337	R$ 3 515
Municipalities	3.0	0.4	2.5	800	R$ 500 *
Private workers	59.6	48.7	10.9	18 643	R$ 2 612
Total	103.7	58.6	45.1	21 698	R$ 2 700

* rough estimate
1999 / per annum
Source: Planning and Budget Ministry

Former Social Security Minister, Reinhold Stephanes, says: "The privileges go to the élite, including the workers' élite, who know how to defend and preserve them, while those who have no voice, and no idea about what is happening, pay the bill." Graph 3 shows the average benefits paid to private-sector and public employees.

Figure 2 - **Expenses with Benefits**
ratio to categories (%)

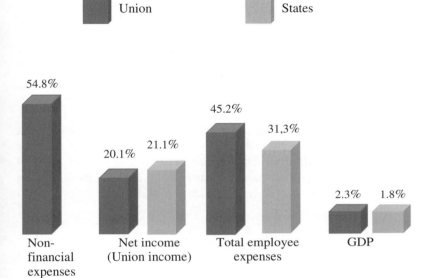

1997, except non financial expenses (1999) – States non available
Source: Financial Ministry and Social Security Ministry

Figure 3 **Benefits Paid to Categories**

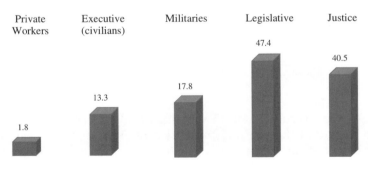

1999
Source: HR Statistic Bulletin – Planning and Budget Ministry

The widening gap generated by the social security system is financed through taxes and public borrowing. If the way in which this money flows from taxpayers to the system is not immediately apparent, still less visible is the relationship between the effort required to finance the deficit and the growing economic and social problems of the country.

One of the principal causes of the present situation was the provision of the 1988 Constitution extending benefits to millions of workers who had never contributed to social security. Almost overnight, for example, more than 400 000 people earned the right to receive 100% of their last salary without having contributed during their working lives.

While other countries around the world have reformed their pension systems in order to set them on a sustainable path, Brazilian authorities have managed only to consistently increase contributions and reduce benefits during the last few decades. It is important to note that these measures have focused primarily on private-sector employees. This has only guaranteed a short-term fragile cash-flow balance.

As the table below shows, practically all the fiscal effort of the government before and after the agreement with the IMF has been jeopardised by social security's negative performance.

Table 2 Federal Government's Primary Result – R$ billions

Item	1998	1999
Treasury	13.4	27.8
Social Security (Union + Private workers)	(18.2)	(26.7)
Unemployment Insurance	3.1	2.4
Federal Govt. Result	**(1.7)**	**3.5**

Source: IPEA – Ministry of Economics

During 1999, the Executive Branch submitted to the Congress three new bills that aimed to reform the social security system. Two of them dealt with the public pension systems, comprising, on the one hand, the Union, states and municipalities and, on the other, of all the government-owned companies and other bodies. The third, and the most important, bill is intended to replace an old law, dated 1977, that regulates the country's entire private pension system.

Graph 4 shows the ratio of pension-fund assets to GDP in the last four years after the period of high inflation. It is clear that the present level of 11% is extremely low compared to that of developed countries or even of other Latin American countries, as Graph 5 shows.

Figure 4 **Pension-Fund Assets/GDP (%)**

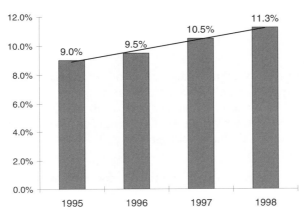

Source: Anapp/ABRAPP/IPEA

Figure 5 **Pensions - Assets/GDP (%)**
selected countries

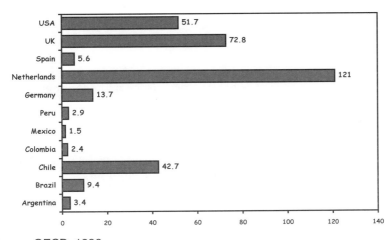

Source: OECD, 1996

The high potential of the private-pensions and life insurance market in Brazil plus the country's economic stabilisation have attracted a significant number of institutional investors to both insurance and banking markets in the last five years. In this period, these sectors were second only to food and beverages in the number of mergers and acquisitions. Right now more than 30 important international financial institutions have begun operations in the country, changing the configuration of those markets from organised oligopoly to extensive competition.

But while the banking market is sophisticated as to both regulations and technology, the same is not true of the private pensions and life insurance market.

The Brazilian pension system is divided into two categories: closed and open pension funds. Approximately 90% of private pensions assets belong to closed pension funds. State-owned companies control about 65% of these assets, and approximately 25% of them are unfounded plans. On the other hand, in the last few years, the open funds have been growing at 40-45% a year due to several factors:

1. The end of inflation and the advent of economic stabilisation

2. Longer investment horizons

3. Entrance of new operators (approximately 25 in the last five years)

4. Permanent coverage by the media

5. The presence of new products compatible with the international market

6. Growing awareness of the possibility of social security bankruptcy

Given the outdated regulations for private pensions, the new law will bring some positive input to the business environment:

1. Portability is now possible between closed and open funds.

2. Defined contributions are accepted for closed funds.

3. Transference of risk riders to insurance companies is allowed.

4. Maximum ratio of employer to employee contributions of 1 to 1 for public sector funds; before there was no limit.

5. The accounts of the public funds will be more transparent.

6. Fiscal benefits are more clearly specified.

Successful reforms in other countries, particularly in Latin America, have several common denominators and point to certain lessons:

1. The technical aspects should be more important than political ones.

2. Commitment on the part of the executive branch is crucial.

3. Social communication should be clear and direct.

4. Legislators should have some familiarity with the subject.

5. Special care should be taken in communicating with people near retirement age.

6. The new system should provide efficient tools to regulate, control, and guarantee its effective operation.

7. There should be no discrimination between entities or sectors.

This agenda is not being heeded in the Brazilian case; as a result, the reforms are inconsistent, the economy is extremely vulnerable, and society is being kept out of the debate.

If it persists in its present path, Brazil risks deepening the public deficit, exacerbating the inequities inherent in the social security system and exposing the economy to a new and more serious macroeconomic maladjustment.

The bright side of this equation is that very recently some segments of the society and some influential voices have entered the discussion. There is now a clear recognition that the new law will not do enough to solve the problems and that a new round of reforms needs to be implemented in the near future.

Part II

THE INSTITUTIONAL SECTOR IN THE OECD

OVERVIEW OF INSTITUTIONAL INVESTORS IN OECD COUNTRIES[1]

by
Stephen Lumpkin[*]

Growth of institutional investors in OECD Countries

Institutional investors are usually defined as financial institutions that invest savings of individuals and non-financial companies in the financial markets. This definition is not very precise and it becomes particularly elusive in dynamic financial markets. Perhaps the key requirement is that funds are being professionally or institutionally managed, as distinct from money managed by retail investors. Examples of institutional investors generally found in most OECD countries are pension funds, insurance companies, open-end funds, hedge funds, closed-end funds, and the proprietary trading activities of investment banks, commercial banks, and securities companies. As a group, institutional investors have enormous financial clout in the world's financial markets, and their importance is growing.

Complete current data on assets under management by institutional investors in the OECD area are generally not available, which hampers efforts to analyse short-term changes in the sector. However, the OECD does publish annually a statistical yearbook that provides detailed data on this sector.[2] Although the data are subject to a lag of a couple years, they are nonetheless quite useful for illustrating the pronounced changes that have occurred in this sector over time. Not surprisingly, the data show that institutional investors within the OECD area have been growing in size dramatically over the past two decades or so. Over the period 1990-96, for example, institutional investors in the OECD area recorded average increases in assets of 9 per cent per year. This gain in the value of assets can be attributed in part to the increase in the volume of individual savings held in institutional form but also reflects some appreciation

---

[*] Principal Administrator, OECD.

in the value of existing holdings. It also provides evidence of the increased institutionalisation of savings that is under way in most countries, as larger amounts of savings are shifted away from regulated and insured banking institutions to entities that are sometimes not insured, and that operate in different regulatory regimes and have different investment objectives.

Pension funds and insurance companies historically have been the most important institutional investors in OECD capital markets, at least in terms of total investment holdings (see Chart 1). This is indicated in the most recently available figures. However, these data also show that, while these institutions control very sizeable (and still growing) asset portfolios, the asset growth of investment companies has been spectacular. Over the 1990-96 period, investment companies recorded proportional increases in assets under management of about 16 per cent per year, compared with growth rates on the order of 10 per cent per annum for insurance companies and pension funds (see Chart 2). As a result of the more rapid growth of investment companies during the period, their total holdings moved into line with the investment levels of pension funds (Chart 1). Partial data for subsequent years suggest that investment companies have continued to record relatively stronger growth in assets under management than other types of institutional investors and, in some cases, have surpassed pension funds in total holdings.

Chart 1. **Total Financial Assets by Type of Investor**

1990

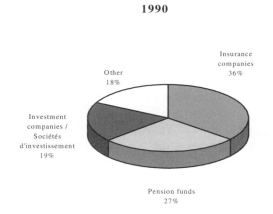

Chart 1. **Total Financial Assets by Type of Investor** (continued)

1996

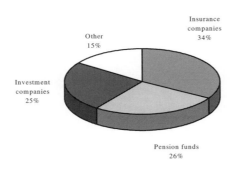

Chart 2. **Average Annual Growth Rate of Financial Assets**
1990 – 1996

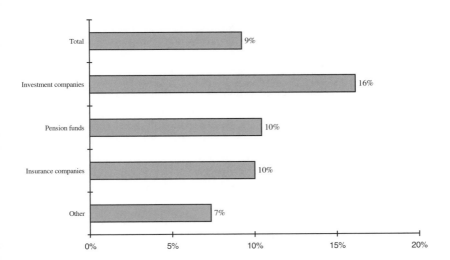

While insurance companies, pension funds and investment companies are clearly the largest institutional investor types, other institutions also collect savings and supply funds to the markets. These include endowment funds, foundations, and other entities. These other institutional investors, found in some OECD countries, represent a non-negligible share of overall investments. For example, in 1996, they accounted for a 15% share, on average, of total assets held by the sector.

Forces shaping the role, structure, and *modus operandi* of institutional investors

Although the various types of institutional investors have each had their own specific influences, several common factors have been crucial in driving the growth of the sector as a whole. As noted in the main issues paper, four are particularly important:

- First, the ageing of the population of the OECD area has produced a rising demand for retirement "products" such as mutual-funds, equity-indexed annuities, asset-backed securities and guaranteed-equity plans on the part of increasingly well-off and sophisticated individual investors. At the same time, the ageing of the baby-boom cohort of the 1940s and 1950s is causing looming fiscal problems for countries relying predominantly on state-financed "pay-as-you-go" pension systems. This projected fiscal shortfall has given major impetus to the introduction of advance-funded pension schemes.

- Second, technological advances in communications and information processing have enhanced the capacity of the financial services sector to provide intermediation and risk-management services by handling vast flows of information at very high speed and low cost. This, in turn, has given rise to a host of sophisticated investment products – a process aided by methodological breakthroughs in the pricing of complex financial instruments.

- Third, deregulation of the banking and securities industries since the beginning of the 1980s has intensified competition between and among banks and other financial institutions. The easing of restrictions on cross-border capital flows and on the entry of foreign financial institutions during this time also served to heighten competition in the financial services sector in the OECD area. These developments, in conjunction with the Basle Accord and the resultant international regulatory capital standards for banks, gave impetus to a spate of strategic acquisitions and defensive mergers among banks and other categories of financial service providers, such as securities dealers, mutual funds, and insurance companies. More recently, the introduction of the common currency in Europe and the spread of asset-quality problems in Asia have acted to further the pace of combinations among financial concerns in those regions. One consequence of this activity is that lines between the various types of service providers have blurred as banks have moved en masse into the fee and commission business associated with capital market transactions.

— Fourth, demand for performance-based investment instruments has soared as individuals have shifted funds from deposit accounts and related savings vehicles at depository institutions in favour of higher yielding assets. This process got its start in the United States but has since spread to other countries as well. For example, in France, cash and deposits as a percentage of total household assets fell from around 65% in 1976 to around 34% in 1996; in Germany the drop over the same period was from 62% to about 43%. Canadian investors also have shown increased willingness to shift from bank deposits and investment products with guaranteed returns to money market mutual funds and instruments with potentially high, but fluctuating, returns. Similar shifts are evident in other OECD countries.

Apart from these broad trends, several other factors have influenced the growth and development of the institutional investors sector in various OECD countries. These factors include the favourable tax treatment accorded retirement savings in most countries; the regulatory and supervisory infrastructure (and changes to it); the rates of return offered on institutional investment products relative to those on traditional savings alternatives; and changes in individual investors' attitudes regarding the various means of saving. In addition, many countries have long had policies that explicitly promote particular types of institutional investors, chief among them private pension plans.

Investment strategies and portfolio composition

Institutional investors generally operate on the basis of well-defined risk-return criteria and rely increasingly on sophisticated investment strategies and techniques. Their investment activities and trading techniques have far-reaching impacts, both in financial markets and in the business sector generally. Of course, the actual investment strategies used by institutional investors may differ considerably across categories of institutions, and across regions and countries. This is not surprising, given that the nature of their liabilities and their fiduciary mandates, as well as the regulatory and tax regimes under which they operate, also differ. As a result of these factors (and the institutions' own risk preferences), different types of institutional investors generally have different investment objectives. Some institutions are highly risk averse, while others are free to invest in riskier assets with higher expected returns. Some investment funds are actively managed; others use passive investment strategies based on indexing to broad market benchmarks. Many pension funds pursue a hybrid strategy, comprising a passively managed "core" portfolio, which typically is an indexed position, and one or more actively managed companion portfolios.

The assets held by institutional investors may be managed in-house, externally, or through some combination of the two approaches. In many countries, it is becoming more common for the funds controlled by institutional investors to be managed by professional fund managers. These fund managers compete actively for mandates to manage funds from pension plans, foundations, life insurance companies and so on, and these are often based on the managers' investment performance. Emphasis has typically been placed on a portfolio's performance against a broad benchmark index, but the current trend is to supplement this measure with an indication of the amount of risk that a portfolio manager has taken to achieve his return.

Inasmuch as individual and institutional investors have increasingly delegated the management of their portfolios to professional fund managers, it is important, when discussing the behaviour of institutional investors, to take into account the professional fund managers who develop asset allocation strategies and make investment decisions on behalf of institutional investors. An analysis of the links between institutional investors and professional fund managers reveals the following broad picture:

> – Fund managers may work in four different basic types of institutional set-up: (1) in the fund or trust departments of banks; (2) in separately capitalised long-term fund (or money) management companies, which may be owned by banks or insurance companies; (3) in independent money management companies that are not affiliated with an insurance company or bank; and (4) in the in-house fund management departments of large insurance companies and pension funds.

- The total amount of professionally managed funds is larger than the portfolios of "classic" institutional investors. Fund management companies, as noted in the introduction, are also involved in the management of portfolios of "high-net worth" individuals, the non-pension fund money of non-financial enterprises, foundations and endowment funds, and non-pension fund money managed by banks, as well as the banks' and securities firms' own portfolios (proprietary trading by banks and securities firms has expanded strongly).

- The number of asset portfolio managers is smaller than the number of institutional investors whose portfolios are professionally managed. The smaller insurance companies and pension funds usually give portfolio management mandates to outside fund management teams. In many cases, fund management companies pool the funds of smaller institutional investors. Institutional investors are increasingly indexing assets, thereby reducing the need for a large number of asset portfolio managers. Finally, to the extent that insurance companies and pension funds invest directly in investment fund shares, they reduce the amount of assets that would have to be invested by the fund's own fund managers in the capital and money markets.

All of the various arrangements are designed to achieve specific investment objectives, consistent with the nature of the institution's liabilities and operating environment. As might be expected, the size and composition of the portfolios of institutional investors in the OECD area varies not only by type of institution but also across countries (see Chart 3). However, upon closer inspection, a few obvious patterns emerge. First, holdings of equities have tended historically to be fairly limited in most OECD countries, although there are exceptions (mainly the English-speaking countries such as the United Kingdom and United States) and the share of equities has been increasing in most countries (see Charts 4 and 5). Second, there tends to be a considerable domestic bias in asset allocation which, partly because of currency-matching requirements and other regulations, has tended to be relatively stronger for pension funds and life-insurance companies than for mutual funds.

Chart 3. **Total Financial Assets: As a Percentage OF GDP**

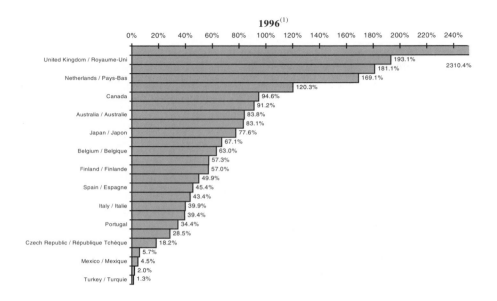

1996[1]

United Kingdom / Royaume-Uni	193.1% / 2310.4%
	181.1%
Netherlands / Pays-Bas	169.1%
	120.3%
Canada	94.6%
	91.2%
Australia / Australie	83.8%
	83.1%
Japan / Japon	77.6%
	67.1%
Belgium / Belgique	63.0%
	57.3%
Finland / Finlande	57.0%
	49.9%
Spain / Espagne	45.4%
	43.4%
Italy / Italie	39.9%
	39.4%
Portugal	34.4%
	28.5%
Czech Republic / République Tchèque	18.2%
	5.7%
Mexico / Mexique	4.5%
	2.0%
Turkey / Turquie	1.3%

(1)   1994 data for the Czech Republic. Data for insurance companies in Luxembourg are not available.

Europe is an interesting example of this phenomenon. The vast majority of institutional investors in most European countries have been "over-invested" in domestic assets. Some analysts estimate that over three-quarters of European fund assets have been invested in instruments offered by entities in the funds' domestic markets, and roughly the same proportion of government debt has been held by domestic investors. To some extent this may simply reflect a preference for instruments issued by local borrowers with which the fund managers have the most familiarity.

However, it probably reflects the desire of investors to avoid exchange-rate risks, as well as regulatory impediments such as asset-liability and currency matching requirements that have limited the amount of foreign currency-denominated investments held by some types of financial institutions. Of course, under the single currency, this changes. Among countries participating in European monetary union (EMU), investments in assets in other EMU-area countries in many cases have been re-classified as domestic currency assets. This enables insurance companies and other previously constrained investors to shift more of their portfolios outside their domestic borders.

Chart 4. **Trends in Financial Assets of Institutional Investors**
1990 – 1996

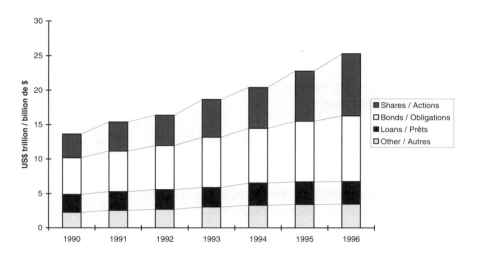

Until now, European asset managers have pursued country-specific investment strategies, with currency positioned at or near the top of the decision ladder, followed by market sector, and then, depending on risk preferences, a yield-curve decision regarding duration/convexity. In the EMU area, the borders of the "domestic" capital market have been expanded, which enables EMU-based investors to switch their strategies from a focus on segmentation by currency to diversification on a sectoral basis. Moreover, with currency concerns diminished, the pricing of assets should become more transparent, which will make any remaining distortions all the more visible, and increase pressures to remove them. Most market participants expect the increased transparency to induce Europe's investors to assign more weight to credit risk in the analysis of investment alternatives, especially in light of historically low interest rates on government paper, and flat term structures which offer little scope for yield enhancement by moving out along the maturity spectrum. In this yield environment, to enhance the returns of their investment portfolios, investors will probably have to turn to higher-risk, credit-driven performance strategies. Exactly what form and size this portfolio re-allocation will take, however, remains to be seen.

Chart 5. **Average Annual Growth Rate of Financial Assets by Type of Asset 1990 - 1996**

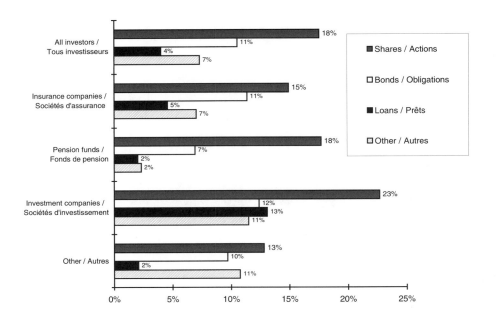

Impact of institutional investors on the financial landscape

The increasing importance of institutional investors (life insurance companies, pension funds, and investment funds) as holders of assets means that their impact on the functioning of financial markets is steadily growing. The involvement of institutional investors in capital market transactions is increasing in tandem with their growing financial clout. A strong community of institutional investors seems to be a precondition for the development of liquid securities markets with sophisticated financial vehicles. For example, countries with a large institutional sector – Canada, the United Kingdom and the United States, for example – tend to have more highly developed securities markets than countries that historically have had a "banking culture" (mainly continental Europe and Japan). The evolution of sophisticated trading strategies and the introduction of new financial instruments are in part a consequence of the requirements of the institutional investor community. A dynamic institutional sector encourages the development of capital markets. Institutional investors, in turn, need well-developed securities markets for the efficient execution of their investment strategies.

The growth of the institutional investor community has had a profound effect on capital market structure. That growth stems from the increased institutionalisation of savings which, in turn, implies a shift in the composition of the portfolios of the household sector toward long-term assets and correspondingly higher returns. These shifts suggest that securities are increasingly being held by large, informed investors whose investment decisions are driven by relative asset returns. Institutional investors make rapid adjustments to changes in relative returns, which aids price efficiency and contributes to a more efficient allocation of funds. As a consequence of the increased demand for long-term assets by institutional asset managers, the increased institutionalisation of savings has led to an increased supply of long-term funds, and may have contributed to an increase in the supply of risk capital as well, stimulating new businesses and facilitating job growth.

Going forward, these shifts in the portfolio composition of the household sector may have a different effect on asset prices. Population ageing in the OECD area may bring about a decline in the prime savers' ratio [3] in around ten years' time. This development could lead to major changes in the portfolios of institutional investors and, thereby, might exert downward pressure on the prices of financial assets, provided the accumulation of financial assets by institutional investors slowed in response to the demographics-induced decline in savings. This outcome is subject to considerable uncertainty, but asset preferences do tend to vary across age groups. Thus, the ageing of the baby-boom generation has the potential to affect both absolute and relative stock and bond prices.[4] In particular, demographic influences on financial market prices could adversely affect the financial performance of pension funds in the coming decades. Pension funds may offset these population-induced effects on performance by increasing their diversification into younger, emerging-market economies. However, this alone seems unlikely to solve fully the basic pension problems of OECD countries.[5]

Regulation and supervision of the institutional sector

As noted previously, the activities of institutional investors convey certain benefits to capital markets. However, the mounting sophistication of the investment and trading strategies used by the institutional investor community evokes a number of regulatory and supervisory issues, such as the rationale of investment restrictions, the role of risk-management standards and systems, and the adequacy of the financial infrastructure in both OECD and emerging market economies. In view of the growing influence that these institutional investors exert on the structure and *modus operandi* of capital markets, and given the importance of such markets for the real economy, for corporate finance, and for income security, policy makers in OECD countries have taken a close look at the functioning and regulation of these investors. The Committee on Financial Markets of the OECD keeps track of developments in institutional investing and monitors other major structural changes in financial markets by regular discussions among members of the Committee as well as through meetings between the Committee and representatives of the financial services sector. Among the policy issues that have been considered are:

- The influence of institutional investors on the micro-structure of financial markets, financial system structure and demand for new financial products.

- The impact of institutional investors on the stability and volatility of financial markets.

- The impact of demography and the regulation of pension schemes on the efficiency of the allocation of savings.

- The influence of the international portfolio diversification of institutional investors.

- The impact of tax regimes on the behaviour of institutional investors.

The different types of institutional investors operate under different regulatory and tax regimes across the OECD area. The regulation of pension funds, for example, varies markedly across OECD countries. A number of countries (Denmark, Germany, and Japan, for example) impose quantitative limits on portfolio investments, while others (mainly the English-speaking countries and the Netherlands) adhere to the "prudent person" rule. There is some quantitative evidence that portfolios subject to quantitative restrictions achieve lower returns than those that are subject to the "prudent person" concept and may be less well diversified. This result and the losses sustained on portfolio holdings of institutional investors during the market turmoil of the past two years suggest that some consideration should be given to the introduction of a supervisory framework that combines a "prudent person" concept with sound risk-management standards, rather than adherence to quantitative restrictions on asset allocations.

The financial services sector of OECD countries is still undergoing fundamental change. This is to some extent due to explicit regulatory reforms, but also reflects the same factors that have been driving the growth of the institutional investor community. On the regulatory front, many of the explicit obstacles to cross-border trade in financial services in the OECD area have been removed through regulatory reforms introduced over the past two decades or so. But while there are fewer outright restrictions than in the past, important legal, regulatory, structural, tax, and other impediments to full integration of securities markets remain. And in some jurisdictions, national laws still protect domestic banks, inhibiting the development of cross-border banking services. If left as is, these impediments raise the risk that institutional investors will be unable to reap sufficient benefits from diversification across broader markets.

However, in all OECD regions, the authorities are reconsidering the legal and regulatory framework in which all financial institutions operate. Some of the policy issues that arise from the current wave of consolidation among banks and other categories of financial service providers are: the size of financial institutions and their impact on markets, including the implications for competition policy and financial stability; the growing complexity of financial conglomerates brought about by the convergence among banks, managed funds, securities firms, and insurance companies; and the problems encountered in supervising institutions that operate on a global basis.

NOTES

1. For a thorough treatment of the topic, see *Institutional Investors in the New Financial Landscape*, OECD Proceedings, 1998.

2. For the latest issue, see *Institutional Investors-Statistical Yearbook*, OECD (1998).

3. The prime savers' ratio is defined here as the ratio of savers in the age range 40-60 years to those in the range 15-60 years.

4. See the discussion by Hans Blommestein in "Pension Funds and Financial Markets", *The OECD Observer*, No. 212 (June/July 1998), pp. 23-27.

5. For a more complete discussion of these issues, see *Maintaining Prosperity in an Ageing Society*, OECD 1998.

THE INSTITUTIONAL SECTOR IN THE OECD: POLICY LESSONS

by
Glorianne Stromberg[*]

The ideas presented here on adapting regulatory systems and structures to meet the needs of the evolving financial landscape were developed in the context of what is happening in Canada and elsewhere. They reflect the changes that I have recommended be made in the regulation and oversight of Canadian investment funds[1].

These recommendations reflect the growing significance of investment funds in the financial services industry and in the economy as a whole. While the issues and recommendations relate specifically to Canada, I believe they also have a global relevance. This is because the strategic forces that dominated the 1990s are much the same worldwide.

It has often been remarked that the 1990s have democratised the investment process. The factors that have played (and continue to play) a role in this include:

- Economic and demographic forces related to an ageing population.

- The growing awareness of individuals that they need to take charge of providing for their own retirement.

- The resulting competition for the right to provide for the needs of these individuals.

- The impact of globalisation.

- The reality of financial services deregulation.

---

[*] Ms. Stromberg served as a Commissioner of the Ontario Securities Commission during the period 1991-1998.

- The impact of technology.

- The impact of advanced communications facilities.

- The strengthening of the free-market economic system.

These factors have converged to empower individuals as well as financial institutions and intermediaries. The emergence of consumer/investors[2] as strategic forces in their own right is placing demands and expectations not only on the market place but also on the regulatory and supervisory framework. In many countries, including Canada, the current regulatory and supervisory framework is simply not structured to meet these demands and expectations. Changes are needed to align the regulatory and supervisory approach and the provision of financial services with the market-place realities that result from:

- Increasing recognition by consumer/investors of the need for sound personal financial management.

- The blurring and, in some cases, the fusion of product, function and advice.

- The "retailisation" of the market place.

These market-place realities are particularly relevant in the Latin American context as governments consider changes to their current regulatory structure intended to enhance the significant social programmes they have had the foresight to implement.

It is important for governments to keep this forward-looking focus very much in mind and not to fall into the trap of using "yesterday's solutions" to address current and future problems.

I believe that it is possible to move directly to the "next-generation" of financial services regulation and, in doing so, to enhance the ability of consumer/investors, financial service providers, regulators and governments to meet their respective needs for economic well-being in the context of an evolving financial landscape.

Of the three market-place realities that I have just mentioned, the first relates to the recognition of the need for sound personal financial management practices. Many people are ill prepared to take charge of planning and providing for their lifetime needs. They often do not appreciate that, by participating in some sort of collective investment vehicle or by owning some other form of structured

210

product, they have accepted more risk than they would knowingly be prepared to accept.

Governments in Latin America have taken this into account in a variety of ways in designing their mandatory pension plans. However, they have also recognised that some provisions designed to protect vulnerable investors are becoming problematical.

In modifying these arrangements, it is important to bear in mind the reasonable expectations of people who turn to a financial service provider for advice and to ensure that the regulatory system and structure is designed to meet these expectations, namely that:

- The advice people will get will be based on a full individualised assessment of clients' needs.

- The person providing the advice will be competent to make that assessment and will be able - and willing - to give advice that is in the best interests of the clients rather than of the financial services intermediary.

- The advice - and the plan to implement such advice - will be based upon the integrated needs of the consumer/investor and upon the availability of a full range of money management services and products.

- The ability to carry out transactions to implement the plan and to provide ongoing monitoring and reporting services is and will be ancillary to the foregoing.

- The costs will be fair and reasonable.

The second "reality" relates to the fusion of product, function and advice. It is important to recognise not only that the fusion has occurred but also that it has resulted from the increased focus of all financial service providers on asset gathering, asset allocation services and asset management.

Banks, insurance companies, trust companies, credit unions, independent mutual fund management organisations, independent mutual fund dealers and full service investment dealers now offer, directly and indirectly, a full range of investment advisory services and products.[3] Many of them have multiple entries into both advisory and distribution channels through equity interests in other segments of the financial services industry or through strategic alliances or networks.

The activities carried on, directly or indirectly, by the various sectors of the financial services industry are virtually indistinguishable to consumer/investors yet they are regulated differently. Regulation (or the lack thereof) varies according to the type of investment product, the institution issuing the investment product and the intermediary involved. The ramifications of these differences are not readily apparent to consumer/investors and are not well understood.

The simple reality is that the activities of financial service providers have outpaced the current regulatory structure and system. The "four pillars" of financial service regulation that regulated insurance companies, banks, trust companies and securities dealers separately and created four different regulatory systems no longer exist except as regulatory fictions. The pillars have converged; their regulators have not. There are major gaps and shortcomings in many of the current regulatory and supervisory structures and systems. These need to be dealt with to meet the needs of consumer/investors in the new financial landscape.

The third reality of today's market place relates to its "retailisation" and to the fact that the market place has become a unitary "instividual" market place rather than one made up of two classes of investors - the so-called "retail investor" and the so-called "institutional investor".

I use the term "retailisation" to refer to the risk-reward consequences that flow from the direct ownership interest that the individual consumer/investor has in his or her investments as opposed to a simple contractual right to receive stipulated payments on stipulated dates. I also use the term to reflect the fact that the individual consumer/investor who holds investments either directly or through some sort of collective investment vehicle is in direct competition with the institutional investor investing for its own account.

In this environment, the need for equality of regulatory treatment takes on another dimension. It is important that the regulatory and supervisory structure and system not favour the "institutional investor" over the individual consumer/investor who traditionally is referred to as the "retail investor". This is particularly so when the institutional investor is also a purveyor of advice, services and products to the individual consumer/investor.

New approaches to regulatory and supervisory strategies

Below I set out ten fundamental proposals aimed at establishing a new approach to regulatory and supervisory strategies.

1.   *Enhance efforts to reduce the knowledge gap.*

We underestimate the negative impact that informational asymmetry has on creating, or at least contributing to, systemic risk. We need to improve people's knowledge and their ability to apply it. There are many suggestions contained in my 1998 report on ways to do this.

Efforts are needed at every level in every country and should involve consumer/investors, employees and senior executives in the public and private sectors and the people charged with the oversight and supervision of the financial service industry.

There is a need for most people, including many regulators - and I can say this because I was one once - to gain a better understanding of economic and market factors, of cause and effect, of risk and how to manage it, and of the behavioural sciences and how to compensate for the "human" element. It is hard to exercise business or regulatory oversight and supervision without this knowledge.

With respect to consumer/investors, measures to enhance their knowledge and awareness should reduce the knowledge gap and equip them with the basic life skills they need for informed decision-making, including the ability to understand information that is communicated to them. Such measures should empower consumer/investors to take charge of their own economic well being. The 1998 report contains many recommendations on how to bring this about.

Information is a critical tool; it is a major equalising force and a valuable commodity. Open and timely access to information is crucial in levelling the playing field. However, if consumer/investors are not equipped to understand or make use of the information that is communicated to them, none of the other consumer protection remedies (particularly those based on disclosure) will work effectively.

This need to enhance knowledge and to build key competencies for consumer/investors, industry participants and regulators alike is a theme underlying all the recommendations in the 1998 report. Were I limited to just one recommendation, it would be to reduce the knowledge gap.

2. *Match the regulatory structure to the reality of the market place.*

There is a need to devise a workable integrated regulatory system that encompasses functional, institutional and prudential regulation of integrated, multi-functional financial service providers. The continued fragmentation of the regulatory system and supervisory oversight threatens to pose a systemic risk despite the co-ordinating efforts of the various "joint forums" that are being established at country level and internationally.

We need to look for better ways to simplify and rationalise the regulatory structure. One would be to create an integrated financial services authority (FSA). This would operate on a national basis, and its regulatory and supervisory focus would include functional, institutional and prudential regulation and oversight of financial service providers, the need being for broad-based advisory expertise (rather than knowledge of individual products). Specific product knowledge would then be subsumed under the framework of advice-giving and related activities.

3. *Adopt new regulatory strategies that match market-place reality.*

Consistent with the need for an integrated regulatory system is the need to bring all aspects of managing money for others under a common regulatory regime. For those countries that divide regulatory oversight between governmental regulators and self-regulatory organisations, there is a need to take a fresh look at the effectiveness of the self-regulatory component. It is simply not working as well as it should. If we want to devise strategies to avert systemic risk, we need to review some of our "sacred cow" assumptions.[4]

It should not automatically be assumed that the regulatory activities of the FSA would be delegated to a self-regulatory organisation. A stand-alone, self-funded FSA could perform these functions directly.

If regulatory activities are to be divided between the government-established FSA and self-regulatory organisations as has been done in many countries, I recommend having only one self-regulatory organisation (the "Single SRO") that would be recognised by the FSA and would require all intermediaries to be members.

Such an arrangement would simplify the registration/licensing system, requiring only a single registration with the FSA and a single membership in the Single SRO. This would eliminate the need for multi-registrations, multi-regulators and multi self-regulatory organisations and would provide for adequate, uniform and functional oversight, supervision and regulation.

This recommendation assumes that the educational and proficiency requirements of the FSA and of the Single SRO will be at the core of their structural and substantive regulatory requirements. These requirements would be centred on advice giving rather than product licensing, with product knowledge being an integral part.

This recommendation recognises that one of the most essential components of consumer protection is that the intermediaries who deal with the consumer/investor must receive adequate education and training. This needs to be based on what the intermediary is actually doing and on what competencies and skills are required for such activity.

4.   Make systemic changes in the regulatory system.

It is time to replace the "closed" system of securities regulation with a simple issuer-based, integrated disclosure model and to level the playing field for all market participants (including consumer/investors) with respect to the timely dissemination of information. Technology and enhanced communications make this feasible. There should, for example, be no more closed analyst calls or meetings.

We should, as a matter of course, use technology to disseminate disclosure and other information such as proxy solicitation materials. We should, as a matter of course, use technology to permit proxy voting and to allow "attendance" at shareholder meetings. If we need to adapt our laws to this end, we should do so.

We need to develop universal principles and common standards for the calculation and use of performance information and to ensure that they are consistently applied. There are many recommendations along these lines in the 1995 report.

5.   Simplify, modernise and harmonise basic laws.

On both a national and international basis we need to simplify, modernise and harmonise our basic laws. We need to make sure that our pension, tax, labour, insurance, securities and insolvency laws work well together. We need to build on efforts to develop uniform legislation and a uniform approach to various concepts such as "netting" which has plagued global transactions for years. The work of the OECD and of IOSCO is an important starting point. The European Union is also renewing its efforts in this domain.

6.   *Increase focus on governance matters.*

We underestimate the importance of good governance in alleviating systemic risk and managing operating risks. With respect to investment funds, there is a need for prudential oversight mechanisms and prudent operating standards and procedures.

Good governance is essential, not just for business and investment enterprises but for regulatory bodies as well. A starting point would be for each organisation to review its own structure in the light of the OECD Principles of Corporate Governance to identify and deal with any gaps.

It is no longer good enough just to talk about the need for internal systems and controls and risk management procedures. There is a need to put them in place and make sure they work. This requires an investment in technology and training and a strong internal oversight plan.

7.   *Increase focus on international regulatory co-operation.*

IOSCO's work is providing some excellent foundations on which to build. With today's technology having effectively eliminated time and distance, creating a "borderless" world, there is a need to develop protocols so those regulators in one country could use work done by regulators in another. Such international mutual reliance protocols, combined with international compliance and enforcement protocols and the work of joint regulatory co-ordination groups, would go a long way towards creating international standards to meet the needs of today's market place.

Complementary activities would include entering into reciprocity agreements so that regulatory action could be taken or judgements enforced in the "home office" jurisdiction for breaches of laws applicable in other jurisdictions.

It is often easier to agree on the adoption of uniform standards than to agree on ceding jurisdiction. Universally applicable common standards should go a long way towards facilitating cross-border activities and minimising the need for regulatory constraints. The importance of creating international standards cannot be overestimated.

8.   *Establish regulatory and supervisory oversight training programs.*

Protocols on international standards, mutual reliance and other matters only work if they are interpreted, applied and enforced consistently in each of the participating jurisdictions. Training is essential for this and should include exchange programmes with other regulators and other countries. This would have the added benefit of increasing the number of trained regulatory and supervisory personnel, a need that the G-7 Ministers have identified in their proposals for a new global financial architecture.

This strategy would complement the recommendations dealing with increasing knowledge and international regulatory co-operation and harmonisation.

9. Establish supervisory oversight training programs for the private sector.

A similar initiative for training in the private sector would be complementary to the recommendation for the public sector training programme referred to above.

10. Enhance compliance and enforcement activity.

To this end, rather than carry a big stick, I would prefer to devise more effective incentives for compliance than those now do in place in most countries. To do this, we need somehow to make it more profitable for people to comply with regulations than not to comply. There have to be serious consequences in case of non-compliance.

While the recommendations in the 1995 and 1998 reports are aimed at preventing problems from arising in the first place, when problems do nevertheless arise, there is a need to deal expeditiously and effectively with those who have caused them. Several suggestions were made by industry participants, and these are included in the 1998 report: the right to deal with the public is seen as a privilege which can only be granted if the person or firm is deemed suitable for registration and if the registration is not objectionable. Continued registration would depend on continuing suitability.

There is also a need to develop more effective ways for consumer/investors to recover losses incurred through negligence or a breach of contractual or fiduciary obligation - at an affordable cost.

The existence of mandatory savings systems of the type found in many Latin American countries would not affect these recommendations. Rather, they enhance the need for the sort of strategies I have outlined, particularly in view of the proposed liberalisation in these countries.

NOTES

1. The term "investment fund" includes open-end mutual funds that are redeemable on demand, pension funds, segregated funds, pooled investment accounts, and other types of collective investment schemes.

2. I use the term "consumer/investor" to describe the dual role of people who participate in today's market place.

3. Examples include insurance companies offering investment products such as segregated investment funds, universal life policies indexed to the performance of a pool of investment securities, guaranteed investment funds and uninsured mutual funds. Banks, in addition to offering traditional products, are now focussing on combining guaranteed deposit obligations with a market-linked return and on issuing debt obligations linked to the performance of designated mutual funds or other identifiable asset pools. They are also providing wealth management advisory services and products. Mutual fund management organisations, in addition to offering conventional mutual funds, are offering mutual fund wrap programmes and mutual funds with a guaranteed return. They are also converting their offering of mutual funds into segregated funds through arrangements with an insurance company for an insurance "wrapper". Independent mutual fund distributors are establishing their own proprietary mutual funds and selling them to their clients; the distributors receive not only the distribution fees but also the investment-advisory and business-management fees charged for the privilege of investing in these sponsored funds.

4. Questions that should be asked in the context of this review include:

    1. Is there too much "self" in "self-regulation"?
    2. Would the regulatory system work more effectively if the focus were to change from "self-regulation" to "self-management" of regulatory requirements?
    3. Have regulators abdicated too many of their functions to self-regulatory organisations?
    4. How effective is regulatory oversight of the activities of self-regulatory organisations?
    5. What is the purpose of self-regulatory organisations?
        Is their purpose to protect the public?
        Are they appropriately structured to do so?

Are their functions focused on protecting the public?

How effectively is the public interest addressed and protected?

6. How effective is the governance structure of self-regulatory organisations?

7. How pro-active are self-regulatory organisations in making timely changes that would benefit the market place?

8. Do competitive interests interfere with or delay the rule-making process of the self-regulatory organisations?

9. Would we be better off to privatise, through outsourcing or otherwise, the performance of certain regulatory activities?

10. Does the self-funding status of securities regulators remove or reduce the necessity for delegating regulation to self-regulatory organisations?

11. With governmental securities regulation now being vested in free-standing, self-funded agencies, would it be possible (assuming appropriate restructuring of what work is done and the way it is done) to eliminate the intervening layer of regulation represented by the self-regulatory organisations?

12. Are consumer/investors well served by the continuation of this two-tier structure of securities regulation?

13. How adequately and effectively are the complaints, problems and concerns of consumer/investors dealt with in this two-tier structure?

14. With respect to career advancement, how dependent are staffs of the self-regulatory organisations on the good will of the members?

15. Are we continuing to design our processes and procedures as if the significant changes resulting from advances in technology and communications and self-funding had not taken place?

16. If we are, how is this serving the needs of consumer/investors?

17. Are some self-regulatory organisations such as stock exchanges, with their existing or proposed electronic trading systems, now in direct competition with the market participants they regulate?

18. Should there be a separation of activities relating to member regulation, market regulation and industry trade association or advocacy?

19. Is the public interest served by having a multitude of self-regulatory organisations for each "pillar" of the industry and/or for each product sold by members of that pillar?

These are all questions that affect consumer/investors regardless of whether they invest directly or through some sort of collective investment vehicle. There are no doubt other questions and issues that need to be addressed.

ACCESS TO LATIN AMERICAN MARKETS FOR INDIVIDUAL CANADIAN INVESTORS

by
Andrew Scipio Del Campo[*]

There is a great deal of direct investment in Latin America by Canadian interests. For example, Canada is the second largest foreign investor in Chile, with over $7 billion[1] invested in this country's mining, telecommunications and energy sectors. Boosted by the July 1997 free trade agreement between Canada and Chile, our trading relationship is continuing to strengthen.

In Canada, the term mutual funds refers to pooled retail funds, usually legal trusts, managed by portfolio managers on behalf of unit-holders. These funds are always open-ended, are redeemable on demand and are sold under a strict regulatory regime including the terms of a mandatory prospectus-selling document. The Canadian mutual fund industry has grown at a tremendous pace over the past decade. We started 1990 with only $24 billion in assets in 430 funds. As at July 30 1999, our industry managed $354 billion in assets in nearly 1200 funds.

Currently about 77% of eligible Canadians, about eight million people, use some type of private pension plan to save for their retirement. Many working Canadians belong to company pension plans, which are designed to provide them with an income when they retire. There is about $450 billion in Canada's top 100 pension funds.

In addition, Canadians can personally save for retirement through Registered Retirement Savings Plans (RRSPs) as an add-on to their company pension income or as an alternative to a company pension if they do not have access to an employer-sponsored fund.

---

[*]   Director and Past-Chairman, The Investment Funds Institute of Canada.

1.   All dollar figures in this paper are Canadian dollars.

About half of the $350 billion invested in mutual funds is held inside RRSPs. With RRSPs, the money Canadians contribute into the plans is tax deductible. The assets inside the plan compound tax-free over time and are taxed as income when withdrawn from the plan.

Canadians are encouraged to diversify geographically by investing portions of their portfolios in other parts of the world. After all, Canada represents only 3% of the world's capital markets.

Canadian mutual fund companies currently offer twelve speciality funds focussed on Latin America. A number of international funds also have a portion of their assets in this part of the world. As at June 30 1999, the speciality Latin American funds held $537 million dollars. The majority of these funds are less than five years old since Canadian fund companies have only recently developed products with broader exposure to non-North American regions of the world.

Unfortunately, the Canadian government limits how much pension funds and RRSPs can invest outside of Canada. Currently the limit is 20% of each plan. In many other countries around the world, including the United States, United Kingdom, Australia, Ireland and the Netherlands, there are no foreign content restrictions. This means that Canadians do not have the full benefits of investing in different sectors and regions worldwide that can potentially increase their portfolio's returns and minimise risk. This restrictive policy is one that the Investment Fund Institute of Canada (IFIC) and many other groups have been lobbying against for a number of years.

In the past, the Canadian government has believed that keeping investment money in Canada keeps Canadians employed and helps Canada's capital markets. However, a study commissioned by IFIC (Conference Board of Canada, 1998) showed that raising the foreign property limit would not affect the economy and would benefit Canadians.

The study concluded that there was no negative effect the last time the foreign property limit was increased - from 10% to 20% in 1991. Even the present limit, it concluded, gives rise to inefficiencies in the financial markets by restricting the movement of capital.

The study also found that raising the foreign property limit does not create concern about the cost of capital for Canadian businesses. As well, the study showed that raising the limit on the foreign property rule would not increase Canada's international debt position.

Actually, the amount of Canadian investment in registered plans, and therefore subject to this rule, is only a quarter of the total Canadian investment pool. This means that those average-income Canadians whose major savings vehicles are RRSPs and pension plans are in a disadvantaged position.

A further study commissioned by IFIC (Ernst & Young 1997) found that a higher foreign content limit would allow ordinary Canadian investors to take advantage of potentially better investment returns in other markets.

This study found that for nearly the entire period since 1970, Canadians would have benefited from both higher returns and greater security through diversification had they enjoyed more investment flexibility as to foreign equities. For example, according to the Morgan Stanley Capital International Indexes Canada lagged behind nine other major stock markets over the past 15 years. Canada's 15-year average annual return was 5.9% compared to 14.6% for the U.S., 16.6% for Germany and even 8.9% for the Far East. (*Source:* Globe and Mail)

Our study found that the current 20% limit can increase annual returns by up to one percent a year. Increasing the limit to 30% would boost the annual improvement to as much as 1.5%.

The bottom line is that all these surveys found that increasing foreign content would help augment the value of financial assets held for retirement, allow more flexibility to Canadian investors for their retirement savings, reduce risk through diversification of investments and provide greater access to the world equities market. A higher limit would allow Canadians to participate in higher-growth economies and in industrial sectors in which Canada is less developed than other countries.

Besides restricting the Canadian population's ability to build their retirement funds, this 20% foreign property rule has stimulated Canadian mutual fund companies to develop innovative new products. Recently they have launched a product that allows investors to skirt the 20% rule and still benefit from investing offshore. We refer to these new products as clone funds. These new funds invest in money market instruments and use a form of derivatives called forward contracts to mimic the performance of actively managed funds – less the additional fee charged on the funds. Instead of investing in the stocks selected by the manager of the underlying fund, they buy futures contracts based on those stocks and hold most of their assets in Canadian treasury bills. The investments are considered Canadian content because their assets are mostly invested in Canadian treasury bills and money market instruments.

With these new products, mutual fund companies are allowing Canadians to get around our government's restrictive policies but, unfortunately, there are additional costs to both the fund company and the investor. Despite the higher cost, these funds have been very popular. In June, the top-selling fund was one of these new clone funds. In July, sales of these funds continued to be robust, as additional companies began to offer this type of option to investors. Total sales of foreign equity funds in July were $665 million with analysts estimating that about half of that was channelled into these new clone funds.

Our government has not yet addressed the fundamental issue of the 20% ceiling. However, our lobbying efforts have shown signs of success, and we are now optimistic that it is not a matter of whether the rule is changed but when.

When that happens, individual Canadian investors will be able to invest to a greater extent in other parts of the world, including, of course, Latin America.

As the vast majority of Canadians believe that our population should be able to invest more of their savings into markets around the world, programmes such as the IOSCO training session in Montreal, held in collaboration with the World Bank Group (September 1999) and the meeting of the Council of Securities Regulators of the Americas (COSRA) in Calgary (also in September) are critical in encouraging consistent regulatory practices throughout the world and helping to shape our global economy.

Part III

SUMMARY OF CONCLUSIONS BY THE OECD SECRETARIAT

The workshop provided a setting for assessing the current state of development of institutional investors in Latin America and for comparing the experience of countries in this region with that of OECD Member countries. It was opened by the Chilean Vice-Minister of Finance, who referred to the innovative nature of the pension reform carried out by his country in 1981. The Chilean experience served as a useful benchmark for describing trends in the institutional investor sector across the region. In all, seven Latin American countries had established private pension industries that closely resembled the one established in Chile.

The next two speakers set the Chilean reform in a broader international context. The OECD representative considered that the complementarity of policy background in OECD countries and in Latin American countries provided a sound basis for an exchange of views and experiences. He referred to the OECD's multidisciplinary work programme, highlighting the recent establishment of the OECD Working Group on Private Pensions. He also expressed the organisation's interest in establishing a policy dialogue with countries of Latin America on the theme of institutional investors. The European Union delegate referred to the prospects for liberalisation of trade in financial services, specifically in the pension and insurance industries, noting that this was an important challenge in EU countries as well as in Latin America. He also mentioned the recent EU Communication on regulation of supplementary pensions and the forthcoming meeting between the EU and Latin American countries in Rio de Janeiro.

The workshop dealt with competition issues as well as regulatory policies and discussed the main challenges Latin American countries have faced in their institutional investor sectors. The common theme that ran through all the discussions was the tension that could emerge at times between choice and competition objectives on the one hand and prudential and protective objectives on the other. Regulations and constraints that sought to protect investors, consumers and workers could at times hamper competition in the institutional investor sector. They could also be counterproductive, since choice and competition can bring benefits to these agents through diversification over financial instruments with different risk-return characteristics, lower commissions, and greater control over firms' corporate governance, hence over returns to financial assets. Yet, competition itself could at times have undesirable effects. Competition between pension fund administrators in Latin America, for example, has certainly brought many costs to consumers in the form of higher fees, as the firms devote large sums to advertising, marketing campaigns and sales forces.

At the workshop, a sharp contrast was drawn between the Latin American experience and developments in OECD countries, where there is a rapidly increasing integration of institutional investors. Brazil stood out as the only country in the region that was following the route of increasing choice in financial services provided by institutional investors and encouraging greater competition and integration among different types of institutional investors. Many reasons were given for these divergent experiences, but two were perceived as critical. First was the fact that private pension systems in most Latin American countries were mandatory, Brazil being an exception. The mandatory nature of these systems had raised the fiduciary responsibility of the government to ensure the financial security of workers' retirement income. Second was the unpopularity of existing financial institutions, in the wake of the region's financial crises. Governments had responded by increasing their demands on the financial system and restricting choice and competition in the pension industry.

Session 1.   The Institutional Sector in Latin America – Assessment, Experience, Comparison

This session looked at recent trends in the development of pension funds, mutual funds and insurance companies. The focus was mainly on pension funds and insurance companies, since there has been very little development of mutual funds in the region, except in Brazil, where the assets held by mutual funds represent over 15% of GDP. The first two speakers (from the International Federation of Pension Funds and the Interamerican Federation of Insurance Companies) considered the general trends in the pension fund and insurance sectors and the interaction between them. By the measure of assets to GDP, Chile showed by far the most developed sectors (40 and 14%, respectively), while other countries were at an early stage in developing these sectors. The contrast is particularly marked if one compares Latin America to OECD countries. Insurance premiums per capita in most countries in the region were below US$ 100, against levels of over US$ 2 000 in many OECD countries.

226

The session centred on three main issues:

- *Choice* in mandatory, private pension systems

- *Competition* in the provision of pension services

- *Complementarities* in the operation and functions of institutional investors.

The design of the new private pension systems, where investment of mandatory savings is restricted to defined-contribution accounts managed by pension fund administrators, had promoted institutional investors to the level of sole providers of all pension services except annuities and other forms of insurance. Insurance companies, meanwhile, had seen the demand for private insurance of disability and survivors' risks increase dramatically, and had sponsored the appearance of markets for annuities. The demand for annuities, in particular, would lead in the near future to rapid growth in life insurance assets. The current situation in Chile, where life insurance assets are greater than general insurance assets, could be replicated elsewhere. The role of insurance companies in the new pension system had also recently become more important in Bolivia, with the introduction of mandatory insurance for professional risks. Ten per cent of workers' salaries would be set aside to pay for insurance premiums. The choice of insurance companies would be made by public bidding, as was the case with pension funds.

While the business activity of insurance companies is increasingly tied to developments in the private pension system, mutual funds are excluded from this rapidly growing sector. They are neither allowed to offer pension accounts nor can they manage pension assets, as they do in many OECD countries. Even indirect effects on mutual funds, via the investment of pension assets, are severely limited. Most countries forbid the related investment of pension assets, and those that do allow it limit such investment to between 5 and 10% of the pension funds' portfolios.

This contrasts with the situation in Brazil. The Brazilian structure is closer to that of some OECD countries, with a broad range of investment instruments for retirement available, heavy involvement of the insurance industry in the provision and management of pension plans, and widespread contracting out of asset management to mutual funds. Pension plans in Brazil are of two types: employer-sponsored closed funds and individual-account open funds. The establishment in 1998 of the PGBL (*Plano Gerador de Beneficio Livre*) and the FAPI (*Fundo de Aposentadoria Programada Individual*), which are similar to the 401(k) and the IRA in the United States, had significantly increased integration between the two types of plan, but some obstacles remained. A private sector representative from Brazil highlighted the different treatment of the two plans. In general, open funds can be transformed into closed funds but not vice versa. The PGBLs also offer less flexibility than 401 (k) accounts.

While it was accepted that increasing choice, competition, and integration were worthwhile ultimate aims, some commentators were concerned about various problems that could arise. Choice could be increased by allowing each participant to invest in more than one pension fund and by permitting the investment of mandatory retirement savings in insurance instruments and other pension products. Competition and integration could be encouraged by allowing different institutional investors to participate in the provision of pension services. For example, mutual funds could become managers of pension fund assets and insurance companies could administer mandatory pension fund accounts.

Problems arising from increased choice

Choice in mandatory pension systems has two facets. One relates to increased choice within the current set-up of individual defined-contribution accounts. Increased choice would involve offering the option of more than one fund in which to invest mandatory savings. This would require a change in the legislation in most countries, except those, like Mexico and Colombia, which are already considering more than one fund in their private pension systems. Chile has recently approved the creation of a second, fixed-income fund. There was general agreement among participants that increasing the number of funds to at least two was a desirable reform.

The second facet relates to choice between retirement instruments. In addition to individual defined- contribution accounts, OECD countries offer other forms of retirement products, including employer pension plans (defined benefit, defined contribution, and hybrid plans), deferred annuities, and with-profits life insurance products. One important problem in increasing choice among products was the danger of individuals taking wrong decisions because of insufficient knowledge or education. Various commentators agreed that efforts to broaden and improve consumer and investor education should precede any attempt to increase individual choice among retirement products.

Another potential adverse impact is higher administrative costs. The introduction of new, more sophisticated pension products could result in more product differentiation and even more active marketing campaigns than are now carried out. One commentator argued that this was already the case in Brazil, where fees charged by open pension funds were very high by regional standards, despite the large size of the domestic market. Introducing the possibility for affiliates to opt out of their employer pension plans and move to open pension funds could in fact lead to higher administrative costs.

In fact, some participants and observers of the pension industry in Latin America feel that fees are excessive already. The debate on pension fund fees has recently heated up in Chile. While switching between pension funds has significantly diminished in the past year, fees have not fallen. This has created a politically explosive combination: high commissions, high profitability for pension fund administrators, and low (negative in 1998) returns to pension fund accounts. Some observers argued that fees could be kept at a minimum by centralising collection and account management, thus taming competition. Contribution collection is centralised in Mexico, but the two functions are combined in a single entity only in the new complementary pension system of public sector workers in Panama. On the other hand, greater competition in the provision of other pension services, such as asset management, could also lower fees.

Concerned by these adverse effects, some commentators argued that the issue of greater choice should, for the time being, focus on the voluntary pillar of a private pension system, through the introduction of favourable tax treatment for all suitable and well-regulated forms of retirement products. The establishment of a level playing field in the voluntary savings sector was a worthwhile policy objective, and would require giving life insurance products fiscal treatment similar to that accorded to the voluntary accounts of pension funds. Otherwise, it was unlikely that the voluntary sector of the insurance industry would grow significantly. Some insurance products, like the *seguro de vida con ahorro* (literally, "life insurance with savings") in Chile, were very attractive as a retirement instrument. Other countries could follow the Chilean lead by offering tax treatment to these instruments that is similar to pension fund accounts. However, there was some controversy as to the potential regressive impact of fiscal subsidies.

Problems arising from increased competition and integration

The main problem is conflict of interest. Uninformed consumers could be exploited by powerful financial conglomerates, which could use their ability to offer mandatory savings instruments to sell additional, and possibly unnecessary, financial products. A conflict of interest could also arise in the ownership of pension fund administrators and the investment regime, since the owners of pension fund administrators could have a vested interest in investing pension fund resources in the assets of companies they control. These problems may justify constraints on the interaction between pension fund administrators and other financial institutions at three levels. First, on the ownership of pension fund administrators by financial conglomerates; second, on the investment of pension fund assets in firms linked to the owner of the pension fund administrator; third, on the retailing of financial products.

To the extent that conflicts could be resolved through adequate regulatory measures, however, there was little reason to exclude insurance companies from the provision of pension products or mutual funds from the management of pension assets. While the limited liberalisation of the insurance industry in the 1980s may have been a good enough reason for this structure, it was asked whether this justification were still relevant. The industry had undergone a process of liberalisation and re-regulation since the early 1980s that placed it in a good position to become a real player in the provision of retirement instruments. Why, it was asked, did countries that had sound and well-regulated insurance industries still follow the Chilean structure when designing their pension reforms?

An additional constraint discussed was the ban on ownership of pension fund administrators by banks, insurance companies and, in general, by financial conglomerates in Chile, Peru and El Salvador. This was defended on grounds that serious conflicts of interest could arise. Such problems could, however, be resolved if a financial conglomerate law was passed that regulated corporate governance of financial institutions. A general law on corporate governance is in fact currently being debated in the Chilean Congress. OECD officials commented on the principles of corporate governance recently issued by the organisation.

Session 2.   The Institutional Sector in the OECD: Lessons for Policies

This session provided an overview of the structure and operation of the institutional investor sector in OECD countries. The experience of OECD countries was compared with that of Latin American countries and policy lessons were drawn. As with the first session, the underlying theme was the conflict that can arise between the twin objectives of choice and competition on the one hand, and financial security and consumer-investor-worker protection on the other. Three main facts about the extent of choice and competition were identified during the discussion:

- The much greater choice among retirement instruments in OECD countries than in Latin American countries.

- The much greater degree of competition between institutional investors in the provision of financial services to final consumers in OECD countries.

- The much greater participation of the three types of institutional investors in the provision of financial services to each other in OECD countries.

Structure of the institutional investor sector in OECD countries

The reliance of OECD countries on public sources of retirement income had meant that the institutional investor sector had developed largely through the voluntary channel. In general, therefore, choice, competition, and integration in this sector were much greater in OECD countries than in those Latin American countries that had introduced mandatory private systems. In most OECD countries, retirement products belong to two main groups or pillars: employer pension plans and personal pension plans. Choice within these was quite extensive, especially in countries like the United Kingdom and the United States. The extent of choice in the 401 (k)s in the United States was in fact greater than in their equivalent products in Brazil, the PGBLs. In the US, regulations require companies to set up at least three different funds, allow switching with a minimum frequency (quarterly), and oblige companies to provide relevant and timely information to affiliates.

Competition between different types of institutional investors in OECD countries operates at two main levels: first, when an employer chooses between administering the company's pension plan internally or sub-contracting to an external administrator, such as an insurance company; second, when the choice is between different providers of personal pension plans. The two main competitors are insurance companies and mutual funds, though the latter only offer defined-contribution schemes. In Latin America, on the other hand, there is no competition between different types of institutional investors in the mandatory private pension pillar. Pension funds, insurance companies and mutual funds, however, compete for voluntary savings in most countries.

The extent of integration of the different institutional investors is also much greater in OECD countries. The role of mutual funds in the management of other institutional investors' assets in the US and Canada was described. In the US, 34% of mutual fund assets belong to retirement plans. In Canada, over half of mutual fund assets are held inside individual retirement plans. The regulatory framework is critical in ensuring the soundness of the industry. Both in the US and Canada, regulations cover reporting, disclosure, valuation, investment and corporate governance.

The regulatory framework

In addition, the session served to discuss the types of regulations that have been implemented in OECD countries, including investor protection and prudential rules. Some speakers and commentators stressed the importance of investor protection in the form of high standards of information disclosure as a means to ensure an adequate functioning of the institutional investor sector. The increased retailisation of the market place required an even greater effort to close the knowledge gap between the sellers and buyers of financial services.

The second part of this session dealt with investment abroad and the role it plays in improving the performance of institutional investors' portfolios. In Canada, the 10% limit on the portion of the portfolio that can be invested abroad was raised in 1991 to 20%. Demand for investment in foreign markets nevertheless is overwhelming. Mutual funds have reacted to this demand by creating innovative products that get around the investment rule. These new products consist of the so-called clone funds, which invest proceeds in money market instruments and enter futures contracts to buy foreign stocks.

Session 3.   The regulatory and supervisory framework and the financial infrastructure

The prudential and protective regulatory framework in Latin America was at the centre stage in the discussions of the third session. In general, the most complete and effectively enforced regulatory framework was that of pension funds in countries with mandatory private pension systems. The new regulatory framework included, for the first time in many cases, standard valuation methods, mandatory risk rating, custody by recognised financial institutions, and high disclosure requirements. Regulatory changes in the insurance, mutual fund and securities markets were in fact largely based on the pension model. In all these countries, also, pension funds tend to be more strictly regulated than either insurance companies or mutual funds. This was certainly the case with investment regulation, performance rules, and information and disclosure requirements. This situation contrasts with that in OECD countries where, in general, regulations applied to pension funds are more lenient than those applied to insurance companies. While it is recognised that different institutional investors may require a different set of regulations, some participants argued that regulators should take into consideration their impact on competition in the sector. Institutional investors require a level playing field if they are to participate on equal terms in the financial market.

The mandatory nature of most pension plans in Latin America as well as the existence of a sizeable informal sector raised issues relating to the regulatory framework. The adequacy of benefit levels and population coverage was highlighted as a major policy issue for regulatory reform.

Four main topics were discussed:

- Performance rules

- Investment regulations

- Financial infrastructure

- Capital market development.

Performance rules

The first two presentations analysed the regulatory regimes of Mexico and Peru. Performance bands and quantitative investment restrictions in the pension fund industry could be called into question, both in theory and in practice. Both seem to have arisen as a result of a political compromise during the reform process. It was argued that government guarantees for poorer households were already provided through minimum pension guarantees. Moreover, the relevant measure of performance in defined-contribution pension systems is the long-term, risk-adjusted rate of return. Relative rate-of-return bands (limits on pension fund returns relative to the industry average) offered no protection against adverse movements in market yields (such as in 1998, when returns to pension funds were negative in many Latin American countries). They could also have perverse incentive effects, exacerbating herding behaviour and investment myopia among pension funds.

Absolute return rules, such as those in place in Peru (0% in real terms over five years) and Brazil (6% real, annual rate of return), were thought as even more distortionary than relative return rules (in place in other Latin American countries). They could be rationalised, however, as a means of limiting the fiscal cost of the minimum pension guarantee. Pension funds, or indeed any other financial institution, can only be expected to provide insurance to the extent that financial products exist allowing them to hedge market and inflation risks. In Brazil, the guarantee was easier to achieve because national savings accounts offer a 6% guaranteed return.

Investment regulations

It was also shown how quantitative investment limits constrain the portfolio efficiency frontier; increasing risks for a given expected return, or lowering expected returns for a given level of risk. The justification for such controls has been based on some notion of "financial security", but, clearly, this objective can come into conflict with that of profitability. In some Latin American countries (Mexico, Uruguay, Bolivia) there is certainly excessive protection of pension fund portfolios, since the only permitted investment instruments are fixed-income securities. As argued by one commentator, too conservative investment regimes could in fact increase risks, especially the risk of not achieving an adequate level of income at retirement.

Most commentators agreed that a relaxation of foreign investment limits was required in Latin American countries, especially in view of the high volatility of capital markets in this region. In Chile, in the space of one year, pension funds had increased their allocation to foreign securities from 1 to 13% of their portfolio, mainly as a response to the negative returns obtained on their portfolios in 1998. This contrasts with the situation in Argentina, where foreign investment is less than 1%. In Peru, Bolivia, and Colombia, investment abroad is permitted by the legislation, but no foreign securities have as yet been approved for investment.

Most participants agreed that the current regime of quantitative restrictions should be only temporary, and that regulations should gradually move to a portfolio perspective, where the risk of the aggregate portfolio, and not just that of individual securities was controlled. Countries that had flexible limits in the law, even if there were tight limits in the regulations, were found to be best prepared for this shift. There was some disagreement, however, as to whether the most suitable risk-control model would be that of prudent-person regimes.

Any new risk-control model would have to take into account the availability of instruments in the domestic capital markets. Peru was a case in point. At the start of the new system in 1993, there were few government securities available. The Treasury responded by issuing short-term paper. Since then, pension funds have increased their exposure to longer-term private sector securities. Except in Chile, however, capital markets in most Latin American countries are still concentrated in the short to medium term of the maturity spectrum. The average maturity of the fixed income portion of investment portfolios is rarely above three to five years. This clearly has severe implications for the extent of risk management feasible in local markets.

The problem is particularly acute for life insurance companies that sell annuities to pension fund administrators. Evidence from Chile showed that even there, insurance companies were not able to carry out full maturity matching after sixteen years. In other Latin American countries the limit would be much less, around three to five years. Since people can expect to live up to twenty or more years after retirement, the lack of adequate maturity matching instruments was worrying. Participants agreed that regulatory agencies should play an important role in helping create long term investment instruments. In Chile, for example, the Securities and Insurance Supervisor was involved in developing the new infrastructure bonds, with maturities as long as twenty-five to thirty years.

Financial infrastructure

A sound and financial infrastructure was also vital in ensuring adequate control of the investment behaviour of institutional investors. One commentator described the Peruvian example, identifying at least four different valuation models for variable income securities: mutual funds, retail banks, private banking, and pension funds each used their own valuation model. These models needed to be standardised to ensure an efficient functioning of the sector.

Brazil now has some of the most liberal quantitative limits in the region for institutional investors. At the same time, however, the country suffers from deficiencies in its financial infrastructure. An important problem is the limited development of risk rating. Pension funds are not required to have even their fixed income securities risk-rated, as is the case in other Latin American countries. The closed fund regulator has recently submitted a proposal to the Central Bank for a new investment control regime that would include risk rating, but a decision has yet to be reached.

Capital market development

The activities of institutional investors bring certain benefits to capital markets. They can help increase the breadth and depth of capital markets and promote the development of subsidiary services; these investors can also exert corporate governance. Institutional investors with a long-term investment horizon, such as pension funds and insurance companies, can also become important providers of long-term finance for domestic enterprises. The strengthening and growth of domestic capital markets can also have important externalities, such as reducing dependency on foreign capital and playing a role in crisis prevention.

Institutional investors have been active players in recent innovations in capital markets in Latin America. A recent development in Bolivia is the introduction of mortgage securitisation. The experience of Latin American pension funds with these instruments, however, has been mixed. While in Chile and Colombia pension funds have become major investors in these instruments, other countries have seen very limited demand for these instruments.

At the same time, the increased presence of institutional investors is presenting some policy dilemmas for policy makers. In countries like Chile, where pension funds have existed for many years, these institutions dominate most long-term fixed-income markets (they own over half the corporate bond and mortgage bond markets) and have become large shareholders of some firms, especially privatised utilities. In two firms, pension funds on aggregate hold over 30% of total equity. Corporate governance is exerted by pension funds via representation and voting in shareholder meetings, but as yet the funds are not able to have a voice in corporate affairs. For example, pension funds are prohibited from commenting on a firm's performance in public.

Pension funds in Chile are in a quandary in regard to their investment in equity holdings. On the one hand, regulations limit the extent to which they can influence management. On the other hand, they are finding that the ultimate threat of selling their stocks is not an easy option. Because of their buy-and-hold strategies, liquidity in the local market has not increased significantly. Hence, pension funds often find it difficult to divest their shares without adversely affecting prices. Liquidity problems have been particularly acute in recent months, including the de-listing of large companies in the main Latin American stock markets (e.g. YPF in Argentina, Endesa in Chile, Telebras in Brazil). This process could turn the virtuous circle of growth of institutional investors and the development of capital markets into a vicious circle of increased illiquidity in stock markets and declining returns to institutionally-held assets.

Session 4. *Opportunities and policy challenges for the growth of the institutional sector in Latin America*

In the last session, the chairpersons summarised the discussions in their respective sessions. Following these reports, the discussion focussed on policy challenges ahead, and explored ways to advance the analysis and formulate policy recommendations. Some specific obstacles to the development of institutional investors and future challenges were mentioned, including:

- Short-termism and over-regulation

- Low level of income and savings

- Low coverage

- Thin capital markets

- A tradition of closed, family businesses

- A taxation system that favours banking finance (dividends are not tax-deductible, interest on loans is)

- Existing contractual law that makes securitisation difficult.

The obstacles discussed affected both the extent of affiliation and the ability to achieve diversified investment portfolios and offer a variety of retirement instruments. Proposals to address the low coverage in contributions included the possibility of making fixed contributions, and to license alternative financial companies to channel pension fund services. In particular, NGOs have established extensive networks in rural areas that could be used to offer the poorer segment of society access to financial services similar to those available to urban workers. Such networks could also bring the advantages of group negotiation with a consequent reduction in administrative costs.

The contrast with the situation in Brazil was again patent. There, new regulations have been proposed which will lead to the introduction of a new entity, the *instituidor*, to administer pension plans. This entity would no longer have to be sponsored by either an employer or a financial institution. In fact, the new regulations would allow trade associations and other non-profit organisations to set up pension plans.

The workshop closed with an appeal by the various representatives to continue discussions on this topic at international level. A specific request was made for the OECD to extend its work on institutional investor databases to developing countries, providing internet access to statistics, regulations, major publications, and potentially a discussion forum for academics, regulators and industry professionals. In this respect, specific reference was also made to the relevance of the new OECD *International Forum on Private Pensions,* and delegates expressed their support for several on-going OECD initiatives, including the setting-up of an OECD internet site on private pensions regulations, the development of an international network of pension regulators and supervisors, and the appropriate collection and dissemination of statistical and regulatory data. Representatives from the AIOS and ASSAL stressed the need to develop further co-operation with OECD in the field of insurance and private pensions. A proposal was also made to organise a workshop for the region's legislators on obstacles to the development of the institutional investor sector.

Some topics of interest to both Latin American and OECD countries were identified for future research:

- Designing multi-pillar pension plans: mandatory, funded, private *systems versus tax incentives for voluntary savings*:

  - Eight Latin American countries and several OECD countries have mandatory private pension systems. This imposes a greater fiduciary responsibility on the state to ensure adequate functioning of financial markets and especially of the institutions that manage retirement plans. Governments in Latin America have responded by imposing restrictions on the structure of the pension fund industry and requiring regulations. The choice between replacing and supplementing the public pillar with private pensions cannot ignore the basic fact that the private industry thereby created will not be the same as one operating in a market with voluntary savings. In countries where a high degree of choice has been permitted, affiliates have sometimes been left worse off.

- Competition between different types of institutional investors:

  - While there may be good justification for limiting choice of financial instruments in mandatory pension systems, it is not clear why different institutional investors should not be able to offer a particular product. In countries where some types of institutional investors are not adequately regulated, the objective should be to improve the regulatory framework rather than exclude them from the provision of retirement products.

- Preconditions for mutual fund involvement in the pension industry:

  - There is a need to identify the regulatory needs of the mutual fund industry, since in countries with mandatory private pensions, mutual funds have not been deemed fit to manage retirement assets. In OECD countries, on the other hand, mutual funds are very active as asset mangers of pension-fund and insurance-company portfolios.

- Risk management in incipient capital markets and the choice between *defined-benefit and defined- contribution pension schemes*:

- Countries differ in the state of development of their capital markets. In most of Latin America, maturity matching with fixed income instruments is practically impossible after ten years, Chile being the main exception. Diversification overseas can help reduce long-term risks, but it exposes asset prices to fluctuations in exchange rates. Hence, in general, defined-benefit plans may currently be more expensive to manage in Latin America than in OECD countries. By the same token, the switch from defined-benefit to defined-contribution schemes has different implications for the welfare of individuals in developing countries than for those in developed ones.

Annex I

LIST OF PARTICIPANTS

Government Officials

Austria

Mr. Johann Elsinger
Manager, Austrian National Bank

Bolivia

Ms. Helga SALINAS
Intendent of Pensions

Brazil

Mr. Paulo KLIASS
Secretary, Secretaria de Previdencia
Complementar

Canada

Ms. Glorianne STROMBERG
Former Commissioner
Ontario Securities Commission

Chile

Mr. Mario BENAVENTE
Vice-President
Foreign Investment Committee
General Direction of International
Economic Relations

Mr. Julio BUSTAMANTE
Superintendent of Pensions

Ms. Mónica CACERES
Intendent of Insurance
Superintendency of Securities and
Insurance

Mr. Claudio CHAMORRO
Director
Financial Studies and Analyse
Superintendency of Banks and
Financial Institutions

Mr. Alejandro JARA
General Director of Economic
Relations, Ministry of Foreign Affairs

Mr. Liselott KANA
Head of International Taxation
Tax Treaty Negotiator and
Interpretation
Ministry of Finance

Mr. Eduardo MOYANO
President
Foreign Investment Committee
General Direction of International
Economic Relations -Chile

Mr. Heinz RUDOLPH
Director
International Finance
Ministry of Finance

Mr. José Miguel ZAVALA MATULIC
Director, Capital Markets Department,
Central Bank

Ms. Maria Eugenia WAGNER
Co-ordinator, International Affairs
Department, Minister of Finance

Dominican Republic

Mr. Edwin GUERRA
Executive Director
Dominican Association of Pension
Funds Managers

Finland

Ms. Liisa MAUNULA
First Secretary
Embassy of Finland in Santiago

Hungary

Mr. Sandor DOGEI
Deputy President
State Supervisory Authority of
Insurance

Mr. Tibor PARNICZKY
Vice-President
State Private Funds Supervision

Korea

Mr. Won-Young YON
Standing Commissioner
Securities and Futures Commission
Financial Supervisory Service

Mr. Gwang-Soo KIM
Director
Legal Co-ordination Div. II
Financial Supervisory Commission

Mr. Yong-Seok OH
Head of Policy Research Team
Financial Supervisory Service

Mexico

Mr. Fernando SOLIS
President
National Commission of Pension
Funds Administrators (CONSAR)

Peru

Mr. Augusto MOUCHARD
Superintendent of Pensions

Mr. Elio SANCHEZ
Superintendency of Private Pension
Funds Administrators

Poland

Mr. Daniel PASSENT
Ambassador

Mr. Dariusz LATOSZEC
Commercial Attaché

Mr. Lech MIODEK
Counselor
Embassy of Poland in Chile

Switzerland

Mr. Jean Jacques JORIS
Chargé d'Affaires a.i.
Swiss Embassy in Chile

United Kingdom

Mr. Tim TORLOT
First Secretary - Commercial
UK Embassy in Santiago

United States

Mr. Everette JAMES
Deputy Assistant Secretary for Service,
Industries & Finance
International Trade Administartion
U.S. Department of Commerce

Ms. Cristina VIDAL
Commercial Specialist / Financial
Services
U.S. Commercial Service
Embassy of the United States of
America

Private Sector

AFP Horizonte - Peru

Mr. José Luis CASABONNE R.
General Manager
Mr. Aldo QUINTANA
Investment Manager

AFP Santa María

Mr. Aldo SIMONETTI
General Manager

Association of Banks -Chile

Mr. Hernán SOMMERVILLE
President

**Association of Mutual Funds
Administrators -Chile**

Mr. Jorge FARAH
President

**Association of Private Pension Funds
Administrators -Chile**

Mr. Guillermo ARTHUR
President

CIGNA international

Mr. Eduardo BOM ANGELO
Vice President Investments and
Retirement Services

European Committee of Insurance

Mr. José MARIN
Delegate
Investment Manager
Chilena Consolidada, Zurich Insurance
International

**FIAP - International Federation of
Private Pension Funds Administrators**

Mr. Pedro CORONA
President
Ms. Gladys Otarola
Executive Secretary

**FIDES - Federación Interamericana
de Empresas de Seguros**

Mr. Francisco SERQUEIRA
President

Kemper Retirement Plans Group

Mr. Thomas BRUNS
President

Peruval SAB

Mr. Lorenzo SOUSA
General Manager

Principal International, Inc

Mr. Luis VALDES
Vice-President
Latin American Operations

Royal & Sunalliance, USA

Mr. Víctor Manuel JARPA
President
Seguros de Vida La Construcción -
Chile

Scotia Securities Inc.

Mr. Andrew SCIPIO DEL CARPIO
President & CEO

243

Consultants and Experts

Mr. Gonzalo DELAVEAU
Consultant Pension and Insurance

Mr. Rodrigo ACUNA
Partner
Prim America Consultores

Mr. Salvador VALDES-PRIETO
Consultant
Universidad Católica de Chile

Mr. Octavio VERGARA
President & CEO
Andueza y Cía Consultants

International Organisations

Inter-American Development Bank - IADB

Mr. Antonio VIVES
Deputy Manager
Infrastructure, Financial Markets and
Private Enterprise

European Commission

Mr. Anton Santos
Head
EU Delegation in Chile

OECD Secretariat

Mr. Rolf ALTER
Counselor
Directorate for Financial, Fiscal and
Enterprise Affairs

Mr. André LABOUL
Head
Insurance and Private Pensions Unit
Directorate for Financial, Fiscal and
Enterprise Affairs

Mr. Stephen LUMPKIN
Principal Administrator
Directorate for Financial, Fiscal and
Enterprise Affairs

Mr. Juan YERMO
Consultant
Directorate for Financial, Fiscal and
Enterprise Affairs

Ms. Carmen VILLEGAS
CABALLERO
Consultant
Directorate for Financial, Fiscal and
Enterprise Affairs

Annex II

AGENDA OF THE WORKSHOP

1 September 1999, Wednesday, Day One

Key Note Speech
- Mr. Manuel Marfán, Vice Minister of Finance of Chile

Opening Addresses
- Mr. Mario Matus, Director of Economic Affairs, Ministry of Foreign Affairs, Chile

- Mr. Anton Santos, Head of Delegation, European Union Delegation in Chile

- Mr. Rolf Alter, Counsellor, Directorate for Financial, Fiscal and Enterprise Affairs, Organisation for Economic Co-operation and Development (OECD)

Session 1
The Institutional Sector in Latin America - Assessment, Experience, Comparison

Experts will consider the implications for Latin America's domestic financial sector, in particular with respect to the pension reform and life insurance and pension products. In addition, obstacles to the development of the institutional sector in the region will be identified. Participants are invited to assess the development of the institutional sector in different Latin America countries and to discuss the necessary efforts for further development. Participants may also wish to discuss the way in which Latin America plays a key role in the development of institutional investors worldwide.

Chair:
- Mr. Antonio Vives, Deputy Manager, Infrastructure, Financial Markets and Private Enterprise, IADB

Overview of the Latin American Institutional Market
- Mr. Francisco Serqueira, President, Interamerican Federation of Insurance Companies (FIDES)

- Mr. Pedro Corona, President, International Federation of Pension Funds Administrators (FIAP)

245

Commentaries

- Mr. Johann Elsinger, Manager, Austrian National Bank, Austria

- Mr. Luis Valdés, Vice-President, Latin American Operations, Principal International, USA

General discussion

Contact Break

Country report and outlook

- Ms. Helga Salinas, Intendent of Pensions, Superintendency of Pension, Securities and Insurance, Bolivia

- Mr. Heinz Rudolph, Director, International Finance, Ministry of Finance, Chile

Commentaries

- Mr. Salvador Valdés-Prieto, Professor, Universidad Católica de Chile

- Mr. Tibor Parniczky, Vice-President, State Private Funds Supervision, Hungary

General discussion

Session 2
The Institutional Sector in the OECD: Lessons for Policies

OECD representatives will outline the recent policy initiatives in the OECD area that have fostered the expansion of the institutional sector for investments. Participants will discuss the implications and relevance for foreign institutional investors in Latin America.

Chair:

- Mr. Everette James, Deputy Assistant Secretary for Service, Industries & Finance. International Trade Administration, US Department of Commerce and Chair of the OECD Working Party on Private Pensions

Introduction by the chairman

Background presentation

- Mr. Stephen Lumpkin, Principal Administrator, DAF, OECD

Presentations

- Ms. Glorianne Stromberg, Former Commissioner, Ontario Securities Commission, Canada

- Mr. Thomas Bruns, President, Kemper Retirement Plans Group, US

Commentaries

- Mr. Sandor Dogei, Deputy President, State Supervisory Authority of Insurance, Hungary

- Mr. Jorge Marín, Delegate, European Committee of Insurance

General Discussion

Contact Break

Presentations

- Mr. Andrew Scipio del Campo, President and CEO, Scotia Securities Inc Expert from Private Sector

Commentaries

- Mr. Aldo Simonetti, General Manager, AFP Santa María, Aetna International, Chile

- Mr. Heinz Rudolph, Director, International Finance, Ministry of Finance, Chile

General discussion

2 September 1999, Thursday, Day Two

Session 3
The Regulatory and Supervisory Framework and the Financial Infrastructure

Experts from OECD and Latin American regulators will discuss the role of public policy in ensuring an adequate framework for the further development of the institutional sector in Latin America.

Chair:

- Mr. André Laboul, Head of Insurance and Private Pensions Unit, DAF, OECD

Introduction by the chairman

Background presentation

- Mr. Juan Yermo, Consultant, OECD

Part I: Investment regulation, financial infrastructure, and competition

Presentations

- Mr. Fernando Solis, President, CONSAR, Mexico

- Mr. Augusto Mouchard, Superintendent, Superintendency of Pension Funds Administrators, Peru

Commentaries

- Ms. Glorianne Stromberg, Former Commissioner, Ontario Securities Commission, Canada

- Mr. Aldo Quintana, Investment Manager, AFP Horizonte, Peru

General discussion (Including on OECD regulatory principles)

Contact Break

Part II Regulation of employer pension plans and life insurance markets

Presentations

- Mr. Paulo Kliass, Secretary, Secretaria de Previdência Complementar, Brazil

- Ms. Mónica Cáceres, Intendent of Insurance, Superintendence of Securities and Insurance, Chile

Commentaries

- Mr. Eduardo Bom Angelo, President, CIGNA Retirement & Investments, Brazil

- Mr. Gonzalo Delaveau, Senior Consultant, Pension and Insurance, Chile

General Discussion (Including on OECD regulatory principles)

Session 4
Opportunities and Policy Challenges for the Growth of the Institutional Sector in Latin America

This session will draw preliminary conclusions of the debate focusing on the opportunities for further growth of institutional investment in Latin America and the policy requirements. This assessment will take into account broader related issues, such as, for example, the adequacy of pensions in Latin America and their coverage given the sizeable informal sector. The session will also identify the scope for further co-operation of Latin American countries and the OECD in this area.

Chair:

- Mr. Rolf Alter, Counsellor, Directorate for Financial, Fiscal and Enterprise Affairs, OECD

Panel Discussion

- Report from the Chairpersons

General Discussion

Contact Break

Closing Address